YOUNG CHILDREN PLAYING AND LEARNING IN A DIGITAL AGE

Young Children Playing and Learning in a Digital Age explores the emergence of the digital age and young children's experiences with digital technologies at home and in educational environments.

Drawing on theory and research-based evidence, this book makes an important contribution to understanding the contemporary experiences of young children in the digital age. It argues that a cultural and critically informed perspective allows educators, policy-makers and parents to make sense of children's digital experiences as they play and learn, enabling informed decision-making about future early years curriculum and practices at home and in early learning and care settings.

An essential read for researchers, students, policy-makers and professionals working with children today, this book draws attention to the evolution of digital developments and the relationship between contemporary technologies, play and learning in the early years.

Christine Stephen recently retired as a Research Fellow at the University of Stirling, Scotland. Her research focuses on young children's learning and in particular on their everyday experiences as they engage with digital technologies.

Susan Edwards is the Director of the Early Childhood Futures research group in the Learning Sciences Institute Australia, Australian Catholic University, Australia.

EECERA
European Early Childhood
Education Research Association

Written in association with the European Early Childhood Education Research Association (EECERA), titles in this series will reflect the latest developments and most current research and practice in early childhood education on a global level. Feeding into and supporting the further development of the discipline as an exciting and urgent field of research and high academic endeavour, the series carries a particular focus on knowledge and reflection, which has huge relevance and topicality for those at the front line of decision making and professional practice.

Rather than following a linear approach of research to practice, this series offers a unique fusion of research, theoretical, conceptual and philosophical perspectives, values and ethics, and professional practice, which has been termed 'Ethical Praxis'.

Other titles published in association with the European Early Childhood Education Research Association (EECERA):

Assessment and Evaluation for Transformation in Early Childhood
Júlia Formosinho and Christine Pascal
2016/PB: 978-1-138-90974-8

Pathways to Professionalism in Early Childhood Education and Care
Michel Vandenbroeck, Mathias Urban and Jan Peeters
2016/PB: 978-1-138-91889-4

Young Children Playing and Learning in a Digital Age
a Cultural and Critical Perspective
Christine Stephen and Susan Edwards
2018/PB: 978-1-138-65469-3

Values in Early Childhood Education
Citizenship for Tomorrow
Eva Johansson and Jóhanna Einarsdottir
2018/PB: 978-1-138-23070-5

YOUNG CHILDREN PLAYING AND LEARNING IN A DIGITAL AGE

a Cultural and Critical Perspective

Christine Stephen and Susan Edwards

Routledge
Taylor & Francis Group

LONDON AND NEW YORK

EECERA
European Early Childhood
Education Research Association

First published 2018
by Routledge
2 Park Square, Milton Park, Abingdon, Oxon OX14 4RN

and by Routledge
711 Third Avenue, New York, NY 10017

Routledge is an imprint of the Taylor & Francis Group, an informa business

© 2018 Christine Stephen and Susan Edwards

British Library Cataloguing in Publication Data
A catalogue record for this book is available from the British Library

Library of Congress Cataloging in Publication Data
Names: Stephen, Christine, author. | Edwards, Susan, 1975– author.
Title: Young children playing and learning in a digital age : a cultural and critical perspective / Christine Stephen and Susan Edwards.
Description: Abingdon, Oxon ; New York, NY : Routledge, 2017.
Identifiers: LCCN 2017034720 (print) | LCCN 2017048500 (ebook) |
ISBN 9781315623092 (ebook) | ISBN 9781138654686 (hbk) |
ISBN 9781138654693 (pbk) | ISBN 9781315623092 (ebk)
Subjects: LCSH: Early childhood education–Computer assisted instruction. |
Computers and children. | Play.
Classification: LCC LB1139.35.C64 (ebook) | LCC LB1139.35.C64 S74
2018 (print) | DDC 372.21–dc23
LC record available at https://lccn.loc.gov/2017034720

ISBN: 978-1-138-65468-6 (hbk)
ISBN: 978-1-138-65469-3 (pbk)
ISBN: 978-1-315-62309-2 (ebk)

Typeset in Bembo
by Wearset Ltd, Boldon, Tyne and Wear

From Christine:
To Olivia and Sam and their Grandpa

From Susan:
To Luke Cosgriff, Noel Edwards and Elizabeth Edwards

CONTENTS

FOREWORD

Introduction to the EECERA Book Series

Tony Bertram and Chris Pascal

Underpinning aspirations

This ground-breaking book by Christine Stephen and Susan Edwards, entitled *Young Children Playing and Learning in a Digital Age: a Cultural and Critical Perspective*, provides the third book in an innovative new book series generated by the European Early Childhood Education Research Association (EECERA). The EECERA Book Series, entitled 'Towards an Ethical Praxis in Early Childhood', offers an innovative and exemplary vehicle for the international early childhood sector to develop transformative pedagogy which demonstrates effective integrated praxis. The EECERA Book Series is designed to complement and link with the *European Early Childhood Education Research Journal* (EECERJ), which is primarily a worldwide academic platform for publishing research according to the highest international standards of scholarship. The EECERA Book Series aims to highlight pedagogic praxis in order to demonstrate how this knowledge can be used to develop and improve the quality of early education and care services to young children and their families. It is also intended to stimulate dialogue about the impact of such research studies.

Pedagogic approach

The approach taken in the book series is not a linear one, but rather a praxeological one focused on praxis, meaning a focus on pedagogic action impregnated in theory and supported by a belief system. It is this fusion of practice, theoretical perspectives, ethics and research which we term 'Ethical Praxis'. This fusion is embodied in all EECERA research and development activity, but we anticipate the book series will have a stronger focus on the development of pedagogic praxis and policy. In addition to offering a forum for plural, integrated pedagogic praxis, the series offers a strong model of praxeological processes that will secure deep improvements in the educational experience of children and families, of professionals and researchers across international early childhood services.

The book series acknowledges pedagogy as a branch of professional/practical knowledge which is constructed in situated action in dialogue with theories and research and with beliefs (values and principles). Pedagogy is seen as an 'ambiguous' space, not of one-between-two (theory and practice) but as one-between-three (actions, theories and beliefs) in an interactive, constantly renewed triangulation. Convening beliefs, values and principles, analysing practices and using several branches of knowledge (philosophy, history, anthropology, psychology, sociology amongst others) constitutes the triangular movement of the creation of pedagogy. Pedagogy is thus based on praxis, in other words, an action based on theory and sustained by belief systems. Contrary to other branches of knowledge which are identified by the definition of areas with well-defined frontiers, the pedagogical branch of knowledge is created in the ambiguity of a space which is aware of the frontiers but does not delimit them because their essence is in their integration.

Praxeological intentions

There is a growing body of practitioner- and practice-focused research which is reflected in the push at national and international levels to add research and analysis skills into the professional skill set of all early childhood practitioners. This is a reflection of the growing professionalism of the early childhood sector and its increased status internationally. The development of higher order professional standards and increased accountability are reflective of these international trends as the status and importance of early education in the success of educational systems is acknowledged.

Each book in the series is designed to have the following praxeological features:

- strongly and transparently positioned in the sociocultural context of the authors
- practice or policy focused but based on research and with strong conceptual/theoretical perspectives
- topical and timely, focusing on key issues and new knowledge
- provocative, ground breaking, innovative
- critical, dialogic, reflexive
- euro-centric, giving voice to Europe's traditions and innovations but open to global contributions
- open, polyphonic, prismatic
- plural, multidisciplinary, multi-method
- praxeological, with a concern for power, values and ethics, praxis and a focus on action research, the learning community and reflexive practitioners
- views early childhood pedagogy as a field in itself, not as applied psychology

- concerned with social justice, equity, diversity and transformation
- concerned with professionalism and quality improvement
- working for a social science of the social
- NOT designed as a text book for practice but as a text for professional and practice/policy development.

This third book in the series exemplifies these underpinning philosophies, pedagogical ethics and scholarly intentions beautifully. We believe it is topical and timely, focusing on key issues and new knowledge, and also provocative and critical, encouraging and opening dialogue about our thinking and actions in developing high quality early childhood services internationally.

ACKNOWLEDGEMENTS

While we take responsibility for the content of this book, we wish to acknowledge the debt we owe to our colleagues for the shared research projects on which we now report. Also, the many remembered debates and conversations we have shared with colleagues, both locally and internationally over time. In particular, Christine acknowledges the substantial contribution working with Lydia Plowman and Joanna McPake made to developing her interest in, and understanding of, young children's engagement with digital technologies. Susan thanks her collaborators Joce Nuttall, Susan Grieshaber and Elizabeth Wood for growing her understanding of the contextual nature of digital play and learning.

Our work has depended on the willing participation of many children, families and educators. We are grateful for the time and insights these participants have gifted us. We extend our thanks to Chris Pascal for inviting us to contribute this book to the EECERA series 'Towards an Ethical Praxis in Early Childhood: from Research into Practice' and for her editorial support and patience. Our families have also been patient and endlessly supportive during the ups and downs of producing this book – thank you.

Finally, we acknowledge the superb formatting and editorial care provided by Carmela Germano with financial contributions from the Australian Catholic University.

1

TOWARDS A NEW KNOWLEDGE PERSPECTIVE

Introduction

As he pretended to be a delivery driver, three-year-old Sam handed over an imaginary parcel and was offered a small plastic card in payment. He tapped it on the corner of the old mobile phone being used as a card reader and having completed this contactless transaction climbed back into his van, turned a key to start the engine and called goodbye. This was a familiar play episode for Sam. He was enacting the kind of transaction he frequently observed during shopping trips. A card is tapped on a small rectangular box and a purchase is handed over. But his grandfather, his partner in the play, noticed his use of the contactless electronic with some surprise, although he would not have commented on Sam accepting pretend coins or even trying to place the card into the old phone and typing in some numbers. He was not surprised either at the use of a pretend motor vehicle and the actions of driving. Contactless payment is a relatively new practice for Sam's grandfather and therefore noteworthy in a way that did not necessarily extend to his own everyday experience of paying electronically with a card and PIN number – and especially with driving a car. Sam's understanding of shopping, communicating and engaging with digital technologies might seem different from that of earlier generations but just like his grandfather's experience it is embedded in his daily life.

Books about young children and technologies often open with observations such as this one describing Sam and his grandfather. Typically, the vignettes are used to highlight what the authors present as the remarkable capacity of modern day children to use technologies. However, in this book we suggest that Sam and his grandfather are quite unremarkable. Culturally, both the child and the grandfather are of their time. Sam's technological practices illustrate the evolution of knowledge, its application in technological innovations and the ways in which new knowledge and technologies transform the everyday practices of adults and children over time. This book is about cultural change, change in what is known and in the technologies made possible by new knowledge and understandings. Here we will argue that it is necessary to make sense of the evolution of changes in society's knowledge and what that means for the technologies at our disposal and our everyday actions and interactions if we are to understand and respond to young children's play and learning in contemporary times.

Culture is central to our thinking in this book. By culture we mean the dynamic nature of knowledge in the practices of everyday life. We explore how the process of cultural-historical change gives rise to contemporary knowledge (conceptual, practical and theoretical) and cultural tools and creates the conditions for transformative future innovation. It is our contention that this cultural perspective enables educators, policy-makers and parents to both understand the nature of the changes in play and learning in the digital age and, importantly, respond to these changes in ways that reflect the values and desires of contemporary times and the opportunities and challenges for future transformations. In order to think about how we can respond to the implications of technological change for young children's play and learning in the digital age we will introduce some theoretical ideas about the relationship between people and technologies. One such important idea is that of taking a critical perspective on technologies. We will argue that adopting a culturally informed and critical perspective empowers educators, parents and all those responsible for caring for and educating young children in the digital age. Thinking culturally and critically is challenging. It requires a proactive and questioning approach that seeks to appreciate the cultural-historical transformations of the past, understand the present and consider future possibilities. However, we argue that just as changes in knowledge have informed technological innovation, so too should knowledge in the field of early childhood education evolve in the digital age. In what follows we seek to demonstrate the value of a cultural and critical perspective on young children's play and learning in the digital age. First, however, to open our thinking and to lead the way in better understanding what we mean by a cultural and critical perspective we open this introductory chapter with an account of how research into young children's engagement with technologies moved from being a predominately niche area of early childhood scholarship into a mainstream concern of early childhood education.

From niche research area to mainstream concern

Ten to 20 years ago, research about young children's play and learning with technologies was a niche area of investigation. Defined as birth to eight years, the early childhood period tended to attract the interest of a committed band of scholars and researchers interested in understanding what types of technologies young children were using and how these technologies were being put to use in children's play and learning (e.g. Haugland, 2000; Marsh *et al.*, 2005; Yelland, 2005). Most of the research about young children's technological experiences was conducted in relative isolation, focusing on what is variously labelled as preschool, nursery or early years education. Other sectors of education, such as primary, secondary and tertiary education, were pre-occupied with their own pedagogical technological issues and paid little heed to what was occurring in the early years (see for example: Collins & Halverson, 2009; Greenhow, Robelia, & Hughes, 2009). The early childhood sector meanwhile – in those moments when it did pay attention to young children's engagements with technologies – tended towards a continuous re-enactment of the 'benefits versus risks' orientation towards the role of technologies in the lives of the very young. This orientation is most evident in the 'Fools Gold' debate occurring between Cordes and Miller (2000) and Clements and Sarama (2002) in the early part of the new century. What and how young children might be playing and learning with technologies was not a mainstream consideration for the field. However, leaders researching in this area continued to establish the empirical evidence base regarding young children's technology use in multiple settings, including at home and in educational contexts (Plowman & Stephen, 2005). New ideas and concepts for understanding young children's digital literacies (Marsh, 2004) and the emergence of digital play were slowly percolating (Zevenbergen, 2007).

Then, in 2010 came the iPad. Arriving with a suddenness that made the iPad seem as if it had arrived from nowhere, the early childhood sector was ill-prepared to greet this new technology in the lives of young children. Putting computing technology literally at the fingertips of the very youngest of children, an explosion of interest in young children's technology use in the early years suddenly occurred. A quick Google search reveals a rapid succession of research publications focused on iPads in the early years. With titles such as 'iPads as a literacy teaching tool in early childhood' (Beschorner & Hutchison, 2013) and 'Touch, type, and transform: iPads in the social studies classroom' (Berson, Berson, & McGlinn Manfra, 2012) technology research in the early years was unexpectedly high on the agenda. There was interest from the popular media too. 'Are iPads and tablets bad for young children?' asked the *Guardian* newspaper (Cocozza, 2014) and 'Toddlers obsessed with iPads: could it hurt their development?' (Chang, Rakowsky, & Frost, 2013). Yet, despite this high profile rush of interest, research into young children's technology use at home and in early childhood education settings had gone on somewhat quietly unnoticed for many years. Indeed, outside of the specifics of early childhood technology research, studies in the areas of media and new media had already provided many important insights and understanding about young children's engagements with technologies – particularly those pertaining to what was once, at some earlier point in time, the newest of the new – first radio, and then television (Buckingham, 1993).

In this book we pay attention to the range of research and thinking pertaining to young children's play and learning in the digital age. We consider both the 'niche' research of the past 20 years, and newer research and theorisation regarding young children's engagements with technologies. In particular, we draw on our own research – some of which was conducted and published during the 'niche' era, and some of which makes a more contemporary contribution. For example, we draw heavily on the ground-breaking work of Stephen and colleagues in their three

Economic and Social Research Council (ESRC)-funded projects ('Interplay' 2003–2005; 'Entering the e-Society' 2005–2007; and 'Young Children Learning with Toys and Technology' 2008–2011) examining young children's technology use in the home. Predominately pre-iPad, this research drew attention to forms of learning with digital technologies that go beyond acquiring new operating skills and established that learning in the digital age was mediated not just by the technology but by the key pedagogical contribution of parents and educators. We also build on the contributions of Edwards (2003), who in this niche area contributed to one of the first-ever publications on touchscreen technology use by young children in early childhood settings – anticipating and describing young children's preference for input devices as culturally acquired skills (Romeo, Edwards, McNamara, Walker, & Ziguras, 2003). Some newer work (e.g. Edwards, 2013) regarding the pedagogical positioning of technologies in early childhood education is also canvassed. Here, we focus particularly on Edwards' (2015) approach to the problem of integrating technologies into early childhood education settings where she argues for an increased focus on understanding, developing and conceptualising digital play over a continued emphasis on teaching teachers to use technologies with children. This work has set in motion a newer body of work in which researchers are now examining how early childhood teachers view technologies as play (Nikolopoulou & Gialamas, 2015; Palaiologou, 2016), and the extent to which technologies are likely to be integrated by teachers into the early childhood curriculum according to their own constructs of digital play (Arnott, 2016).

Now that the topic of 'young children playing and learning in a digital age' appears to be the concern of so many writers, researchers, teachers, families, policy- and decision-makers we seek to do more in this book than simply broaden the existing scope of this once niche area of interest. While a summary of the relevant literature and a distillation of 'tips' for teachers and parents may seem superficially attractive, it is our firm belief that the field of early learning both deserves, and needs, more than this to guide our thinking regarding young children's engagements with digital technologies. Distilled literature and tips will not help teachers, parents, policy-makers and even researchers understand how it is that iPads 'suddenly' arrived in the lives of the very youngest of children. Nor will such a summative approach help researchers and teachers attend to what is significant and important about young children's play and learning in a digital age and their own role in contemporary childhoods as they evolve in a digital context. Even further, concentrating on tips for technology use in families and early-learning settings denies the field a comprehensive understanding of what actually comprises the digital age and how this 'digital age' came into existence. It is our contention, that to teach children growing up within a particular 'age' we must at the very least, have a basic cultural-historical understanding of how things came to be in order to inform what it is we decide to do next.

Thus this book is different to many books that consider young children's play and learning in a digital age. We do not begin with breathless claims about the brave new world of digital media. Nor do we commence with arguments pertaining to the digital native-hood of very young children. We know that for some people digital technologies are a source of anxiety and regret. Technologies may be viewed as threatening historically valued 'developmentally appropriate' approaches towards learning and as substituting virtual engagement for face to face interaction with adults and peers. Perhaps technologies are understood as encouraging inactivity and closing down experiential learning, collaborative problem-solving and creative engagement. Other people may well favour the power of digital technologies to extend children's horizons and communicative power and value the motivating influence of on-screen activities and the opportunities which they offer for person-alised leisure and sharing of digital media content. For some commentators digital technologies matter because they are part of the 21st century knowledge environ-ment (e.g. Parette, Quesenberry, & Blum, 2010). They argue that young learners have to acquire familiarity with using digital resources and the competencies that will allow them to enter and make good use of the knowledge economy afforded by evolving technological developments.

Discussion of these approaches is common enough now in the literature about young children and digital technologies. The justification for much of the inclusion and recognition of the digital in early years education increasingly comes from claims that the children of today live in a technological world and therefore must be educated and brought up to effectively use these technologies (e.g. Parette, Quesenberry, & Blum, 2010). While we sympathise with this form of justification, we also view this rationale as a somewhat superficial reason for including technolo-gies in the early years. Instead, we argue that it may be more productive to under-stand that a particular 'age', whether digital or not, will always contain within it the cultural-historically developed practices and technologies that characterise what people of that time period *do*. Young children playing and learning in a digital age is not about *including* technologies in the early years because children are now living in a technological world. Young children playing and learning in a digital age is about understanding what it is that people – both adults and children – *do with* technologies to communicate with each other, to be entertained, to create and share digital media and content, and even to make money. In avoiding dichotom-ised debates about the benefits and/or limitations of technologies for young chil-dren's play and learning in the digital age we try to circumvent the replication of what technological historian Colin Divall (2010) calls 'techno-tales'.

Beyond techno-tales

Techno-tales are the explanations people develop about technologies to account for what they see happening around them in society. In the seven years since the release of the iPad, early childhood as a sector, both educational and in the arena of 'parent-ing' literature has begun to develop its own series of techno-tales about young chil-dren and technologies. These tales already make somewhat familiar reading – as discussed by Plowman and McPake (2013) as a series of 'myths' about young chil-dren and technologies. 'Young children naturally learn to use technologies' is one such story. This story is captured in the popular catchphrase 'digital natives' as first proposed by Prensky (2001). In fact, the research of Stephen and colleagues shows that, while it seems children naturally learn to use technologies, the process of technological learning is clearly socially and culturally situated (e.g. Plowman, McPake, & Stephen, 2008; Stephen, Stevenson, & Adey, 2013). Children learn to use the technologies to which they are exposed in their family and community settings. The use to which they put these technologies relates to how they are applied by older family members and peers. Furthermore, social learning practices, that have gone on for generations, are evident in the learning process – parents, siblings and peers model technology use, actively scaffold children's developing technology skills, mediate access to newer technologies and digital media and explicitly teach children the skills required to operate given technologies.

Yet another techno-tale in the field of early childhood education is that 'young children get enough technologies at home – they don't need more of them in their early learning settings'. Again, there is research that speaks against this tale. Young children do not all equally experience access to technologies. Even where research shows that children across different socio-economic statuses have access to similar types of technologies – the practices to which these technologies are put clearly differ. Children from lower socio-economic groups tend to use technologies in ways that are orientated towards the consumption of digital media, whereas children in higher socio-economic groups access technologies for the generation of digital media, searching for information and communicating with families and friends (Harris, Straker, & Pollock, 2017; Yuen, Lau, Park, Lau, & Chan, 2016). Furthermore, newer research from Estonia (Nevski & Siibak, 2016) shows that parents of young children are noticing the discrepancy between home and centre technology access and beginning to question why digital technologies are not more frequently used in early childhood settings. Thus, while techno-tales may be a powerful way for us to make meaning from what we see happening with technologies in our lives, and the lives of very young children, they are not necessarily a grounded basis from which to think about and respond to young children's play and learning in a digital age.

So, if we are keen to avoid telling too many techno-tales in this book – on what do we base our thinking and writing that differs from existing available resources? The answer is two-fold. First, we draw on the cultural-historical argument regarding the cultural transformation of knowledge over time as shaping the developmental niche in which the children of any age, including the digital age, grow up. We understand this cultural knowledge to be most appropriately thought of as largely multidisciplinary in its construction and application to the innovations that characterise cultural transformation. We therefore consistently draw on multiple perspectives to inform our understanding of how young children play and learn in the digital age. Second, we maintain a critical perspective on the human relationship with technologies considering how and why technologies are used by people in context.

The cultural transformation of knowledge over time

Culture is an increasingly familiar term in writing about children's development in the early years. However, in the Western-European early childhood literature, culture was not commonly evident in the ideas pertaining to young children's learning and development during the 1900s. The post-developmental period in early childhood education, occurring in the late 1990s and early 2000s (Nolan & Kilderry, 2010), evidenced a shift in thinking about constructivist-developmental ideas about young children's learning away from accounts that were concerned with articulating a universal biologically or developmentally driven learning pattern to a strong focus on the role of culture in shaping young children's learning outcomes, and consequently the notion of culturally defined developmental expectations.

Sociocultural theory, particularly the cultural-historical tradition derived from the thinking of Vygotsky, is amongst the most dominant of culturally based ideas used in early childhood education. Vygotsky's (1997) central premise, the concept of cultural mediation, is a breathtakingly simple explanatory mechanism for understanding the relationship between people, activity and their sociocultural situation. Cultural mediation holds that all people (or the 'subject') typically have an object of activity with which they wish to engage. The achievement of any object of activity is obtained using a tool. Tools are culturally derived and can be physical or conceptual. Because tools are culturally derived they always have a history of development over time according to the context in which they have developed. Using a tool to master an object of activity leads to the achievement of a desired outcome which at the same time transforms the knowledge capacity of the subject. For example, a person uses a hammer to insert a hook into the wall because they wish to hang a picture. The hammer is the tool used to achieve the object of inserting the hook in the wall. The outcome is the successful hanging up of a picture. Having mastered the tool, the person is transformed in their capacity to realise a similar goal into the future. As a cultural tool the hammer has a 300-million-year-old history of development – beginning life as we know as a nicely shaped rock, prior to gaining a handle in 30,000 BC and in the Bronze Age being made of melted and harden metal. The historical development and transformative capacity of tools over time is a key concept in sociocultural theory because it attends to the *role of history in understanding the present*. History is always evident in the use of tools presently employed and therefore in the capacities of people to transform knowledge for current and future purposes. From a cultural-historical perspective, tools are not just physical tools – such as a hammer or a technological device like an iPad. Tools also comprise language and the concepts embedded in theoretical ways of thinking. As tools, language and concepts also develop over time within cultural communities, and in doing so transform the capabilities of people such that new innovations and ways of achieving different objects of activity and outcomes are achieved.

The historical evolution and transformative capacity of tools over time is one of the key reasons for framing this book within a concept of culture. To understand play and learning in the digital age we need to understand that culture is not a static experience. Rather, culture is always connected to the past and the past is always evident in the tools with which we engage in the present. In this book, the significance of this claim for young children's learning in a digital age emerges first within Chapter 2 when we examine the profound implications conceptual knowledge about solid state physics had on the emergence of the sheer range and capacity of technologies enabled by the consequent invention of the transistor which transformed human capabilities for the distribution of information via the microprocessor. In Chapter 3 we go on to explore the invention of the internet, and how conceptual knowledge regarding the connection of computer systems enabled the first forms of online communication. Also in Chapter 3, we reflect on the cultural thinking and values of the 1960s regarding freedom of access to information and how this thinking informed the later development of the World Wide Web. In examining from a cultural-historical perspective, these three knowledge components of: 1. solid state physics; 2. interconnected computing; and 3. access to information, we are able by the end of Chapter 3 to provide the background knowledge that helps us to better understand young children's play and learning in a digital age. This cultural-historical framing illustrates how the digital age fostered alternative patterns of communication amongst people, changing communication technologies from being primarily point to point (this being single-line telephony) to being predominately distributed (that is shared over the World Wide Web). The use of knowledge as a tool to achieve the objectives of technological innovation therefore led to new communicative outcomes – again, transforming human capabilities so that more information and knowledge could be shared with more people over time and space than had previously been possible. This is illustrated by contemporary communication through digital social media such as Facebook and Twitter which were in fact derived through the activity of applying and developing prior knowledge from a variety of fields to the object of communicating simultaneously with many people, as opposed to being restricted to sending messages to a single listener or reader.

New communicative processes and products are accompanied by new opportunities and practices and these novel ways of operating within a society require new kinds of knowledge and build expectations of what play and learning is required of the contemporary world. For example, the translation of the Bible into English, along with the advent of the printing press and agreement to distribute these new texts, is credited with advancing literacy in 16th and 17th-century England. This pattern of shifting towards mass or popular literacy as a result of the availability of new translations of biblical texts into home languages, driven by the desire to have independent and direct access to the scriptures, was replicated in many societies. As literacy became a more widespread capacity and mass communication through written texts became possible, a different status was conferred on those who could read over those who could not. Being able to read and write became a necessity for effective functioning in the culture of a society where information to be shared was written down and people were expected to access knowledge through written texts rather than through inherited practices and oral traditions.

In recent times, as we explain in Chapters 2 and 3, prior to the advent of the World Wide Web children were taught the fundamentals of reading, writing and talking that enabled them to engage in what was then primarily point-to-point information exchange. Prior to the digital age, people would talk directly to each other, tended to read material intended for one main audience, and if writing, would typically write to one person (e.g. a letter) or for one identified audience (e.g. attendees at a particular lecture or readers on a specified topic). Distributive patterns of communication made possible by the World Wide Web mean that young children today do not need to master point-to-point communication in exactly the same way as they have previously – rather they need to acquire the skills required for distributed communication. Reading and writing are still necessary skills, but so is the capacity to create content that can be shared online and to access and understand material 'posted' and distributed on the web. Here the popularity of child-created digital channels on YouTube Kids in which children themselves narrate and record episodes for consumption and commentary by peers from around the world is an example in which interests as widely drawn as Baby Alive through to Playdough are shared daily. In Chapter 4, we cite the cultural-historical theorist Bert van Oers (2008), who beautifully sums up the cultural-historical pattern of knowledge development, and the way in which historical patterns of knowledge shape the current context and therefore the play and learning requirements of any given generation:

> [W]e can maintain that learning is indeed transformed during cultural history in accordance with the prevailing psychological, epistemological, and scientific points of view, in accordance with pedagogical, sociological, and cultural views on the child and its position in the world. So it is not only the descriptions that change but also the process of learning itself.
>
> (p. 7)

Thus, the notion of 'culture', understood as the way in which a group of people act, express ideas, share values and communicate, offers an explanatory mechanism for understanding young children's play and learning in the digital age. In this book, instead of focusing on how to use or 'integrate' technologies in early childhood education, we will consider the historical transformation of knowledge informing the range of technological innovations that shape the cultural context for young children today. Thus far we have attended principally to the transformative aspect of culture as expressed over time, and within the current generation in terms of the available tools that shape consequent practices. However, our thinking is not only concerned with accounting for the past but also with implications for the future of this dynamic process of cultural change and innovation.

To examine the dynamic nature of culture we draw on the ideas of cultural theorist Raymond Williams. Williams (1958) was influenced in his thinking about culture by the work of Vygotsky. Williams (1958) famously argued that 'culture is ordinary' (p. 10). By ordinary, he meant that culture comprises the purpose and meanings of people engaged within a community that gives rise to society. Much like Vygotsky, Williams (1958) understood the relationship between people and culture as dialectically related:

> Every human society has its own shape, its own purposes, its own meanings. Every human society expresses these, in institutions, and in arts and learning. The making of a society is the finding of common meanings and directions, and its growth is an active debate and amendment under the pressures of experiences, contact, and discovery, writing themselves into the land. The growing society is there, yet is also made and remade in every individual mind. The making of mind, is first, the slow learning of shapes, purposes, and meanings, so that work, observation and communication are possible. Then, second, but equal in importance, is the testing of these in experiences, the making of new observations, comparisons and meanings.
>
> *(p. 11)*

The making and remaking of society within the individual and the consequent making of new cultural meaning by the individual is powerfully told in this book in the story that is the invention of the iPad. At the beginning of this chapter, we noted that the iPad seemingly arrived in the midst of the early years from nowhere. The cultural-historical research we conducted for this book shows that this is not the case. The iPad did not suddenly land in the lives of young children, their educators and families from nowhere. By taking a cultural-historical perspective on young children's play and learning in the digital age, we are able to show in Chapters 2 and 4 of this book that the invention of the iPad has a history very closely tied to the theories and philosophies of play and learning used in early childhood education for over 100 years.

Prior to the 2010 release of the iPad, tablet computing already had a history of development, beginning in the early 1970s with the work of a computer scientist called Alan Kay. Kay (1972) proposed a personal computer for every child, that in effect was portable, had a built-in keyboard, would be connected to inter-networked information sites and allow children to be actively involved in driving their own learning through guided exploration with adults. Kay's (1972) computer was called the 'DynaBook'. In developing the DynaBook concept Kay was heavily influenced by his reading of key works in the early years, including those by Bruner, Dewey, Montessori, Piaget and Vygotsky. In fact, the paper in which Kay (1972) outlines his DynaBook concept directly cites the work of these theorists.

In 1984 Kay joined Steve Jobs, the founder of Apple computers and inventor of the iPad, as an Apple Fellow. The 'makings of society' under the 'pressures of experiences, contact, and discovery' so described by Williams (1958), were made and remade by Kay in the evolution of the theoretical and philosophical ideas of Bruner, Dewey, Montessori, Piaget and Vygotsky – thus giving rise to his Dyna-Book. Later the collaboration between Kay and Jobs was to continue this story of making and remaking. Here, the individual learning of the 'purpose and meanings of society' (Williams, 1958), such that these can be re-offered in 'the making of new observations, comparisons and meanings' (Williams, 1958) was applied by Jobs through his collaboration with Kay in the ultimate invention of the iPad. The cultural stance on young children's play and learning in the digital age that we take in this book has led us to argue for a new interpretation of the rapid and enthusiastic adoption of tablet technologies in early childhood contexts (at home and in educational settings). We suggest that the iPad appeals to children and meets their developmental needs because its historical development is located in the theory and thinking that has informed generations of early childhood teachers and researchers.

In this way, the cultural-historical interpretation of the iPad we offer in this book helps to attend to some of the many concerns or 'techno-tales' expressed about using technologies, such as tablet computers with young children. Chief amongst these concerns is the worry that technologies take children away from the hands-on exploratory tasks of 'real-world' activity considered necessary to promote learning and development. Instead, tablet technologies may be effectively reconsidered as a cultural product of thinking about young children's learning that capitalises on technological innovations in micro-processing and touchscreen interfaces transformed by people over time. As Williams (1958) so aptly described 'Culture is ordinary, in every society and in every mind' (p. 23).

Culture as a base concept for driving forth our understanding about the digital age provides an additional benefit for our thinking and writing beyond that enabled by a consideration of what the past offers our interpretations of the present. Culture as a concept encompasses knowledge. Knowledge, in any given culture is not only historically comprised, but simultaneously directed towards the problem of engaging with complex situations in order to solve a problem or to reach a conclusion, a decision of some type, a framework for thinking or understanding. Knowledge thus understood, responds to what Williams (1958) describes as 'an extreme diversity of situation, in a high and moving tension'. At any point in time, people are likely to face some type of complex situation – such as that with which we engage in this book – the problem of better understanding young children's play and learning in the digital age. Frameworks for thinking are, for Williams (1958), 'as diverse as our starting points'. Thus cultural knowledge itself requires multiplicity otherwise people will have no means with which to respond to the range of situations in which they find themselves at any given point in time. One set of knowledge will not necessarily be adequate for dealing with the diverse starting points of any of our problem situations. Thus we turn to the second idea informing this book – that of multidisciplinarity, this being the idea that more than one area of disciplinary knowledge can be used to inform thinking about complex situations.

Multidisciplinarity

Young children playing and learning in the digital age is not a simple topic. As we have already canvassed in this introduction, multiple forms of knowledge have been brought to bear on the tools and concepts that gave rise to the digital age in the first instance. For example, we have talked of solid state physics, of theories of learning and development and, quite broadly, of 'technologies'. In this book we consequently draw on a range of disciplines 'placing them relationally to deepen our understanding' (Brooker & Edwards, 2010) of young children's play and learning in the digital age. Multidisciplinary knowledge is increasingly considered appropriate for dealing with the social and cultural complexities of a field such as education (McCarty, Mancevice, Lemire, & O'Neil, 2017). In Chapter 4, we explore the significance of multidisciplinary knowledge for the early childhood sector by returning to the writing of Brooker and Edwards (2010) in the Introduction to their book *Engaging Play*. In this book Brooker and Edwards used the idea of Mode 1 and Mode 2 knowledge as proposed by Nowotny, Scott, and Gibbons (2001) to explain the application of multiple forms of knowledge to the complexity of problems in situated contexts. Mode 1 knowledge, according to this line of argument, focuses on the incremental development of knowledge in a specific field over time. Mode 2 knowledge, in contrast, brings different forms of knowledge to bear on a problem situation to better understand and respond to the contextual demands creating or shaping the situation in the first instance. Brooker and Edwards (2010) argued that Mode 2 knowledge was an appropriate means for scholars and teachers to engage in thinking about play as it reduced the typical reliance on a single definition or way of thinking about the role of play in the learning of very young children.

In this book, we likewise draw on multiple disciplines around the common cause of thinking about young children playing and learning in the digital age. For this book, which engages a cultural-historical perspective on knowledge, we have been exposed in our research to a range of diverse knowledge fields that collectively feed into our understanding of young children playing and learning in the digital age. Our reading and research has taken us to the field of computing science so that we could better understand the historical development of the technologies children of today use. From an examination of computer science, we found our way to solid state physics needing to comprehend how this form of knowledge contributed to the range of technologies now used in our daily lives. From computing science we have necessarily considered the sociological implications of the knowledge society, and from here we have engaged with key ideas in the philosophical realm of thought known as the theories of technology – a body of work that seeks to position or describe the relationship between people and technologies in society over time (Webster, 2017).

As we move through the various chapters of this book we continue to draw on multiple knowledge domains to frame our thinking about children's play and learning in the digital age for the consequent chapters. Here, in Chapters 6, 7 and 8 we draw on ideas from the fields of media studies, the Learning Sciences and cultural studies to better appreciate the nature of children's play and learning in the digital age – how, where, why and with whom do young children normally use technologies? In our writing of both the earlier and later chapters, we typically flag the discipline area from which our various references to multiple fields of knowledge derives. We cite the work of key theorists from those fields and explain the contribution we see their work making to our understanding of young children playing and learning in the digital age. However, from the range of disciplines that we draw on in this book, we understand two to be of particular use for understanding young children's play and learning in the digital age. These are the theories of technology and the Learning Sciences.

Theories of technology

Attempts to theorise technology are infrequently referenced in discussions about young children's play and learning in the digital age. A notable exception is the work of Gibbons (2010) who argues that theories of technology should be inscribed in all considerations of young children's play and learning in a digital age. This is because theories of technology consider the relationship between people and technologies in society. An absence of theory pertaining to technology, so argues Gibbons, leaves early childhood researchers and teachers in a philosophical vacuum – an engaged understanding of the role and use of technologies by young children in the digital age is not possible if we have not first considered our relationship with technologies. We note here that we ourselves are guilty in our own published work of lacking a strong theoretical grounding in thinking about technology (e.g. Edwards, 2014; Stephen & Plowman, 2008). While our own research has been strongly located in theories of learning and development, we, like other researchers and scholars in the area of early learning with technologies, have not necessarily made explicit our stance regarding the relationship between people and technologies. Thus in this book, we draw to our own attention some of the key thinking associated with theories of technology.

Broadly speaking, theories of technology encompass three main bodies of thought. The first body of thought describes technologies as responsible for generating social change. As new technologies are invented, they cause change in social practices. This vein of thinking is described as technological determinism (Dafoe, 2015). For example, a type of technological determinism commonly cited today is that the iPad has caused an increase in the amount of screen time experienced by young children with associated increases in sedentary behaviour leading to weight gain. As the new form of technology, the iPad is viewed as 'determining' new social practices, such as increased levels of sedentary behaviour which in turn generate social change manifest in increased levels of childhood obesity. When we live in a society in which technologies are used and invented, it is easy for us to see how technologies seem to drive change in social practices. Marx and Smith (1994) argue that a tendency of the technological determinist orientation is to describe a relationship between the appearance of a technology and a change in social practices. For example, in our own lifetime, we have seen the invention of the mobile telephone. We can ascribe changes in social conditions and practices directly to this technological invention, such that it seems the mobile phone itself has determined new ways of being. Technological determinism may lead us to think that it is the technology that has forced a change from talk to texts, or changes in the ways that news is shared and in the content that is shared by using Facebook on a smartphone or the substantial decline in the sales of cameras as we rely on our mobile phones to take and store photographs. This perspective of technological determinism attends to the social consequences of the technology and not necessarily the cultural-historical genesis of the innovation itself (Marx & Smith, 1994, p. xiii). And while such a view acknowledges the role of material objects in behaviours and outcomes it does not consider the values, motives and practices that adults and children bring to the technology–human nexus.

The second body of thought is that represented by a substantive view of technologies. The substantive theory of technology attributes a particular value to technologies. A technology may be valued because it helps people attend to mundane tasks or increases efficiency. The value attributed to a technology informs the extent to which it is used in society. Heidegger (1954), the most significant of substantive technology theorists, argues that as technologies are used by people they shape our cultural systems. As cultural systems are shaped by technologies people lose sight of the technologies per se and begin to operate within those systems without necessarily thinking about the technology any more. There are many examples of the substantive view in practice: for example, the use of technologies to automate daily tasks such as using a washing machine, banking using an automated teller machine or cooking with a microwave oven. On a daily basis, these technologies shape the cultural systems of being clean, obtaining money or cooking – yet the technologies themselves are not necessarily noticed as the driving agents of the system itself. We simply think 'I am doing the washing' or 'I will go to the teller machine to withdraw some cash'. Our focus in these instances is on what technologies allow us to do in much the same way as we think about that ubiquitous invention of an earlier age – the car – without considering the processes of a combustion engine.

The third way of thinking about technology takes a critical perspective. Critical theory of technology contrasts with technological determinism because it does not see technologies in terms of social cause and effect. Like the substantive view, the critical view accepts that technologies are value laden. As people, we attribute a value of some kind or another to any given technology. We see this attribution of values occurring in early childhood education all the time, for instance when plain wooden blocks are chosen over brightly coloured plastic or when in early years settings traditional retellings of fairy stories are preferred over Disney cartoon versions. This recourse to value positions is particularly evident in the moral panic about children's technology use. Computers, for example, are described as 'bad' for children's social development or as 'good' for promoting problem solving. However, unlike substantive views of technology, critical theory characterises a greater degree of human agency in relation to the use of technologies in society. Here, the idea is that people engage with technologies and the invention of technologies according to 'purposes and practices already in mind' (Williams, 2004, p. 7). A critical view, directing our attention to a more humanely agentic relationship with technologies emphasises that the known 'purposes and practices' to which we put the use of technologies are 'not marginal but central' (Williams, 2004, p. 7). A critical view of technology therefore highlights that technologies do not suddenly arrive into a social situation and cause change. Nor do technologies necessarily always sink from our view and come to shape our cultural practices. From a critical perspective, technologies always come from somewhere, are informed by intended social needs and purposes and hold humanely ascribed values.

We believe that the critical view holds potential for those researchers and teachers occupied with early childhood education. It offers an empowering means of thinking about young children's play and learning in a digital age. This is because the critical view acknowledges technologies in context and technologies in context concern the historical development of technologies as the transformative expression of cultural knowledge. From a critical perspective, teachers or researchers are able to consider what knowledge transformation in relation to technologies means for how and why current and future generations of children engage with the digital resources of their time.

The Learning Sciences

The Learning Sciences is not a widely used term in the field of early childhood education. As far as we are aware, this body of knowledge has not previously been used in systematic thinking about young children's play and learning in the digital age. In Chapter 4, we detail how the Learning Sciences evolved as a discipline area in its own right in response to the complexities facing researchers and teachers providing educational opportunities for older learners (primary, secondary and tertiary-aged) in the digital age. Ideas about teaching and learning previously used in the industrial age, such as behaviourism or direct instruction, were increasingly considered inadequate for teaching and learning in an age in which multiple forms of knowledge access and representation were being made available to students globally. Following the logic of multidisciplinarity, the Learning Sciences accepts that no one description is adequate for explaining how people learn. Instead, the Learning Sciences draws on multiple disciplines, including those of constructivism, social constructivism, educational technology, sociology, computing science, neuroscience and knowledge work to articulate core explanations for how learning is achieved. Many of these core explanations are likely to be very familiar to readers of the early childhood literature, including as they do ideas about building from the existing knowledge base of learners and highlighting the role of social interactions in fostering learning.

Central to the notion of the Learning Sciences is the emphasis paid to the idea of *sciences*. In Chapter 4, we explain how Kalantzis and Cope (2014) direct attention to what is meant by the idea of sciences. Explaining that science derives from the Latin 'sciens' or 'to know', Kalantzis and Cope (2014) argue that the Learning Sciences is not about learning as hard science. Rather, the focus is on knowing more about learning. The Learning Sciences is therefore orientated towards understanding as much as we can about learning. In this book we explore the idea that Alan Kay, the inventor of the DynaBook, may have been amongst the most original of Learning Scientists. This is because his ideas were located in the cultural-historical knowledge he held of both technologies (e.g. the potentiality for the forthcoming touchscreen technology) and core learning theory, including the ideas of Bruner, Dewey, Montessori, Piaget and Vygotsky. Kay's (2013) DynaBook was a technology he viewed as capable of amplifying the possibilities for learning. From his acknowledged concern to address children's learning as a social need and the value he ascribed to the possibility of amplifying cognitive capacities, Kay's understanding of learning in relation to technology prompts us in the rest of the book to consider from a critical perspective the 'central purposes and practices' (Williams, 2004, p. 7) of young children's play and learning in the digital age. In Chapters 6, 7 and 8 we therefore consider the empirical literature about young children's play and learning with technologies in their families and communities, questions of equity and the access young children have to technologies, and importantly, the relationship between the social and cultural contexts in which children are playing and learning with technologies.

Conclusion

This book is arranged in three broad sections that follow the development of our thinking about the value of a cultural and critical perspective on young children's play and learning in the digital age. Part I offers a cultural-historical understanding of the transformation of knowledge over time and of the technological innovations afforded by evolving knowledge. Here too we raise the possibility of adopting a critical perspective on the current and future relationship between people and technologies. In Part II we consider the knowledge resources and ways of thinking about play and learning on which we can draw to enable a cultural and critical perspective on the digital age. Part III focuses on empirical studies of the contemporary experiences of young children growing up in the digital age, employing our cultural and critical approach to explore the nature of the practices involved in engaging with technologies in the early years and the purposes and outcomes of these encounters.

The book concludes with Chapter 9 in which we review our argument for a cultural and critical perspective on young children's play and learning for the digital age. In this articulation, we extend our thinking about the benefits of a cultural-historical understanding of technological change and the value of a critical stance for contemporary responses to these changes by making a case for the transformation of the knowledge base informing early years research, policy and pedagogy. We suggest that new knowledge, informed by a cultural and critical perspective, is needed by the sector so that our knowledge base for young children's play and learning is transformed alongside the knowledge innovations shaping the developmental niche in which the young children of today are growing up.

References

Arnott, L. (2016). An ecological exploration of young children's digital play: framing young children's social experiences with technologies in early childhood. *Early Years*, *36*(3), 271–288.

Berson, I., Berson, M., & McGlinn Manfra, M. (2012). Touch, type, and transform: iPads in the social studies classroom. *Social Education*, *76*(2), 88–91.

Beschorner, B., & Hutchison, A. (2013). iPads as a literacy teaching tool in early childhood. *International Journal of Education in Mathematics, Science and Technology*, *1*(1), 16–24.

Brooker, E., & Edwards, S. (2010). *Engaging play*. Maidenhead: Open University Press.

Buckingham, D. (1993). Introduction: young people and the media. In D. Buckingham (Ed.), *Young people and the media* (pp. 1–24). Manchester: Manchester University Press.

Chang, J., Rakowsky, C., & Frost, M. (2013, 1 April). Toddlers obsessed with iPads: could it hurt their development? *ABC News*. Retrieved from http://abcnews.go.com/Health/toddlers-obsessed-ipads-hurt-development/story?id=18855537.

Clements, D. H., & Sarama, J. (2002). The role of technology in early childhood learning. *Teaching Children Mathematics*, *8*(6), 340.

Cocozza, P. (2014). Are iPads and tablets bad for children? *Guardian*. Retrieved from www.theguardian.com/society/2014/jan/08/are-tablet-computers-bad-young-children.

Collins, A., & Halverson, R. (2009). *Rethinking education in the age of technology: the digital revolution and schooling in America*. New York, NY: Teachers College Press.

Cordes, C., & Miller, E. (2000). *Fool's gold: a critical look at computers in childhood*. College Park, MD: Alliance for Childhood.

Dafoe, A. (2015). On technological determinism: a typology, scope conditions, and a mechanism. *Science, Technology, & Human Values*, *40*(6), 1047–1076.

Divall, C. (2010). Mobilising the history of technology. *Technology and Culture*, *51*(4), 938–960.

Edwards, S. (2003). New directions: charting the paths for the role of sociocultural theory in early childhood education and curriculum. *Contemporary Issues in Early Childhood*, *4*(3), 251–266.

Edwards, S. (2013). Digital play in the early years: a contextual response to the problem of integrating digital technologies and play-based learning in the early childhood curriculum. *European Early Childhood Education Research Journal*, *21*(2), 199–212.

Edwards, S. (2014). Towards contemporary play: sociocultural theory and the digital-consumerist context. *Journal of Early Childhood Research*, *12*(3), 219–233.

Edwards, S. (2015). New concepts of play and the problem of technology, digital media and popular-culture integration with play-based learning in early childhood education. *Technology, Pedagogy and Education*, *25*(4), 513–532.

Gibbons, A. (2010). Reflections concerning technology: a case for the philosophy of technology in early childhood teacher education and professional development programs. In S. Izumi-Taylor & S. Blake (Eds.), *Technology for early childhood education and socialization: developmental applications and methodologies* (pp. 1–19). Hershey, NY: IGI Global.

Greenhow, C., Robelia, B., & Hughes, J. E. (2009). Learning, teaching, and scholarship in a digital age Web 2.0 and classroom research: What path should we take now? *Educational Researcher*, *38*(4), 246–259.

Harris, C., Straker, L., & Pollock, C. (2017). A socioeconomic related 'digital divide' exists in how, not if, young people use computers. *PloS One*, *12*(3), e0175011. doi: 10.1371/journal.pone.0175011.

Haugland, S. W. (2000). What role should technology play in young children's learning? Part 2. Early childhood classrooms in the 21st century: using computers to maximize learning. *Young Children*, *55*(1), 12–18.

Heidegger, M. (1954). The question concerning technology. *Technology and Values: Essential Readings*, 99–113.

Kalantzis, M., & Cope, B. (2014). Education is the new philosophy to make a metadisciplinary claim for the Learning Sciences. In A. D. Reid (Ed.), *A companion to Research in Education* (pp. 3–13). Dordrecht, Netherlands: Springer.

Kay, A. C. (1972, August). A personal computer for children of all ages. In *Proceedings of the ACM annual conference – Volume 1* (p. 1). ACM.

Kay, A. (2013). The future of reading depends on the future of learning difficult to learn things. In B. Junge, Z. Berzina, W. Scheiffele, W. Westerveld, & C. Zwick (Eds.), *The digital turn: design in the era of interactive technologies.* Chicago: University of Chicago Press.

Marsh, J. (2004). The techno-literacy practices of young children. *Journal of Early Childhood Research*, 2(1), 51–66.

Marsh, J., Brooks, G., Hughes, J., Ritchie, L., Roberts, S., & Wright, K. (2005). *Digital beginnings: young children's use of popular culture, media and new technologies.* Literacy Research Centre: University of Sheffield.

Marx, L., & Smith, M. (1994). Introduction. In M. Smith & L. Marx (Eds.), *Does technology drive history: the dilemma of technological determinism* (pp. ix–xv). Cambridge, MA: MIT Press.

McCarty, T. L., Mancevice, N., Lemire, S., & O'Neil, H. F. (2017). Introduction: education research for a new century: a renewed vision of interdisciplinarity. *American Educational Research Journal*, 54(Suppl. 1), 5S–22S. doi: 10.3102/0002831216687340.

Nevski, E., & Siibak, A. (2016). The role of parents and parental mediation on 0–3-year old's digital play with smart devices: Estonian parents' attitudes and practices. *Early Years*, 36(3), 227–241.

Nikolopoulou, K., & Gialamas, V. (2015). ICT and play in preschool: early childhood teachers' beliefs and confidence. *International Journal of Early Years Education*, 23(4), 409–425.

Nolan, A., & Kilderry, A. (2010). Post developmentalism and professional learning: implications for understanding the relationship between play and learning. In E. Brooker & S. Edwards (Eds.), *Engaging play* (pp. 108–122). Maidenhead: Open University Press.

Nowotny, H., Scott, P., & Gibbons, M. (2001). *Rethinking science: knowledge and the public in an age of uncertainty.* Cambridge, MA: Polity Press.

Palaiologou, I. (2016). Teachers' dispositions towards the role of digital devices in play-based pedagogy in early childhood. *Early Years*, 36(3), 305–321. doi: 10.1080/09575146. 2016.1174816.

Parette, H. P., Quesenberry, A. C., & Blum, C. (2010). Missing the boat with technology usage in early childhood settings: a 21st century view of developmentally appropriate practice. *Early Childhood Education Journal*, 37(5), 335–343.

Plowman, L., & McPake, J. (2013). Seven myths about young children and technology. *Childhood Education*, 89(1), 27–33.

Plowman, L., McPake, J., & Stephen, C. (2008). Just picking it up? Young children learning with technology at home. *Cambridge Journal of Education*, 38(3), 303–319.

Plowman, L., & Stephen, C. (2005). Children, play and computers in pre-school settings. *British Journal of Educational Technology*, 36(2), 145–157.

Prensky, M. (2001). Digital natives, digital immigrants. *On the Horizon*, 9(5), 1–6.

Romeo, G., Edwards, S., McNamara, S., Walker, I., & Ziguras, C. (2003). Touching the screen: issues associated with the use of touch screen technology in early childhood education. *British Journal of Educational Technology*, 34(3), 329–341.

Stephen, C., & Plowman, L. (2008). Enhancing learning with information and communication technologies in pre-school. *Early Child Development and Care*, 178(6), 637–654.

Stephen, C., Stevenson, O., & Adey, C. (2013). Young children engaging with technologies at home: the influence of family context. *Journal of Early Childhood Research, 11*(2), 149–164.

van Oers, B. (2008). Learning and learning theory from a cultural-historical point of view. In B. van Oers, W. Wardekker, E. Elbers, & R. van der Veer (Eds.), *The transformation of learning: Advances in cultural-historical theory* (pp. 3–15). Cambridge, UK: Cambridge University Press.

Vygotsky, L. S. (1997). *The collected works of LS Vygotsky. Vol. 4, The history of the development of higher mental functions.* R. Rieber (Ed.). New York: Plenum Press.

Webster, M. D. (2017). Philosophy of technology assumptions in educational technology leadership. *Educational Technology & Society, 20*(1), 25–36.

Williams, R. (1958). Culture is ordinary. In J. Higgins (Ed.) (2001), *The Raymond Williams reader* (pp. 10–25). Oxford: Blackwell.

Williams, R. (2004). *Television: technology and cultural form.* Abingdon, Oxon: Taylor and Francis.

Yelland, N. (2005). The future is now: a review of the literature on the use of computers in early childhood education (1994–2004). *AACE Journal, 13*(3), 201–232.

Yuen, A. H., Lau, W. W., Park, J. H., Lau, G. K., & Chan, A. K. (2016). Digital equity and students' home computing: a Hong Kong study. *The Asia-Pacific Education Researcher, 25*(4), 509–518.

Zevenbergen, R. (2007). Digital natives come to preschool: implications for early childhood practice. *Contemporary Issues in Early Childhood, 8*(1), 19–29.

PART I

The evolution of the digital age

In this first section of *Young Children Playing and Learning in a Digital Age: a Cultural and Critical Perspective* we explore the evolution of the digital age, paying attention to the key knowledge ideas informing technological innovation and the social and cultural contexts in which these innovations in understanding developed. Chapter 2 is primarily concerned with knowledge changes that informed the development of microprocessors and enabled the consequent human capacity for digitalisation. This is also the chapter where we consider the practical and theoretical understandings that led to the development of tablet computing early in the 21st century. Chapter 2 concludes with the introduction of the societal theorising that informed the shift from what was understood as the industrial age to what is now known as the digital age. The technological advances reviewed in Chapter 3 build on the advances outlined in Chapter 2 for building computer-to-computer connectivity, instant global communications, mass participation and consumption of media production and the embedding of connected devices in everyday objects and locations.

2

A HISTORY OF KNOWLEDGE TRANSFORMATIONS AND TECHNOLOGICAL INNOVATION

Introduction

In this chapter we provide an account of the evolution of the digital age and in the chapter that follows we look at the development of a distinct characteristic of that age, the changes in communication and information sharing that have accompanied the development of the internet, the World Wide Web and spreadable media. Typically, writing concerned with young children and technologies does not invest time and effort in understanding the history of the digital age. However, the grounding of this book in the notion of 'culture' as outlined in the Introduction highlights that culture is both temporal and dynamic. Sociocultural theory tells us that the past is always in the present (Davydov, 1982). To make sense of the experience of children playing and learning in the digital age and what growing up in this new age requires of supportive adults we contend that a basic historical frame of reference is required.

While located in a temporal definition of culture, this chapter is also multidisciplinary in its informants. To explain the historical evolution of the digital age we necessarily draw on knowledge from solid state physics, computing science, sociology and history. We commence with a brief definition of the term 'digital age'. We then turn to developments in physics for an account of the innovative thinking that informed the invention of the transistor, an innovation fundamental to what we now think of as the digital age. We move between physics and computer science to consider the consequent development of the microprocessor and the ways in which this technology drove forth developments in the miniaturisation of computing and developments in the person/technology interface. Finally we turn to sociology, in particular the contributions of two key sociologists, Daniel Bell (1976) from America and Yoneji Masuda (1980) from Japan, to understand the relationship between technologies and the dawning of the new information or digital age. Along the way, at various points in this chapter we reflect on the dimensions of play and learning required of children in different cultural and temporal eras.

The account we provide of the evolution of the digital age in this chapter identifies three significant changes in cultural knowledge and understanding. These are:

- Advances in scientific understanding harnessed for the enhancement of communication processes.
- Increases in the capacity to gather, store and share information derived from the innovative process of digitisation.
- Playing and learning in the digital age is informed by a disposition towards exploration, knowledge generation and re-generation.

What is the digital age?

The 'digital age' represents a way of thinking about a complex new period of time in human history. Broadly speaking, the digital age is differentiated from two earlier periods of time. The first period, known as the agricultural age, dawned approximately 10,000 years ago and focuses on the use of farming tools to capitalise food production, such as growing wheat or rice. The second, known as the industrial age, occurred as little as 300 years ago. The industrial age saw the application of machinery to raw materials in the production of new goods, as seen in the new capacity to mass produce textiles or fabricate metals. Culturally speaking, movement from one age to another is characterised by the application of new knowledge to existing systems of activity such that new technologies are developed. As new technologies are created, the 'purposes and practices' (Williams, 2004, p. 7) to which they may be put are examined, considered and implemented by people. Alongside technological implementation occurs adjustment in social and cultural systems of activity generating new forms of communication and patterns of work, as seen for instance when factory production rapidly replaced small-scale craft workplaces during the 19th century in England. These shifts to new forms of communication and patterns of work are evident in the learning (e.g. education), leisure, economic and environmental practices of any given society. At the same time, reshaped practices highlight consideration of the values that will be (or are) attributed to the newly emerging technologies. Are these technologies seen as harbingers of a brave new world of opportunity? Or do they challenge all the previous ways of 'being' or practising in a society such that people feel confused or displaced by cultural change or even drawn to acts of resistance such as those exercised by the Luddites who feared for their livelihoods as cotton and woollen mills developed in the early 19th century?

Solid state physics, conductivity and enhanced communications

Solids state physics is the new knowledge that informed the development of the digital age. Solid state physics began to be studied in the early 1940s as a sub-field of condensed state physics. Condensed state physics studies the properties of matter in solids. Solid state physics seeks to understand the electromagnetic and structural properties of matter. This is achieved by examining how atoms in different materials move by working out the influence of heat on levels of atom movement. Einstein (1907) showed that the expected level of energy in a given material could be determined according to a particular temperature. This is known as quantum mechanics (Sanchez-Ron, 1994). Einstein's idea was important because it meant that physicists could determine the range of movement that would occur within the atoms of a given material according to the amount of heat applied. This meant people of the time knew how to manipulate the matter of solid materials to achieve movement in them at the atomic level. Solid state physics gave rise to solid state electronics – a field of research investigating the electromagnetic properties of metals. Here knowledge of how heat influenced atom movement in different metals, and in conductors of electricity (e.g. germanium and silicon) was a particular focus of attention. The 21st century phenomenon of Silicon Valley, home to global technology companies such as Apple, Facebook and Google, evolved from these advances in knowledge about the conduct of electricity through different forms of matter.

This summation of solid state physics and its contribution to solid state electronics does very little justice to the breadth and novelty of Einstein's (1907) thinking about matter. Yet we provide it here, to illustrate the nature of the claim we made in the introduction to this book – that culture, and the historical developing nature of knowledge over time within a culture, serves to shape the practices of consequent generations – in terms of knowledge itself, and in the application of knowledge to the evolution of new technologies. Writing in 1951, the well-known and often controversial cultural theorist, Marshall McLuhan wrote of the attention being paid at the time to solid state physics. Pre-empting the emergence of the digital age, he described how knowledge innovation in this area would become embedded into society in the years to come:

> Physics are not a fad. They have provided new facts about the world, new intelligibility, new insights into the universal fabric. Practically speaking, they mean henceforth this planet is a single city. Far from making for irrationalism, these discoveries make irrationalism intolerable for the intelligent person. They demand much greater exertions of intelligence and a much higher level of personal and social integrity than have existed previously.
>
> (McLuhan, 1951, p. 3)

Solid state electronics was a new field of physics in which the knowledge McLuhan (1951) described as providing 'new facts about the world' was applied to the development of materials that were capable of conducting electricity. Research into solid state electronics began to boom in the early 1950s following the end of World War II and it is the application of this new knowledge to meet the desire for improved communication processes that is most significant for the evolution of the digital age. During World War II, communication systems had undergone advancement, but at this time mostly relied on what were called vacuum tube amplifiers. Vacuum tubes were used in tele-communication systems to amplify sound. The problem with these tubes was that they needed a great deal of heat to operate them, but at the same time the tubes did not last for very long at high temperatures. This meant that existing telephone systems were unreliable and unstable because the very heat needed to operate the vacuum tubes eventually destroyed them. Despite this problem, the very first transatlantic cable capable of carrying telephone conversations was established between America and Europe in 1956 by placing vacuum tubes every 70 kilometres along a cable from America to Europe.

Although this was a remarkable feat of transatlantic communication, the limits of vacuum tube technology had been reached and new technologies were required to support communication systems. Meanwhile, in America the Bell Telephone Company, founded in 1877 by the inventor of the telephone, Alexander Graham Bell, was moving towards increased investment in solid state electronics. In 1945, the Bell Telephone Company (later to be called the American Telephone and Telegraph Company or 'AT&T') established a new industrial research laboratory directed to this effort. Mervin Kelly, the Vice President of the company at the time, established a directive that:

> All research activity in the area of solids is now being consolidated in order to achieve a unified approach to theoretical and experimental work in the solid state area ... for obtaining new knowledge that can be used in the development of completely new and improved components of communication systems.
>
> *(Gertner, 2012; cited in Hopfield, 2014, p. 3)*

The new Bell Laboratory and Mervin Kelly's directive set the scene for the birth of the transistor – a powerful new electronic component that would facilitate later development of the microprocessor that gave rise to communicative computing. This is because the microprocessor is the technology that enables information to be digitised, a key activity for the digital age. As microprocessors became increasingly powerful, more and more innovative communication technologies evolved. The uptake of these technologies by people (initially in the area of industry and commerce and then in the domestic sphere), later came to inform the nature of the digital world now occupied by the young children of today. This includes the advances in touchscreen technologies that we described in Chapter 1 of this book as literally putting computing at the fingertips of babies, toddlers and preschoolers.

The transistor, microprocessor and digitising information

In 1946 three researchers, William Shockley, Walter Brattain and John Bardeen, under the direction of Mervin Kelly at the Bell Laboratories, focused their attention on developing a new electronic component to increase the range and reliability of existing telephone communication systems. This new component would be called the 'transistor'. Shockley led the research group, but worked chiefly at home on his own, while Brattain and Bardeen established a close working relationship in the lab.

Brattain and Bardeen went on to create the very first basic transistor using strips of gold that made contact with an element called germanium. Germanium had been established during World War II as a 'semi-conductor' meaning that it could transmit electricity. The first transistor was able to conduct electricity from one point to another and was therefore called the 'point-contact transistor'. Shockley was frustrated by the advance his colleagues had made in the invention of the point-contact transistor without his direct contribution. While Brattain and Bardeen were busy completing the patent application for their point-contact transistor he immediately set about inventing a new type of transistor based on their findings which he called the 'sandwich transistor'. The sandwich transistor was more robust than the one invented by Brattain and Bardeen because it literally 'sandwiched' a base metal between two levels of silicon as the semiconductor.

Shortly after it was developed by Shockley, the invention of the sandwich transistor was announced by the Bell Laboratory at a press conference on 30 June 1948. For an invention that would later come to reshape the face of worldwide patterns of communication, the announcement attracted little attention. Brinkman, Haggan, and Troutman (1997) in their paper 'A history of the invention of the transistor and where it will lead us' wrote of the announcement:

> It is interesting to note that the impact of this discovery went on deaf ears as far as the public was concerned. The *New York Times* carried a very small article on a back page and did not have too much else to say about it. In some sense that is understandable. It is very hard to see the full implication of something like this, unless you are a scientist or engineer, and have some appreciation for the consequences. No one could have dreamed that the transistor would have the broad social consequences it has had.
>
> *(p. 1860)*

Beaten by Shockley to the invention of the sandwich transistor, Brattain and Bardeen left the research group at Bell Laboratories amongst much acrimony and by 1950 were working elsewhere. Shockley also left Bell Laboratories in the early 1950s to establish a new company building transistors in Palo Alto, California. This company was the beginning of Silicon Valley as it is now known. With recognition of the potential of the transistor to transform electronics, Shockley, Bardeen and Brattain were later jointly awarded the 1956 Nobel Prize in Physics: 'for their researches on semiconductors and their discovery of the transistor effect' (Nobel Media AB, 2014). About the same time, several researchers left Shockley's new company, finding him too difficult to work with, and established original companies of their own. These companies were the Fairchild Semiconductor Company and the now well-known Intel Corporation. Both of these companies focused their attention on the application of the transistor to the development of the microprocessor.

The invention of the microprocessor was a game changer for the electronics industry. For the first time in human history, large amounts of information could be communicated via a very small micro-programmable computer on a chip. This technological capability would in time be embedded in millions of technologies worldwide. The capacity to digitise information on small 'chips' or 'microprocessors' meant that computing and communicative computing would become possible. Computing began to focus on new ways in which people could store, share and access information. Noyce and Hoff (1981), both employees at Intel, wrote a paper titled 'A history of microprocessor development at Intel'. With early insight into the influence the microprocessor was to have on society they wrote (from a somewhat technologically determinist perspective):

> The impact of the microprocessor goes far deeper than new and improved products. It is altering the structure of our society by changing how we gather and use information, how we communicate with one another and how and where we work. The changes are just beginning and it will take decades to assess fully the microprocessor's impact on society. It is certain though, that a world with hundreds of millions of computers will be different from the world we have known.
>
> *(p. 8)*

Like Brinkman *et al.* (1997) reflecting on the social implications of the invention of the transistor, it is difficult now to think back to a time when the microprocessor did not exist. Prior to the advent of the microprocessor information could not be digitised. Without digitisation information was not readily accessible at the swipe of a screen, could not be quickly called up, posted, shared or communicated in a fast and convenient way. Noyce and Hoff's (1981) ideas were largely predictive – a different world to what was known at the time did eventuate. In this new digital world, alternative perspectives about young children's play and learning would be needed, because information would henceforth be generated, stored, used and made available on a scale and level of accessibility that had never before existed.

The microprocessor is so fundamental to the adaption and use of digital technologies by people in society that it is useful to understand its function at the most basic of levels. A microprocessor is like the 'brain' of any given technology. A microprocessor processes information on a small single chip. Microprocessors are used in many different types of technologies – from those we consider 'old' technologies, including phones, television and radio, through to 'newer' technologies such as touchscreen tablets, gaming consoles and computers. Information or data is processed by different combinations of transistors located on a single chip. Electricity flowing through a transistor can be turned on and off. A binary system of 0 or 1 is used to indicate when the transistor is turned on and off. This system controls the flow of electricity through the microprocessor. Multiple combinations of transistors at the 0 or 1 positions on a chip allow unlimited numbers of 'instructions' to be processed by the chip. Micro-processors are also called 'central processing units' or CPUs because they 'centrally process' data. The first microprocessor was invented in 1971 by the Intel Corporation – one of the companies established by Shockley's disgruntled colleagues. The first microprocessor was called the 'Intel 4004'. It processed only two types of information – adding and subtraction. It was used to develop one of the first known portable calculators. By 1979, manufacturers were selling 75 million microprocessors a year (Noyce & Hoff, 1981).

Advances on the first microprocessor came rapidly. CPUs became smaller, faster and capable of managing increasingly large amounts of information – giving rise to the miniaturisation of electronics. Early computers that were as large as a room became small enough to fit onto a 'desktop'. Small-scale computing became increasingly affordable and new user interfaces and input devices were designed that enabled non-experts to easily navigate a computer. In 1976 the first Apple computer was released, and by the 1980s Microsoft was developing and releasing Graphical User Interface (GUI) software – basically icon-based instructions that people could easily 'click' to operate a computer. As computers became smaller and easier to use, the digitisation of information for economic and entertainment purposes became increasingly commonplace – particularly in what were known as 'first-world' economies.

Tablet computing: interface innovation

Common perceptions of tablet computing focus on the advent of the Apple iPad in 2010. However, as we have illustrated throughout the early chapters of this book, technological innovation is rarely as simple as it first appears. Tablet computing has an evolving history of its own – of which the iPad is amongst one of many innovations. Two technological ideas are important for understanding the evolution of the tablet technologies. First, the notion of Graphical User Interfaces or GUIs, and second the role of input devices in computer use. GUIs are quite simply the combination of text and images presented on a screen that easily allow a user to manipulate a computer. Input devices are the hardware typically used by a person to input their instructions into a computer. The most well-known input devices are the keyboard and the mouse. While the keyboard was associated with the earliest of desktop computers, the invention of the mouse by Douglas Englebart in 1973 came to shape user engagement with technologies in relation to the GUI. This is because Englebart designed his mouse as an input device that would operate in conjunction with a cursor on the screen. Users would manipulate the mouse to direct the cursor prior to clicking to confirm an action. The intuitive relationship between the mouse and the on-screen cursor drove GUI design, such that the notion of clicking, dragging, pointing and scrolling via icons, menus and information bars became accepted computer practices.

The development of tablet computing depended not only on technological innovation from computing science. It drew on the integration of existing theoretical ideas about learning into the pre-iPad concept known as Alan Kay's DynaBook. The DynaBook – a neologism for 'Dynamic Book' – was conceived by Alan Kay (1972) in a now-famous paper describing his vision for 'a personal computer for every child'. Strongly located in the literature of the time pertaining to young children's learning and development, Kay was influenced in his thinking by the work of Dewey, Bruner, Piaget, Montessori and Seymour Papert. He effectively described a constructivist approach to learning in which the active construction of knowledge by children engaged in meaningful activity was central to his thinking about personalised computing for very young children:

> With Dewey, Piaget and Papert, we believe that children 'learn by doing' and that much of the alienation in modern education comes from the great philosophical distance between the kinds of things children can 'do' and much of 20-century adult behaviour.... Piaget's and others' work on the bases and forms of children's thought is a fairly convincing argument for believing that computers are an almost ideal medium for the expression of a child's epistemology.
>
> *(Kay, 1972, p. 4)*

Kay's description of the DynaBook was of a small portable and networked computer with an attached keyboard. The DynaBook would be the size of an A4 notebook and children would be able to use the computer to solve problems, search for information and program their own games. Adults would also be able to use the DynaBook for work purposes, such as filing information, accessing databases and communicating with other people. Kay sketched an image of two children using his DynaBook in a park (Figure 2.1) – an image which was to come to life less than 50 years later in the form of the iPad.

Kay was also interested in the work of Vygotsky (1986) as this pertains to the nature of the social environment for learning. Just as Vygotsky (1986) argued for the social construction of knowledge by children, so Kay (2013) indicated that 'gently guided' learning is necessary for children. Kay (2013) argued that it is not possible for 'human beings to come up with good ideas from scratch' (p. 8). Rather he believed that some guidance is always necessary to support learning. According to Kay, the central activity of the learner should always be the bringing together of new information in the discovery of knowledge under guidance. Kay believed that his DynaBook could facilitate opportunities for children to access guidance beyond that afforded only by adults in their immediate social environment – thus making the technology an enabler of learning.

Kay's dedication to the concept of the DynaBook drove thinking about the development and capacity of tablet technologies – particularly as sites enabling the manipulation of information by people for particular purposes. Kay later worked at Apple, commencing as an Apple Fellow in 1984, and during this time collaborated on a range of projects with Steve Jobs, the ultimate inventor of the iPad (Greelish, 2013). That the resultant iPad came to be of such interest to both young children

FIGURE 2.1 DynaBook sketch – a portable inter-connected computer for every child drawn by Alan Kay, fall 1968.

Source: Kay, 1972, p. 2.

and those now involved in the education and care of young children in the digital age is no accident – the vision that drove innovation in tablet technologies was rooted in Kay's understanding of the very philosophical and theoretical ideas that have informed the provision of play-based learning in early childhood education for generations.

The concept of portable touchscreen technology that is responsive to young children's exploratory and social learning needs drove Kay's thinking about the DynaBook and consequently influenced the design and invention of the iPad. Today, research continues to highlight the rapid uptake of tablet technologies by very young children, including those aged under 12 months (Troseth, Russo, & Strouse, 2016). This research, while acknowledging the interactive appeal of touch-screen technologies, does not yet consistently trace the historical knowledge influ-ences of the technology to key educational thinkers in the early years as evidenced by Kay's (1972) repeated references to Bruner, Vygotsky, Piaget and Montessori. Rather, current research tends to discuss the release of the Apple iPad as the starting point for increased digital media engagement by very young children, for example:

> The launch of the iPad in April 2010 was followed by a rapid and unregu-lated release of more than 80,000 tablet applications or 'apps' tagged as educa-tional in the App Store (Apple, 2016). These inexpensive and accessible programs can easily be downloaded onto touch screen enabled phones and tablets. As such, use of touch screens during early childhood is increasing at a rapid pace.
>
> *(Zack & Barr, 2016, p. 1)*

Understanding Kay's engagement with key thinkers in the social and constructivist approaches to learning, positions the attractiveness of touchscreen technologies for young children in a new light. Touchscreen technologies are a cultural innovation derived from a subset of knowledge commencing with solid state physics that enabled digitalisation that was later subsumed within a particular way of thinking about the role of social 'guidance' in the exploratory play-based learning of the very young. Interestingly, Kay does not believe the iPad has entirely achieved the goal of his DynaBook (Greelish, 2013). The adaption of the iPad to 'apps' means the generative capacity of the DynaBook to engage children in their own thinking and problem solving was not entirely realised as per his vision. Nonetheless, the appeal and 'ease of use' factor associated with the iPad and very young children, remains a chief rationale in research regarding the very rapid uptake of the technology amongst this age group. Today, consequent to the iPad and the attraction of the iPad for very young children, research is shifting from the use of Graphical User Interfaces (GUIs) to the notion of Natural User Interfaces (NUIs) which are described as remediating the way children interact with computers (Jayemanne & Nansen, 2016).

Following Kay's contributions to computing science, technological development in the tablet computing space continued throughout the 1980s and into the early 2000s. Many tablet computers were trialled and taken to market. Amongst these were the GRiDPad, Intel Web Tablet, Palm Pilot, Microsoft Tablet PC, Nokia Internet Tablet and Apple iPod touch. Input devices for tablet technologies at the time included detachable keyboards and the use of styluses. Innovation in touchscreen technologies saw the application of touchscreens to mainstream computers. Early research in the field of education considered the use of touchscreen technologies in early childhood settings. For example, Romeo, Edwards, McNamara, Walker and Ziguras (2003) investigated young children's use of a touchscreen on desktop computers provided in the early childhood classroom and in the first year of school. This research showed that children in fact had a preference for the mouse – a situation described at the time as relevant to young children's previous experience and exposure to using a mouse and the inadequate alignment of the touchscreen with the GUI on the software typically available to teachers at the time. Indeed these findings were consistent with the sociocultural argument that young children learn to use the technological tools of their time. Romeo et al. (2003) described how children addressed limitations in correspondence between the touchscreen and the GUI by using the rubberised end of a pencil as a stylus. They noted, that 'the ingenuity of this discovery by the children should not be underestimated' (p. 335) – and in doing so unwittingly identified the capacity of young children to effectively manipulate touchscreen technologies to their own developmental advantage.

In 2010 Steve Jobs, founder of Apple computers, launched the Apple iPad. While not the first tablet computer to reach the market, the iPad combined high-level touchscreen sensitivity with mobile internet computing and the capacity for users to take photographs and store and use video and music. The iPad also enabled easy connection with the new App store – and the consequent uptake of 'applications' or apps designed to interest users from maps, to recipes to games. At the time, Jobs argued that to be useful the new iPad had to fill a void between the existing mobile phone and desktop computer – it needed to blend the tasks of both and make using the technology a seamless in-life experience. The iPad achieved its goal and by 2015 had sold over 250 million units. A new generation of research focused explicitly on the use of iPads in multiple and diverse educational contexts emerged. In early childhood the iPad was rapidly credited with putting technologies and the internet at the fingertips of the very youngest of children – infants and toddlers included (e.g. Kabali *et al.*, 2015).

Theorising transition to the digital age

The digital age is understood to have commenced in the two decades between 1950 and 1970. This is the period we described earlier, whereby research in solid state physics was moving on to the invention of the transistor and later the microprocessor enabling the digitalisation of information. From a technologically determinist perspective, the social, cultural and economic impact of the transistor and microprocessor on society has been profound. Riordan, Hoddeson and Herring (1999) described the invention of the transistor as 'transformative' for society:

> The transistor discovery has clearly had enormous impact both intellectually and in a commercial sense, upon our lives and work. A major vein in the corpus of condensed-matter physics quite literally owes its existence to this breakthrough. It also led to the microminiaturization of electronics, which has permitted us to have powerful computers on our desktops that communicate easily with others via the internet. The resulting globalization of science, technology, and culture is now transforming the ways we think and interact.
>
> *(p. 343)*

With electronics and computing companies developing and producing ever-new means of managing and representing information, the role of digitisation at a societal level was beginning to be recognised. Two important thinkers described the emergence of a new age, in which the movement from a predominately industrial means of working to a more information, or 'digitally based' engagement with the world of work and leisure was examined (Mansell, 2009). Daniel Bell, an American sociologist from Harvard University, and Yoneji Masuda, a Japanese sociologist writing for the Japanese government, both considered the influence of technologies on society.

In 1976, Bell published a now extensively cited paper titled 'The coming of the post-industrial society'. In this paper, Bell described Shockley's discovery of the transistor as 'the basis of miniaturization', and went on to call this invention 'the most remarkable achievement of the inter-twined science and technology of these

[1950s-1970s] decades of the century' (p. 577). Digitisation, argued Bell (1976) allowed the processing of information to be more important and significant in human endeavour and exchange than those processes of mass production that characterised the preceding age. Industrial societies, in which people had previously focused on the production of saleable goods, was considered 'technical' such that effort was expended on making the machines and the items they produced as efficient as possible. In this way, 'the art of making more with less' (p. 576) was important because mass production resulted in the greatest economic good for producers.

According to Bell, living and working in an industrial age required people to adhere to routine-based tasks and chronological time management so that mass production could be facilitated. Factory production necessitated repetitive assembly-line work, conducted by workers gathered in one place and working for set hours during specified times of day and days of the week. Towns grew around factories to service the needs of mass production and working lives and time for leisure were governed by shift patterns arranged to suit the manufacturing process. In contrast, in the 'post-industrial' age the development of digitisation and microprocessors allowed for a focus on the manipulation of information. Societies were now not only able to produce products for mass consumption, they had ready access to multiple forms and combinations of information offering economic opportunities which depended on the capacity of people to engage with information to create new ideas and services that other people would require – and consequently purchase. Bell called this new development 'the codification of theoretical knowledge' (p. 576). Bell's (1976) conception of the post-industrial society, was somewhat technologically deterministic in its orientation as technologies were attributed with the capacity to generate a new service economy, with knowledge workers needed in areas such as education, health, research and development and data processing.

Masuda (1980), like Bell before him, focused on the transformative impact of digitisation on society in the latter part of the 20th century. However, holding a slightly more critical orientation towards technologies he tackled this impact by considering the *processes of transition* involved for societies as they moved from an agricultural, industrial to information or 'digital' age. His most famous book, *The Information Society as Post-Industrial Society* (1980) is credited with being amongst the earliest of published texts to use the term 'information society' such that Masuda is sometimes known as the 'Father of the Information Age'.

Masuda (1980) proposed a new theory to explain the process of transition from one age to another. His theory was called the 'theory of societal technology'. He argued that technological change could be seen to have consistently influenced societal development from the agriculture to the industrial, and now the 'new' information age. Four key principles underpinned Masuda's theory of societal technological change (directly quoted below):

1. Many different technological innovations are joined together to constitute one complex system of technology.

2. These integrated systems of technology spread throughout society as a whole and gradually take root.
3. As a result, a rapid expansion of a new type of societal productive power occurs.
4. The development of this new societal productive power has an impact great enough to transform traditional society and to establish new norms and values.

(Masuda, 1985, p. 269)

Masuda (1980) argued that the agricultural age was transformed by two main technological innovations. The first innovation saw advances in knowledge of measurement and design that informed the invention of irrigation. Joined with the use of agricultural implements, such as ploughs, hoes and sickles, irrigation spread through society as a dominant mode of food production allowing people to capitalise on what the environment provided in terms of edible plants and animals on a large scale (p. 269). An increase in food production moved societies away from localised hunter/gatherer constructions, generating new power structures in which groups of people (typically peasants) were overseen in their efforts by feudal lords. Local and long-established villages became the social norm, and daily and yearly life was governed by both the seasons and expectations of feudal law. In this predominately pre-print era, learning was mediated by the transmission of knowledge between generations, with knowledge and skill necessary for food production and daily life shared amongst people as children grew up within their communities and craft skills were acquired during apprenticeships. Children did not need to learn to read and write, rather the focus was on learning about the seasons, knowing when to plant crops and how to capitalise on irrigation for increased food production and making the vessels and tools needed for everyday living.

Using his theory of societal technological change, Masuda (1980) showed how the shift from the agricultural to industrial age was achieved via innovations in the sciences such as chemistry and physics that allowed the conversion of natural materials into highly useable products. For example, much of the industrial age was characterised by the use of iron ore abstracted from rock and converted into steel using high levels of heat generated by coal. Ayn Rand's (1957) classic novel *Atlas Shrugged* powerfully illustrates the significance of steel and the evolution of new techniques for creating and developing steel within the political and industrial structures of society. During the shift to the industrial age, innovative ideas and new knowledge about the workings of the cylinder and piston meant that steel could be used to create steam engines. Steam engine power was initially applied to factory and mill work. Previously reliant on water power and manual labour for their productivity, these industries benefited from the application of steam power to their outputs because steam power meant they did not need to be located near a water source for their operation. Steam power was also faster, more reliable and cheaper than human manual labour. With the advent of steam power industrial work no longer needed to operate near a river and was able to spread throughout many different regions, including the cities. New urban settlements sprang up around industrialised sites as workers moved from rural areas to take up the opportunities for employment the industrial age afforded. Mass concentrations of people generated new economic opportunities for servicing the domestic and entertainment needs of the population in the form of food stores, clothing shops, hotels and theatres. The steam engine also facilitated high-level change in the travel patterns of people and the transportation of material goods across the country as steam trains replaced older modes of horse-drawn transportation.

Masuda (1980) argues that as steam engine technology took root within society a new economic order focused on the pursuit of profit and free competition emerged. Combined with changes in work and travel patterns, this new economic order drove developments in the movement of labour (e.g. people working in more closely populated townships located near factories) and increased population-level interest in parliamentary democracies as a form of governance. New norms and values regarding the right to leisure and life in urbanised communities replaced previous ideas in which life had predominately been conducted according to the seasonal laws of nature. Urbanised life and the mass consumption of goods and services driven by the move away from dependency on the land that characterised the agricultural age were accompanied by changes in the approach to education. The industrial age influenced both the content and methods of learning for the majority of people who now lived in urban areas and were expected to move to factory-based work when they reached adulthood. Unlike the previous agricultural age in which skills and knowledge were handed down generationally and focused on knowledge of the seasons and the best time to plant crops, industrial-age education shifted towards the simultaneous transmission of the knowledge deemed necessary to large numbers of children at the same time. Age-level segregation in education commenced as a common practice as it was thought to be more efficient to teach large numbers of children of the same age the same information at the same time. The curriculum arose from ideas about what the workforce needed to know. With the parallel increase in print literacy associated with the industrial age, literacy and numeracy skills at the minimum level required for later workforce participation became the main goal of learning for children growing up in the industrial age.

The dawning of the information or 'digital' age can be explained in terms of Masuda's (1980) theory of societal technology. As we have outlined in the earlier parts of this chapter, the emergence of the digital age is associated with the cultural transformations in knowledge about physics that gave rise to the invention of the transistor and the consequent application of the transistor to the creation of the microprocessor. Drawing from what appears to be a critical, rather than a technologically deterministic orientation towards technology, Masuda (1985) explains how the direction of resources by governments into programmes of defence and space research fast-tracked technological developments in computing. Echoing Williams' (1958) claim that technologies always come from somewhere, this advancement by governmental investment in defence and space research occurred at the same time as computers were increasingly being used to manage and systemise large amounts of data in industry. Once established in the workplace, computing rapidly became personalised at a domestic level, a process supported by the invention of the Apple computer and the development of easily used Graphical User Interfaces (GUIs) by Microsoft.

Masuda (1980) claimed that the rapid increase in computing across society supported a new social order in which synergistic relationships between people were enabled by the rapid and easy exchange of digital information. Writing in 1980, 10 years before the advent of the World Wide Web and social media, Masuda was before his time, arguing that the new digital age would engage people in joint production of knowledge and information, and in the shared utilisation of technological resources via a global information network. According to Masuda, this joint engagement and sharing of information would be possible because the driving force of society would be the amplification of mental labour *by people using technologies.* We note here Masuda's (1980) placement of people before the technology and the notion of people using technologies to enhance and extend human processes and motives. This description of the role of technologies in the digital age contrasts with the more technological deterministic orientation in which technologies are said to have caused the arrival of the digital age. Comparing the steam engine of the industrial age to the computer of the information age, Masuda (1980) wrote:

> The prime innovation technology at the core of development in industrial society was the steam engine, and its major function was to substitute for and amplify the physical labour of man. In the information society, 'computer technology' will be the innovation technology that will constitute the developmental core and its fundamental function will be to substitute for and amplify the mental labour of man.
>
> *(p. 31)*

The notion of 'amplifying mental labour' is critical to understanding the nature of the digital age and why consideration of young children playing and learning in this new age is now necessary. This is because the *amplification of mental labour by people using technologies modifies what it is possible for a society to create.* Sociocultural theory shows us that the possibility for social creation, in terms of knowledge and tools generates change that creates new conditions for learning amongst people (Davydov, 1982). Masuda's theory of societal technology evidences the possibility of social creation from the agricultural through to the industrial age. For the informational age, Masuda (1980) argued that the value placed on technologies would be vested in the personal use of computers for self-representation, knowledge acquisition and self-actualisation. Masuda argued that this increased capacity for and valuing of personal development would be accompanied by a movement towards participatory democracy (p. 35).

In the new digital age, educational learning needs would necessarily change. The delivery of the same information, to the same age cohort of children at the same time would no longer be entirely necessary. The use of computers for personalised learning and knowledge acquisition, combined with an increased capacity for people to communicate with each other across space and time would mean that children would need to learn more than the basics of reading and writing. Furthermore, given Masuda's claim that the amplification of mental labour would increase the possibilities for what society would create, the children of this new age could not necessarily be guaranteed long-term stability in current knowledge and work practices. The increased possibility for social creation would instead instigate consistent and constant change. As the digital age emerged into a daily reality, new educational research began to point to the learning needs of current and future generations of children. Siemens (2014) wrote of this change:

> Learners as little as forty years ago would complete the required schooling and enter a career that would often last a lifetime. Information development was slow. The life of knowledge was measured in decades. Today, these foundational principles have been altered. Knowledge is growing exponentially. In many fields the life of knowledge is now measured in months and years.
>
> *(p. 3)*

The simple achievement of literacy and numeracy skills at the level required for industrialised participation would no longer suffice for the children of the digital age. Instead of identifying only content knowledge – that is, *what* children would learn at a given age, educational aims and descriptions began also to focus on the dispositional aspects of learning so that learners could continue to grow as they experienced changes in and challenges to much of the knowledge they would encounter. Creativity, the ability to solve problems and a critical capacity to evaluate the quality of the growing bodies of knowledge to which they would be exposed were increasingly considered necessary learning dispositions for children (Resnick, 2002). Learning in the digital age would require of children a confluence of content knowledge, skill acquisition in the fields of literacy and numeracy, and a disposition towards knowledge development that orientated towards the inquisitive and exploratory.

Conclusion

The digital age, as described in this chapter represents a period of time in human history in which distributed forms of communication and the mass storage, sharing, retrieval and manipulation of information is made possible by the cultural evolution of knowledge and technical tools. In the digital age young children need to understand and manage alternative sources and forms of information, to be able to differentiate, explore, see synergies and re-create in order to make use of the cultural tools at their disposal in the form of currently available technologies. In the next chapter of this book we continue to provide some further historical context regarding the background against which we believe young children playing and learning in the digital age may be most productively considered. This includes the development of the internet and the innovation of the World Wide Web, leading to the prevalence of social media and the ubiquity of digital connectivity in daily life.

References

Bell, D. (1976). The coming of the post-industrial society. *The Educational Forum, 40*(4), 574–579.

Brinkman, W., Haggan, D., & Troutman, W. (1997). A history of the invention of the transistor and where it will lead us. *IEEE Journal of Solid State Circuits, 32*(12), 1858–1865.

Davydov, V. (1982). Translated by S. Kerr. The influence of L. S. Vygotsky on education, theory, research and practice. *Educational Researcher, 24*(3), 12–21.

Einstein, A. (1907). Plancksche Theorie der Strahlung und die Theorie der Spezifischen Wärme [Planck's Theory of Radiation and the Theory of Specific Heat]. *Annalen der Physik, 4*(22), 180–190. doi:10.1002/andp. 19063270110.

Greelish, D. (2013, 2 April). An interview with computing pioneer Alan Kay. *Time Interviews*. Retrieved from http://techland.time.com/2013/04/02/an-interview-with-computing-pioneer-alan-kay/.

Hopfield, J. J. (2014). Whatever happened to solid state physics? *Annual Review of Condensed Matter Physics, 5*(1), 1–13.

Jayemanne, D., & Nansen, B. (2016). Parental mediation, YouTube's networked public, and the 'Baby-iPad Encounter': mobilizing digital dexterity. *Jeunesse: Young People, Texts, Cultures, 8*(1), 133–153.

Kabali, H. K., Irigoyen, M. M., Nunez-Davis, R., Budacki, J. G., Mohanty, S. H., Leister, K. P., & Bonner, R. L. (2015). Exposure and use of mobile media devices by young children. *Pediatrics, 136*(6), 1044–1050.

Kay, A. C. (1972, August). A personal computer for children of all ages. In *Proceedings of the ACM annual conference – Volume 1* (pp. 1–11). ACM.

Kay, A. (2013). The future of reading depends on the future of learning difficult to learn things. In B. Junge, Z. Berzina, W. Scheiffele, W. Westerveld, & C. Zwick (Eds.), *The digital turn: design in the era of interactive technologies* (pp. 1–12). Chicago: University of Chicago Press.

Mansell, R. (2009). *The information society: critical concepts in sociology*. London: Routledge.

Masuda, Y. (1980). *The information society as post-industrial society*. Tokyo: Institute for the Information Society.

Masuda, Y. (1985). Three great social revolutions: agricultural, industrial, and informational. *Prometheus, 3*(2), 269–274.

McLuhan, M. (1951). *The mechanical bride: folklore of industrial man*. Boston: Beacon Press.

Nobel Media AB (2014). The Nobel Prize in Physics 1956. *Nobelprize.org*. Retrieved from www.nobelprize.org/nobel_prizes/physics/laureates/1956/.

Noyce, R. N., & Hoff Jr, M. E. (1981). A history of microprocessor development at Intel. *IEEE Micro, 1*(1), 8–21.

Rand, A. (1957). *Atlas Shrugged*. New York: Dutton.

Resnick, M. (2002). Rethinking learning in the digital age. In G. S. Kirkman, P. K. Cornelius, J. D. Sachs, & K. Schwab (Eds.), *The global information technology report 2001–2002: Readiness for the networked world* (pp. 32–37). New York: Oxford University Press.

Riordan, M., Hoddeson, L., & Herring, C. (1999). The invention of the transistor. *Reviews of Modern Physics, 71*(2), 336–345.

Romeo, G., Edwards, S., McNamara, S., Walker, I., & Ziguras, C. (2003). Touching the screen: issues associated with the use of touch screen technology in early childhood education. *British Journal of Educational Technology, 34*(3), 329–341.

Sanchez-Ron, J. (1994). Reviewed works: out of the crystal maze: chapters from *The History of Solid-State Physics* by Lillian Hoddeson, Ernest Braun, Jurgen Teichmann and Spencer Weart. *Isis, 85*(4) (December 1994), 735–736.

Siemens, G. (2014). Connectivism: a learning theory for the digital age. *International Journal of Instructional Technology and Distance Learning, 2*(1), 3–10.

Troseth, G. L., Russo, C. E., & Strouse, G. A. (2016). What's next for research on young children's interactive media? *Journal of Children and Media, 10*(1), 54–62. doi: 10.1080/17482798.2015.1123166.

Vygotsky, L. (1986). *Thought and language, Revised Edition.* Cambridge, MA: MIT Press.

Williams, R. (1958). Culture is ordinary. In J. Higgins (Ed.) (2001), *The Raymond Williams reader* (pp. 10–25). Oxford: Blackwell.

Williams, R. (2004). *Television: technology and cultural form.* Abingdon, Oxon: Taylor and Francis.

Zack, E., & Barr, R. (2016). The role of interactional quality in learning from touch screens during infancy: context matters. *Frontiers in Psychology, 7,* 1–12.

3

A COMMUNICATION EVOLUTION – THE INTERNET, WORLD WIDE WEB AND PARTICIPATORY MEDIA

Introduction

In the last chapter we focused on the ways in which developments in scientific understandings were employed to make changes in the hardware underpinning communication processes and the digitisation of information (and all that these developments meant for access to and engagement with knowledge sources, knowledge management and knowledge creation in the digital age). In this chapter, we turn our attention to the scientific and social developments that created the internet, providing immediate and direct engagement with others across the world. In examining the path of this innovation we note two particular socio-political cultural conditions that influenced the computer scientists involved. The advent of the internet was followed by the invention of the World Wide Web as a new and powerful medium of interactive communication. This shift to interactive engagement with information was extended to new and more participatory media possibilities when technological developments located the capacity to create messages and broadcast them within one tool, typically a smartphone. An account of two further innovations completes this chapter – the semantic web and the Internet of Things. We argue that the developments outlined in this chapter have changed the ways in which adults and children can engage with information and knowing. Acting on these substantive possibilities requires new thinking about the why, what and how of young children playing and learning in the digital age and also raises significant areas for critical debate as innovation builds on and re-configures the cultural context of everyday life.

The internet

Microprocessors and the miniaturisation of computers provided the technical capacity informing the invention of the internet. However, as we have emphasised thus far throughout this book, technologies are not self-created. Rather, technological innovation is always culturally and historically located. Flew (2014), a new media scholar, considers an historical analysis of the internet necessary for understanding its role in the generation and sharing of digital media. Furthermore, Flew (2014) argues that an historical engagement with the internet brings to light the 'particular ideas and values' associated with the development of the internet as a significant technological innovation in the history of humankind (p. 6). In this section of the chapter, we therefore briefly describe the history underpinning the invention of the internet, and in common with a critical, rather than deterministic perspective on technological innovation, note the ideas and values informing its creation from a political and social perspective.

According to historian Roy Rosenzweig (1998) the birth of the internet is located in two political and social movements in Western-European history that at first glance appear completely incompatible – these being the Cold War and the counter-cultural ('hippy') revolution of the 1960s. The Cold War provides the contextual justification, in particular the political reason, for creating an interconnected communications system, while the people-powered philosophical basis of the counter-cultural revolution explains why open access to computing was valued as an issue of worldwide human rights. In beginning with the Cold War, we note Flew's (2014) concern that the history of the internet is very American-centric. This centrism, argues Flew (2014), 'reflects the fact that US government dollars, US institutions and US universities were central to the internet's early development' (p. 11).

The Cold War saw America and Russia in a tense stand-off regarding the release of the first nuclear missile to herald a worldwide nuclear holocaust. In the USA, concern was high amongst the Department of Defense that a nuclear incident would render existing communication systems obsolete in a matter of seconds. This was a problem because without a workable communication system the President of the USA would be unable to operate a chain of command for a retaliatory attack, or necessarily be able to respond to the demands of a country in the grips of a significant war-time crisis. The existing communication system was basically telephony, and therefore relied on the point-to-point transmission of voice as data from a centralised point. Destruction at the centralised point would render all points of transmission useless. Any nuclear explosion was likely to wipe out the capacity of the existing communication system to be operable in any form. A new approach towards communication was a critical element in not only responding to a potential attack, but minimising the possibility of an attack in the first instance by making Russia aware that the USA had the communications capacity to respond in a retaliatory fashion. Communication mattered.

In the early 1960s, Paul Baran, a researcher at the USA-based think-tank known as the Research and Development (RAND) Corporation began to engage with the problem of centralised communication systems. In a world first, he conceived the idea of an inter-networked system of nodes across which packets of information would travel according to the fastest possible available pathway. Instead of voice data being transmitted from point to point via a centralised system he envisioned a distributed system that would still operate even if parts of it had been damaged or obliterated. Packets of information containing voice and textual data would travel in the system like 'hot potatoes'. As each hot potato reached a node in the system the node would work as hard as it could to send the potato to the next node. If a node was damaged, non-existent or already busy with another 'hot potato' the node would continue searching the system for the next available node until the packet reached its final destination:

> Each node will attempt to get rid of its message by choosing alternate routes if its preferred route is busy or destroyed. Each message is regarded as a 'hot potato' and the nodes are not wearing gloves. Rather than hold the 'hot potato' the node tosses the message to its neighbour, who will now try to get rid of the message.
>
> *(Baran, 1962, p. 29)*

Packets of information would be reassembled at the end destination to comprise their final form. In this way, larger amounts of data could be sent through the distributed system than would otherwise be possible. Figure 3.1 shows Baran's (1962) original sketches indicating a centralised, decentralised and distributed system.

Baran (1962) tested his concept on the available telephony technology at the time showing that his packets of data could not be sent over the existing telephone wires. What was required was a radical overhaul of existing infrastructure to decentralise the system. Baran's concept did not meet with a receptive audience. When

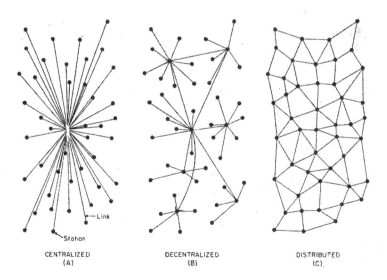

FIGURE 3.1 Baran's (1962) original sketch illustrating three different communication systems.

the USA Airforce approached the major provider of telephone services in America, the American Telephone and Telegraph (AT&T) Company, with an invitation to test Baran's distributed system the idea was met with disbelief. Many people at the time were unable to make the conceptual leap in thinking required to understand distributed rather than centralised communication systems. This was because telephony was the predominate form of communication. Telephony relied on people talking directly to each other and so reinforced the notion of a centralised point-to-point system as the norm. Today, from a substantive view of technology, we have become so accustomed to distributed forms of communication it is difficult to make the same conceptual leap backwards and to understand how entrenched the notion of point-to-point communication really was – Baran's idea would have seemed quite radical. The irony of AT&T rejecting Baran's concept was that this company had previously been the Bell Telephone company – the very company where Mervin Kelly had established the laboratory in which the transistor was invented. Baran, however, was already light years ahead of his contemporaries, foretelling a communication system that in time would enable the mass transmission of information amongst people:

> Is it time now to start thinking about a new and possibly non-existent public utility, a common user digital data communication plant designed specifically for the transmission of digital data among a large set of subscribers?
>
> *(Baran, 1962, p. 40)*

Meanwhile, as Baran was theorising his distributed communication system, a new research agency called the Advanced Research Project Agency (ARPA) was established by the USA government. Echoing Masuda's (1980) theory of societal technology, the establishment of ARPA was in direct response to Russia launching Sputnik as the first satellite in space. ARPA was tasked with fast-tracking developments in communications, space and missile research so that the USA could keep up with Russia. Several researchers at ARPA, including Joseph Licklider, Bob Taylor and Lawrence Roberts engaged with the concept of computer networking. Licklider was interested in the capacity of computers to increase the efficacy of command and control in military operations. Taylor and Roberts were tasked with making the many different computers used at ARPA capable of talking to each other, capitalising on the potential of computing power to amplify human endeavour. This second task was primarily one of efficiency and budget so that ARPA researchers located at different sites could benefit from access to multiple computers. Roberts became aware of Baran's (1962) work and used Baran's ideas as a conceptual framework for establishing nodes of connected computers at ARPA. In 1968, ARPA commissioned a small computing company known as Bolt, Beranek, and Newman (BBN) to extend the network outside of itself and into other research agencies – including most notably universities. BBN connected computers at Stanford, University of California Santa Barbara, UCLA and University of Utah in that same year.

The host computer at each university site was connected to a smaller computer responsible for processing packets of information on the system. This was so that the power of the host computers would not be reduced by having to deal with packet processing and reassembly of data. The small computers were considered the 'middlemen' of the host computers within the system, and were called Interface Message Processors or IMPs for short. With the establishment of a distributed series of hosts and IMPs across four university sites and connected to the ARPA, networked computing was possible. The problem now was to work out how to make networked computers on different systems able to talk with each other. This was because some computers were networked on a satellite, others on a radio and some were embedded in ARPA. An engineer called Bob Kahn from BBN worked on the 'Internetting Project' in response to this problem. He developed the concept of Transmission Control Protocol (TCP) as a new way for networked computers across different nets to talk with each other. The development of TCP meant that for the first time in human history an inter-network of networked computers was now possible. From a cultural knowledge legacy that commenced with Einstein's thinking about matter, through to the invention of the transistor, then the microprocessor and the consequent miniaturisation of computing the internet was born. TCP later came to be called Internet Protocol or IP, and is still in use today as the primary mechanism of communication between networks.

An early purpose to which the internet was put was email. Email later came to be one of the most powerful forms of communicative practices on the internet. Email was invented in 1972 by a BBN engineer called Ray Tomlinson as a way of sending messages across the ARPA net. Tomlinson selected the @ symbol as a way of identifying where on the system an email was to be sent. By selecting the @ symbol, the name of the person 'at' their network address could be used to send the message. Within one year of its invention, email comprised three quarters of the messages sent through the ARPA net. The rapid communicative potential of the internet had been realised. Children born after this time would grow into digital forms of communication that no longer relied on point-to-point telephony. Communication henceforth could be distributed relatively instantly across time and space via 'networked networks' of computers.

Rosenzweig (1998) maintains that the political situation creating the context for the invention of the internet evolved simultaneously with the Western-European counter-cultural revolution of the 1960s. As a large-scale social response to changing social norms following the end of World War II, the counter-cultural revolution focused attention on notions of participatory democracy and anti-authoritarianism. These democratic and anti-authoritarian values were also held by many of the members in the computer science community of the time. Participants in this community believed that knowledge of technological innovation should be shared and be freely available to all. This belief was in sharp contrast to what was happening with the development of the ARPA net. The ARPA net was largely closed to people outside the network and gaining access to the network required payment of a significant monetary fee. The closing off of the ARPA net to the broader community was viewed by members of the computer science community as anti-democratic and highly authoritarian.

Accordingly, a group of students from Duke University used a new operating system called Unix to set up an alternative system for exchanging files with others. Their connected group was called Usenet or the 'poor man's ARPA net' (Hauben & Hauben, 1998) and allowed users to post a newsletter about any given topic to which any other connected member of the group was able to reply. Usenet grew rapidly – initially it was three connected computers, then 150 and within eight years it involved 11,000 connections (Rosenzweig, 1998). As Usenet grew, more and more people became interested in the concept of networked computing. Many people tried to access or 'hack' the ARPA net. Eventually an American graduate student established a connection between Usenet and the ARPA net. Recognising that the ARPA net was no longer secure for sharing military research, the USA Defense established a separate net called MILNET and the ARPA net became more widely available. In doing so, the concept of a widely available computing network began to expand across the globe. The internet is now accepted to have almost global reach. For example, World Internet User Statistics show that as of June 2016, 50 per cent of the world's internet users were based in Asia (www. internetworldstats.com/stats.htm). This is a remarkable feat of human cultural endeavour when we consider that it is only about 50 years ago that vacuum tube amplifiers were being used as the primary system enabling point-to-point communication between people. For young children growing up in a digital age playing and learning would in some form or another necessarily involve their contact and engagement with this new technological infrastructure called the internet which had transformed global communication and information sharing and exploration. The next important historical piece in understanding the evolution of the digital age is the story of how the World Wide Web came into being.

The World Wide Web

The advent of globalised computer networking (otherwise known as the 'internet') gave rise to the World Wide Web in 1989. Invented by Tim Berners-Lee, the World Wide Web provided the user-friendly interface to the internet that allowed people without a computer-programming background to readily access materials and information posted on the network. Berners-Lee was working as a software engineer at the Conseil Européen pour la Recherche Nucléaire – colloquially known as 'CERN' (European Council for Nuclear Research). He noticed that it was difficult for people at CERN to share information with each other. He cited a new term coined by Ted Nelson in the 1950s called 'hypertext' – described as 'human-readable information linked together in an unconstrained way' (Berners-Lee, 1989). Using hyper-text would allow multiple forms of information on the CERN network to be connected with each other and to be searchable using different terms. This would increase productivity because people would no longer have to rely on knowing who held certain pieces of information in order to do their job – they could look it up on the network using hyper-texts.

Berners-Lee (1989) wrote his ideas about hyper-text in a proposal he submitted to his supervisor at CERN in a document called *Information Management: A Proposal*. Like the earlier invention of the sandwich transistor by Shockley, and the concept of networking by Baran, Berners-Lee's paper also met with little initial interest. His supervisor wrote on the cover of his proposal 'interesting but vague'. The proposal was not taken up as an official project at CERN. However, Berners-Lee's supervisor did provide him with some time and resources to continue the development of his ideas. By late 1990 Berners-Lee had established the three fundamental codes that would enable the World Wide Web to operate. These were: 1) HyperText Markup Language (HTML) – the coding language that formats language for us on the internet; 2) Uniform Resource Identifier (URI) – the unique address that is given to all the resources located on the web; and 3) Hypertext Transfer Protocol (HTTP) – used to retrieve information that has been posted on the web.

With these three codes Berners-Lee created and posted the first ever web-page in human history. The page is still available on the World Wide Web and can be seen today at http://info.cern.ch/hypertext/WWW/TheProject.html. Interest in the World Wide Web grew rapidly. People from all walks of life were interested in its use and application. Businesses saw potential in reaching new customers and the Higher Education sector was quick to capitalise on the potential of the World Wide Web for sharing research and resources. Berners-Lee was committed to the realisation of a resource that would be open to people worldwide. Like others concerned with participatory social values, he believed that the web was only possible with the continued contributions of many people and was against the idea of the web being corporatised. He directed his efforts towards ensuring that the coding that operated the web would be available to people royalty-free forever. In 1994 Berners-Lee left CERN and went to the Massachusetts Institute of Technology (MIT) where he established the World Wide Web consortium – known as the W3C. The W3C is a group dedicated to maintaining open standards of the web and continues to operate today.

Reflections on the impact of the World Wide Web are influenced by the three perspectives on technological change which we advanced earlier. From a technologically determinist perspective the World Wide Web may be described as transforming existing patterns of communication, and ways of thinking and sharing information. From a substantive perspective the capacity of the World Wide Web to store and retrieve information represents a technological innovation that has shaped a range of social practices, such as the move from paper-based to email communication, online shopping and presenting corporate identities. However, Berners-Lee's commitment to ensuring the World Wide Web would be an open source technology reflects a more critical and value-based orientation towards the technology. Here, the value attributed to the web by Berners-Lee was in the freedom of access people would have to information from others on which they could consequently collaborate. While the web is frequently described somewhat deterministically as a new technology with such 'potency' that 'it has made individuals change their information access methods and organisations to change their business strategy' (Moon & Kim, 2001, p. 217), we argue, that the cultural knowledge base giving rise to the invention of the internet and the consequent values guiding Berners-Lee in the creation of the World Wide Web should not be denied or overlooked. To do otherwise, is to limit our thinking about young children playing and learning in the digital age to a deterministic orientation towards technology which denies us the human agency to make choices about our purposes in employing digital technologies (deciding when and why to engage with them) and about the value of particular technological practices when considered from a cultural and critical orientation.

From Web 1.0 to participatory media

The first version of the web invented by Berners-Lee is often described as Web 1.0. Web 1.0 is considered a 'read-only' generation of the World Wide Web. This is because when the web was first developed it only allowed people to post information that others could read. The first generation web did not yet possess the capacity to host video, photography or audio. Nor did the early web allow people to provide commentary on the information posted by others. Web 1.0 was quite literally a 'read-only' experience. The shift from Web 1.0 to the second generation of the web commenced with the uptake of Web 1.0 by industry. This occurred as industry became interested in the potential of the web to increase the audience to which their products could be exposed. Because the web was read-only, the most business could do was to promote their products online and coalesce this promotion with a home delivery service.

Pets.com – the most famous business based on this early model – was founded in 1998. Pets.com promised to deliver pet food and products to the family home under its well-known motto 'Because pets can't drive!' Pets.com was built on large-scale contributions by investors who viewed it as a ground-breaking initiative in the brave new world of web-based business. Money flowed into other new 'start-up' online businesses, such as grocery deliveries, that were also listed on the stock exchange. Often these listings doubled their value overnight as people rushed to be part of the new 'dot.com' boom. Many of these new businesses failed to achieve their goals. The rush to be online had not been accompanied by thoughtful planning. For example, the cost to Pets.com of delivering heavy bags of pet food to the family home could not be outweighed by what was a feasible cost to charge pet owners for the product in the first instance. While Pets.com had an exciting online presence and promised user convenience, these attributes could not compensate for what it cost to provide its own service. By 2000, Pets.com, along with many other businesses, was a victim of the bursting of the 'dot.com bubble'. At the time, some analysts argued that the failure of dot.com business was proof that the web would have little influence on existing social, cultural, government, economic and educational practices (Abelson, 2000).

However, this early failure was overcome as cultural innovation driving the evolution of the web continued. Innovation occurred in both technological developments pertaining to the use of the web, and conceptualisation of the web as a new communicative medium located alongside existing 'mass' or traditional 'broadcast' media such as television or radio. From a communicative perspective, the web shifted from being a place of publication to a place servicing user need. Tim O'Reilly (2005), during a conference hosted by his company the O'Reilly Media Group, first proposed the notion of Web 2.0 when he argued that the companies that had successfully survived the bursting of the dot.com bubble were characteristically different to those that had failed. Successful dot.com businesses, he argued focused on attracting people to their sites by attending to their needs – understanding that the more people that came to their site the more they had to offer other services in terms of a captive audience for advertising. For example, successful businesses such as Google provided a 'free' search engine service to internet users. Software upgrades to the service occurred in the background – users never had to download new software or manage their operation of Google to use the service. Google was simply there and enabled people to search the internet for the information of their choice (O'Reilly, 2005). As more and more people used the service provided by Google, the company was able to capitalise on their audience share to entice advertising dollars. O'Reilly's argument meant that one of the first ideas underpinning the movement from Web 1.0 to Web 2.0 was one of *service provision* rather than read-only publication. Interestingly, this notion of service provision aligns with Williams' (1958) claim that technologies themselves do not drive societal change – rather it is the purposes and practices to which technologies are applied that shape their evolution.

Technological developments in computer programming reflected the shift in thinking which regarded the web as a 'service orientated' rather than a 'read-only' space. Engaging with the web was seen as an *interactive* rather than a passive experience. These developments included the invention of Really Simple Syndication (RSS) feeds and permalinks (O'Reilly, 2005). RSS feeds were important because in Web 1.0 there was no way for a site visitor to know that information had been updated in their absence. A user would have to make a conscious decision to go back to the site and check if anything had changed. RSS feeds meant that websites could 'push' or 'feed' information to the email account of regular users about any changes made to a website. RSS feeds gave birth to weblogs whereby any change or update to a weblog would be announced to the readers of the log – thus increasing the frequency of user engagement with the site. Permalinks were the next important development in the evolution of Web 2.0. Short for 'permanent links', permalinks enabled bloggers to connect the content of their weblogs to those of other bloggers. Once these connections were enabled a rapid spike in conversations and communication across and between blogs' users occurred.

Web 2.0 quickly captured the attention of media scholars. Media scholarship had traditionally attended to the role of mass and traditional broadcast media in the social and political lives of people living in different types of political systems –

communist, socialist and democratic. A key tenet in media scholarship was the notion of participatory media. Participatory media referred to the role of people engaging with media to 'speak back' to those ideas or information promoted by the mass media. Mass or broadcast media was typically defined as radio, television or print in which information, entertainment, opinions and/or political messages would be sent from one main dominant media form (e.g. radio) to the main 'mass' of people. Enzenberger (1970), a significant thinker about media, argued that media should enable the full participation of citizens in their society rather than be used solely as a means of mass information delivery. The notion of 'participatory media' drove early media scholarship in Web 2.0 thinking. This was because Web 2.0 practices such as service provision and the capacity to post user-generated content were viewed as a vehicle for realising participatory media in a way that had not been possible with television or radio. Anyone with a computer and access to the internet could create their own blog, post to a blog made by another person or connect one or two blogs together – they could in fact 'participate' in their own media making.

As Web 2.0 became entrenched in the media landscape alongside more tradi-tional media, such as television, radio and the newspapers, media scholars began to talk about the possibilities of web media as a form of 'new' rather than participatory media. This is because the new web media involved people in the self-creation of combinations of text, audio, photography and video that they could self-publish online. In this way, the media was 'new' rather than only participatory because people could create their own digital media representations. However, the capacity for this new media to be easily communicated with others by creating shared links and commentary generated fresh thinking in media studies. Thus, the idea of 'new media' merged with the notion of 'collective intelligence'. Proposed by well-known new media scholar Henry Jenkins (2006), collective intelligence was related to the concept of new media because it allowed people operating within 'net-worked' communities to 'develop knowledge systems that are not only greater than the sum of their individual parts, but which also grow, evolve and collectively learn through ongoing participation' (Flew, 2014, p. 79). Early examples of web-based collective intelligence include Wikipedia and YouTube.

Collective intelligence provided the cultural repertoire for social media. As the technological capacity for people to create connections amongst themselves was realised (e.g. through permalinks) new sites were established with the primary func-tion of servicing social engagement. Social engagement contrasts starkly with the original purpose of the web which was to host searchable information accessible to many people across time and distance. Instead, of hosting 'read-only' data, the web had evolved to accommodate people in the creation of their own content – through the posting of self-recorded written commentary, video footage and photographs. Commenting upon and further sharing personalised digital content enabled the practice of social networking – thus witnessing the rise of now-famous social media sites such as Facebook. The generational difference between Web 1.0 and Web 2.0 was noted in educational research in which the read-only version of the web had attracted attention for changing the *way* children learned from *what* they learned (Lankshear & Knobel, 2006). Now that digital media could be self-created and widely shared, the learning needs of children in the digital age were once again under consideration (e.g. Burnett & Merchant, 2015).

A focus on social servicing contrasted directly with the original goal of Web 1.0 which was to network or make accessible information. Social media sites allowed people to create their own content – through the generation of written commentary and posting of video footage and photographs. Sharing personalised digital content gave rise to the practice of social networking – thus witness the rise of Facebook. Web 1.0 and Web 2.0 came to be characterised by qualitatively different digital practices and purposes. Web 1.0 was considered a read-only repository for information, while Web 2.0 became a noted location for the consumption and sharing of collectively generated multi-modal content (Greenhow, Robelia, & Hughes, 2009). The readily produced and shared content can be seen as having characteristics akin to those of the 'unofficial' programme of public instruction, carried on by commerce through the press, radio and movies, first identified by McLuhan (1951) as in competition with 'official' or state education programmes. In education circles the capacity to share collectively generated multi-modal content was reflected in calls for 'New Learning' and 'New Literacies' to meet the needs of children consuming and contributing to social media sites (The New London Group, 1996). However, perhaps because of the developing status of traditional literacy competencies, there was no parallel play-based learning movement in early childhood education to help educators engage with the increasing presence of social media in the lives of young children (Edwards et al., 2015).

Spreadable media

The rise of social media via Web 2.0 is credited with what some authors describe as the uptake of 'new new media' (Levinson, 2009). 'New new media' incorporates the notion of 'convergence' (Lash, 2007). Convergence reflects the idea that the boundary between the technology used to access and engage with a given media and the media itself is increasingly blurred. For example, a smartphone is used to take photographs and record video footage, and yet it simultaneously enables immediate access to social media for posting, sharing and commentary. Edwards (2013) regards convergence as increasingly characteristic of young children's digital play arguing that the distinction between the use of the technology by the child to play a game and/or engage with digital media is increasingly difficult to decipher. A commonly described consequence of convergence is the ubiquity of technologies and digital media in daily lives. Jenkins (2006) first described the implications of ubiquitous technology and digital media in terms of transmedia. Transmedia refers to the multiple forms of media available to people on a day-to-day basis. This includes television, radio, online video, traditional texts and digital texts. Transmedia storytelling is a frequently used strategy for engaging contemporary audiences, including young children in the consumption of media. Research by Edwards

(2014) shows that young children can follow the story of Peppa Pig jumping in muddy puddles in media that includes online videos, television, books, gaming and apps. 'New new media' therefore encapsulates the dialectical relationship between convergence and collective intelligence as expressed via the use of social media.

More recently Jenkins, Ford and Green (2013) have raised the notion of spreadable media. Spreadable media conceptualises the common practice of 'liking' and 'sharing' on social media sites and the capacity for people to develop, create and 'mash-up' shared media. Jenkins *et al.* argue that the concept of spreadable media attends to the most recent iteration of the web because it follows the use of information by people across multiple platforms and in many conversations – conducted both online and offline. From our cultural and critical perspective spreadable media is neither inherently good nor bad. Rather, like Jenkins *et al.* we argue that spreadable media is a manifestation of cultural practices driven by the use of available technologies. As evolving web technologies have been developed, they have been adapted and co-opted by people for particular purposes. Jenkins *et al.* argue that people have always shared media – through scrapbooks, re-telling radio broadcasts and/or distributing newspaper clippings. However, the main contribution of technology in this respect is the extent to which it has significantly hastened the process of sharing media over space and time.

While Jenkins *et al.* acknowledge the ubiquity of spreadable media in daily life, other commentators attend to the implications of spreadable media on personal, civic and cultural participation and growth. For example, researchers now actively engage with questions regarding the role of spreadable media in identity formation, issues of privacy, political engagement and even fund-raising through platforms such as 'Go fund me' (Baym & Boyd, 2012). The first two issues in this list are perhaps most pertinent in the lives of young children as their images and experiences are shared by their parents, and oftentimes educators on social media (Feeney & Freeman, 2015).

A significant consideration in the digital age pertaining to spreadable media is the role of algorithms in shaping what and how people are exposed to their daily media engagement. Beer (2009) describes how algorithms shape the flow of information we are exposed to during our interactions with spreadable media. Typically offered via 'recommendations for you' algorithms are step–by–step instructions followed by a technology that provides almost unnoticed services for users. For adults on Facebook, this could be the sudden appearance of advertising for fitness services after once or twice liking the post a relative has made about going to the gym. For young children, this could be the offering of similar videos after watching several episodes of the popular craft programme 'Mister Maker'. Beer (2009) argues that spreadable media is in fact sinking into daily life such that what we are exposed to online gradually and imperceptibly shapes our world-view and knowledge. He reports how even his own research into social media and algorithms is ironically shaped by this process, noting literature searches conducted for his work rely on algorithms and that he has in certain situations even cited books that appeared on his 'recommended for you' list by Amazon. Web 2.0, argues Beer

(2009), requires consideration of how knowledge is used, appropriated and re-constructed, both digitally and by people:

> Web 2.0 technologies are clearly close-up technologies that are on the inside of the lives of users. The acts of participation and collaboration that define the Web 2.0 area are generating information, sensitive and private information, to be harvested and used in the algorithmic process of sorting and the like. As data 'comes to find us' (Lash, 2007), so the things we encounter and consequently our experiences and views of the world, will be shaped by the sorting and filtering of algorithms.
>
> *(p. 998)*

Spreadable social media suggests new requirements of young children playing and learning in the digital age. First, there is actual engagement in spreadable media. Australian research shows that children aged birth to five years commonly use touch-screen technologies to access digital media (Nansen, 2015). Of this use, social media intended for very young children, such as YouTube Kids, is likely to be dominant. From a young age it is probable that consumption is shaped by algorithms. Second, is the concern for learning that engages children in understanding the structure of spreadable media and the way in which this functions to shape media experiences for people. Not all people experience the same media. For very young children both engagement with spreadable media and learning about the structure of media presupposes a conception of the internet and World Wide Web as an interconnected network of technologies enabling social communication. In the early years, new play and learning may not necessarily be immediately attendant on the concept of algorithms, but increasingly require attention to the facilitation of what and how very young children understand the internet as foundational for later social media learning. Research into the pedagogical development of young children's concepts of the internet remains limited. Chaudron (2015) suggests preschoolers are 'little aware' of when they are online. Edwards *et al.* (2016), following Vygotsky (1987), have shown that young children are capable of holding everyday concepts of the internet – such as the purposes to which the internet is put by themselves and family members. They argue that, like play-based science education in early childhood settings, young children's everyday concepts of the internet may be facilitated for development into what Vygotsky (1987) describes as 'mature concepts'. Mature concepts are fostered as children are supported to understand their everyday concepts in relation to academic explanations of given phenomena. In the digital age, this relates to young children's play-based learning opportunities about the internet such that they are supported to understand the networked nature of technologies for social purposes.

Semantic web and the Internet of Things

Beyond Web 2.0 are discussions regarding the semantic web and the Internet of Things. Both the semantic web and the Internet of Things speak to the continued integration of technologies and information with the activities of daily life. The semantic web is predicated on the idea that linked data is more powerful than listed and shared data. Web 2.0 operates using posted and shared data. Computers on the internet communicate with each other using Hypertext Transfer Protocol (HTTP). HTTP is like the syntax of language. It helps computers understand *where* information posted and shared by people is located. However, the semantic web operates by enabling machines to understand the *content* of information posted on the web – it tries to understand meaning. Current search engines respond according to words and phrases whereas the semantic web is orientated towards creating and showing relationships between data as a form of meaning.

When machines are able to link data in terms of meaning, they can create bigger databases for people to use. For example, a search of the terms 'technologies and young children' in Google lists the American-based National Association for the Education of Young Children's (NAEYC) position statement on Technology and the Young Child as the first three items. This information is useful, but as Beer (2009) describes, it has the effect of shaping our knowledge ecology such that we may be unaware of other ways of thinking about the topic 'children and technologies'. However, using the semantic web a search according to these terms could provide linked data regarding technology use by children in the global south and global north. Linked data is considered more powerful than posted data because it creates new relationships for people to explore beyond those which they can initiate through their search processes. In this way, the topic 'children and technologies' does not necessarily just include the NAEYC position statement, but provides insight into how technology use occurs in non-privileged and privileged settings. However, the issue of living in a technologically shaped knowledge ecology is not necessarily made redundant by the semantic web – it is more that the knowledge available is created at greater potential depth and coherence. The need for critical knowledge skills in a digital age corresponds with the evolutions in technologies and associated means of thinking of information and data (whether this be Web 2.0 or semantic web), posing questions about how this is to be taught, learned and developed for young children. Again, the development during the early years of young children's concepts about the internet is pertinent.

The Internet of Things (IoT) explains the increasing enfolding of the digital with what was once entirely analogue. The Internet of Things works using a technology called Radio Frequency ID (RFID) chips. An RFID chip is like an internet address and emits a signal that connects it with the internet. Technically, an RFID chip is small and mobile enough to be placed on literally any item. This means that objects or 'things' commonly used in daily life, such as heating and cooling appliances, clothing, toys and cars can all be connected to the internet – thus resulting in an Internet of Things. Plowman (2015) has been amongst the first early childhood scholars to attend to the implications of the IoT for children's engagements with technologies. She argues that the embeddedness of IoT in commonly used children's objects, such as toys, requires re-thinking 'flat' descriptions of children's engagements with technologies as either online or offline. Instead, Plowman recommends a 'more fluid, emergent and multiscalar understanding of context without boundaries, to think differently about the relationships between practices, people and things' (p. 191). Plowman goes on to argue that the advent of the IoT prompts an awareness of the cultural context as possibly situated, embodied and influenced by actions of the material technologies, rather than always shared but distinct and at a distance from individual actors. Cole's (1996) suggestion that the cultural context can best be conceptualised as a weaving of distinct threads into one relationship in the moment has much to offer here.

This fluid notion characterises thinking about the IoT more broadly, seeing the boundary between the digital and non-digital as increasingly non-existent. Like Beer's (2009) ideas of information sinking into daily life, Floridi (2007), an internet philosopher, describes how the IoT contributes a new informational ecology in which people are always generating, connected to and using data for multiple purposes. These purposes range from the mundane, such as using a 'robot' (e.g. a dishwasher) to complete daily tasks, to the cognitively complex, such as searching for and abstracting information via an online search engine to create a new digital work. Manches, Duncan, Plowman, and Sabeti (2015) describe how IoT toys enable Disney Infinity and Skylanders characters to become alive on the screen such that young children's physical tools integrate with the digital. Floridi (2007) calls this new informational ecology the 'infosphere' arguing that it has emerged as the nature of reality or the ontological perspective we hold about the world has gradually been reshaped by our immediate access to digitalised information. According to Floridi (2007), the 'reontologization' of the environment means that people are now as likely to become cyborgs, as they are to become inforgs:

> What I have in mind is a quieter, less sensational, and yet crucial and profound change in our conception of what it means to be an agent. We are all becoming *connected informational organisms* (*inforgs*). This is happening not through some fanciful transformation in our body, but, more seriously and realistically, through the reontologization of our environment and of ourselves.
>
> (p. 62)

Both the semantic web and the IoT thus hold implications for the nature of the world in which young children are growing up in the digital age. Information that sinks into daily life, agentic technologies, the semantic web that creates and provides access to connected data and the experience of living within an IoT all suggest new informational and knowledge patterns and relationships between technologies, individuals and their cultural context that mean that attending only to children's *use of technology* will be increasingly inadequate for their life and cultural needs. Instead, new ways of thinking about technology in society and children's engagements with technologies will be required of the early childhood sector – from educators, through to researchers, policy and decision-makers. It is our contention that these developments should not focus so much on how technologies are being employed or what they can be employed to do as on the development of the understandings and skills needed for everyday life in the digital age. One such new understanding we argue is that of development of young children's conceptions of inter-networked technologies and the social dimensions of the World Wide Web in the early years. Not previously required of young children, such understanding is now central to their participation in a world in which they are highly likely to engage with spreadable media and/or the IoT.

Conclusion

By the end of this chapter we have located the play and learning of young children in the digital age within the widespread cultural use and application of interconnected technologies that allow an ease of distributed communication amongst people alongside significant capacity for the storage, retrieval, representation and sharing of information. The Internet of Things extends this collection, storage and analysis of information from computers to objects and actions across the everyday lives of children within their families, communities and their experience of educational settings. The semantic web raises questions about the relationship between individuals and knowledge and the act of knowing and learning. These innovations suggest to us that thinking about young children learning in the digital age requires a shift away from a focus on the 'what, when, how and what outcomes' of encounters with technologies to a more culturally orientated and critical engagement with the digital era that takes account of context, history, roles, forms of engagement and technology usage for building the inter-networked knowledge young children require for their informed participation in the digital age.

References

Abelson, R. (2000, 8 November). Technology; pets.com, sock puppet's home, will close. *New York Times.* Retrieved from www.nytimes.com/2000/11/08/business/technology-petscom-sock-puppet-s-home-will-close.html.

Baran, P. (1962). *On distributed communications networks.* Santa Monica, CA: RAND Corporation.

Baym, N. K., & Boyd, D. (2012). Socially mediated publicness: an introduction. *Journal of Broadcasting & Electronic Media, 56*(3), 320–329. doi: 10.1080/08838151.2012.705200.

Beer, D. (2009). Power through the algorithm? Participatory web cultures and the technological unconscious. *New Media & Society, 11*, 985–1002. doi: 10.1177/1461444809336551.

Berners-Lee, T. (1989). Hypertext and CERN. Retrieved from www.w3.org/Administration/HTandCERN.txt.

Burnett, C., & Merchant, G. (2015). The challenge of 21st century literacies. *Journal of Adolescent and Adult Literacy, 59*(3), 271–274.

Chaudron, S. (2015). Young children (0–8) and digital technology: a qualitative exploratory study across seven countries. Luxembourg: Publications Office of the European Union. Retrieved from http://publications.jrc.ec.europa.eu/repository/handle/JRC93239.

Cole, M. (1996). *Cultural psychology: a once and future discipline.* Cambridge, MA: Harvard University Press.

Edwards, S. (2013). Digital play in the early years: a contextual response to the problem of integrating digital technologies and play-based learning in the early childhood curriculum. *European Early Childhood Education Research Journal*, *21*(2), 199–212.

Edwards, S. (2014). Towards contemporary play: sociocultural theory and the digital-consumerist context. *Journal of Early Childhood Research*, *12*(3), 219–233.

Edwards, S., Nuttall, J., Lee, S., Wood, L., Mantilla, A., & Grieshaber, S. (2015). Digital play: what do teachers see? In S. Bulfin, N. Johnson, & C. Bigum (Eds.), *Critical perspectives on education and technology* (pp. 69–84). New York, NY: Palgrave Macmillan.

Edwards, S., Nolan, A., Henderson, M., Mantilla, A., Plowman, L., & Skouteris, H. (2016). Young children's everyday concepts about the internet: implications for cyber-safety education in the early years. *British Journal of Educational Technology*. doi: 10.1111/bjet.12529.

Enzenberger, H. (1970). Constituents of a theory of the media. *New Left Review*, *64*, 13–36.

Feeney, S., & Freeman, N. K. (2015). Smartphones and social media: ethical implications for educators. *YC Young Children*, *70*(1), 98–101.

Flew, T. (2014). *New media* (4th edn). Oxford: Oxford University Press.

Floridi, L. (2007). A look into the future impact of ICT on our lives. *The Information Society*, *23*(1), 59–64.

Greenhow, C., Robelia, B., & Hughes, J. E. (2009). Learning, teaching, and scholarship in a digital age Web 2.0 and classroom research: what path should we take now? *Educational researcher*, *38*(4), 246–259.

Hauben, M., & Hauben, R. (1998). Netizens: on the history and impact of Usenet and the Internet. *First Monday*, *3*(7).

Jenkins, H. (2006). *Convergence culture: where old and new media collide*. New York, NY: New York University Press.

Jenkins, H., Ford, S., & Green, J. (2013). *Spreadable media: creating value and meaning in a networked culture*. New York, NY: New York University Press.

Lankshear, C., & Knobel, M. (2006). Researching new literacies: Web 2.0 practices and insider perspectives. *E-Learning*, *4*(3), 224–240.

Lash, S. (2007). 'New new media ontology'. Presentation at Toward a Social Science of Web 2.0, National Science Learning Centre, York, UK, 5 September.

Levinson, P. (2009). *New new media*. Boston: Allyn & Bacon.

Manches, A., Duncan, P., Plowman, L., & Sabeti, S. (2015). Three questions about the Internet of things and children. *Tech Trends*, *59*(1), 76–78.

Masuda, Y. (1980). *The information society as post-industrial society*. Tokyo: Institute for the Information Society.

McLuhan, M. (1951). *The mechanical bride: folklore of industrial man*. Boston: Beacon Press.

Moon, J., & Kim, Y. (2001). Extending the TAM for a World Wide Web context. *Information and Management*, *38*, 217–230.

Nansen, B. (2015). Accidental, assisted, automated: an emerging repertoire of infant mobile media techniques. *M/C Journal*, *18*(5).

O'Reilly, T. (2005, 30 September). *What is Web 2.0? Design patterns and business models for the next generation of software*. Retrieved from www.oreilly.com/pub/a//web2/archive/what-is-web-20.html.

Plowman, L. (2015). Rethinking context: digital technologies and children's everyday lives. *Children's Geographies*, *14*(2), 190–202.

Rosenzweig, R. (1998). Wizards, bureaucrats, warriors and hackers: writing the history of the internet. *The American Historical Review*, *103*(5), 1530–1552.

The New London Group (1996). A pedagogy of multiliteracies: designing social futures. *Harvard Educational Review*, *66*(1), 60–93. doi: 10.17763/haer.66.1.17370n67v22j160u.

Vygotsky, L. S. (1987). Problems of general psychology. In R. Rieber, A. Carton, & N. Minick (Eds.), *The collected works of L. S. Vygotsky* (Vol. 1). New York, NY: Plenum Press.

Williams, R. (1958). Culture is ordinary. In J. Higgins (Ed.) (2001), *The Raymond Williams reader* (pp. 10–25). Oxford: Blackwell.

PART II

Play and learning

Part II is concerned with two areas of young children's experience that are central to early years research and theory – play and learning. Continuing with the cultural and critical perspective we have adopted throughout this book we turn in this section to consider ways of thinking about learning that make sense in contemporary contexts and question the notion that technologies determine learning outcomes. Chapter 4 begins by challenging the dependence on technological potential that can arise when educators, policy-makers and parents debate the place of digital resources and activities in the lives of young children. We go on to suggest that the multidisciplinary approach of the Learning Sciences with its concern with Mode 2 or context- and problem-related learning offers an appropriate base for considering play and learning in the digital age. Chapter 5 is about the emergence of the concept of digital play. We look first at the ways in which conceptualising traditional play has been applied to play with digital technologies, before turning our attention to new thinking about digital play. We highlight the cultural meaning of digital play for children and observe the blending of digital and non-digital play in young children's everyday experiences.

4

LEARNING AND TECHNOLOGIES

Introduction

In this chapter we begin by taking a critical look at the oft mentioned 'potential' of technologies to make a difference to children's learning. We advance a more cultural and critical perspective as an alternative to the deterministic orientation towards technological potential before considering the value understandings from the Learning Sciences, and in particular the work of Alan Kay, have to offer as a framework for understanding young children's learning in the digital age.

Assumptions about technological potential

Young children's learning in the digital age is sometimes tied to assumptions about the potential of technologies to enable children's learning in newer or more effective ways. Assumed relations between technologies and learning tend to mirror technological determinist notions of cause and effect. Here, technologies themselves are often described in the literature as having an almost inherent potential for informing young children's learning – often for the better with respect. For example:

> In their review of the literature, Vernadakis, Avgerinos, Tsitskari, and Zachopoulou (2005) indicated that computer-assisted instruction (CAI) in preschool holds much promise as the technology becomes more accessible. CAI offers pictures and sounds to support the natural ways that young children learn. Engagement in the learning process is directly linked to motivation, as illustrated in Haugland's (1999) study, which found the motivation of kindergarten and primary-aged children increased when academic instruction was paired with the use of computers.
>
> *(Couse & Chen, 2010, p. 76)*

Also, Flewitt, Messer, and Kucirkova (2015):

> Empirical research has begun to piece together evidence regarding the teaching/ learning potential of new technologies, including phonological awareness, vocabulary learning, reading comprehension and language development.
>
> *(Burnett, 2010; Flewitt et al. 2015 citing Burnett et al. 2012, p. 4)*

Focusing on the potential of technologies to enhance young children's learning is seductive. First, technological potential can be a way for researchers, teachers and policy-makers to respond to the imperatives of a digital age. Believing that technologies have the potential to enhance children's learning provides a justification for technological provision in the early years. This justification becomes particularly important in the face of fierce opposition to the role of technologies in early childhood settings (e.g. House, 2011) – such as that customarily characterised by the range of moral panic we examine later in Chapter 7. Second, technologies are attractive to young children. Research by Stephen, McPake, Plowman, and Berch-Heyman (2008) shows that technologies have high levels of status appeal to children. Young children frequently observe adults, older children and siblings using technologies and quite reasonably wish to engage with them as well – if adults are able to justify young children's engagement with technologies in terms of 'learning potential' and children enjoy using them it is easier to establish a pedagogical rationale for their role in learning. Third, technologies allow adults to create digital content for children that can feel comfortingly familiar in terms of realising learning potential. Games and apps designed to help children learn in traditional content areas, such as literacy and numeracy, feature activities pertaining to size, shape, number, colour and letter recognition that appear to fulfil the promise that technologies can help children learn.

However, we contend that operating from a perspective of technological potential incurs difficulties in early childhood education. This is because an emphasis on potential places the responsibility for learning on the technology. As we discussed in the preceding chapter, technological innovation from radio, to television and now digital media are neither good nor bad for learning. Technologies are located in historical and cultural contexts, and contexts comprise people engaged in human activities. Placing responsibility for learning on the technology, instead of seeking to understand the relevant cultural context is a reoccurring trope in early childhood education. This trope tells a story of technological possibility in which young children's learning will be transformed by using listening posts, desktop computers, digital cameras or, most recently – iPads (Bebell & Pedulla, 2015). In a comprehensive review of the literature about technologies in early childhood education, Bolstad (2004) recognised the extent of this dependency on the idea of technological potential. She found that there was more literature arguing for the potential of technologies to transform learning in the early years than there was literature grounded in empirical evidence about the outcomes of encounters with technologies in early childhood education settings. Ten years later in 2014 that potential was still being claimed as a report from the RAND Corporation illustrates (Daugherty, Dossani, Johnson, & Oguz, 2014). The RAND report frames the potential of technologies to contribute to learning in terms of 'may' and 'can' and suggests that, as the early years are known to be an important period for developing academic skills, they are probably also a good time to enhance technological literacy. Turvey and Pachler (2016) identify assertions about the apparent self-evident benefits of engaging learning technologies in educational settings as problematic and go on to suggest that this belief is compounded when technologies are sold to schools as 'solutions' without acknowledging that they can significantly disrupt existing pedagogic practices.

Making technologies responsible for learning also leads to the creation of the games and apps that replicate the value of existing forms of knowledge for children instead of seeking to realise the alternative patterns of communication and thinking associated with the semantic web and the IoT. Much of the content of the digital games that children are provided with in educational settings (and at home) involves practising and extending the same cognitive operations they experience with traditional educational materials. As they engage with these games children are invited to sort, label, count, match and categorise – all important operations, but not necessarily stretching their capacity to use technologies and digital media for the range of communicative reasons with which they are familiar in their daily lives, let alone helping children reflect on or develop critical capacities for responding to how knowledge is presented and shaped by technologies (e.g. Beer's (2009) concept of algorithmically generated knowledge sinking into daily life).

Additionally, and perhaps most significantly, making technologies responsible for learning deflects attention from pedagogical concerns. When teachers, administrators, researchers and policy-makers are focused on technological potential they can be distracted from understanding how children learn. This is because the technology becomes the focus of attention rather than what and how children and adults will learn together with technologies in a given setting. As Edwards (2015) notes, the need for new pedagogical ideas about young children's learning with technologies has been an enduring concern in the early childhood literature for decades. In the late 1970s and early 1980s Kay and Goldberg (1977) and Papert (1980) promoted computer programming as a vehicle for young children's learning *with* technologies. But learning with technologies via computer programming arguably involves children in a unique set of problem-solving activities that are not necessarily enabled by apps directed towards teaching children concepts about shape, number or letter. By 1993 Cuban (1993) was still talking about the lack of pedagogical development in the ways in which technologies were being used to support learning for young children.

By 2008, with the exception of work by Stephen and Plowman (e.g. Stephen & Plowman, 2008) on the need for distal and proximal guided interaction when children engage with digital technologies in early education settings, little progress had been made in the development of new pedagogical knowledge about learning with technologies. Marsh *et al.* (2005) in their oft-cited *Digital Beginnings* report suggested that the main problem facing the field was the lack of progress in developing new pedagogical knowledge about how to use computers and digital media with young children in early childhood settings. A few years later and little had changed. In Australia, Nicola Yelland (2011) lamented a lack of progress in better understanding early learning with technologies. Meanwhile, in America a report released by the Digital Age Teacher Preparation Council (Barron *et al.*, 2011) claimed that the most pressing professional development need facing early childhood teachers in the digital age was about early learning *with* technologies. In 2012 the American National Association for the Education of Young Children (NAEYC, 2012) position statement on technologies and digital media in the early years indicated an urgent need for research about early learning with technologies. So aside from a deterministic perspective on the potential of technologies to enhance learning, or a position of moral panic rejecting their use entirely, what is available to those researchers, educators and policy-makers seeking to make sense of the learning needs of young children in a digital age?

A critical perspective on technologies

Neil Selwyn, a leading thinker about technologies in education and society, argues that a critical perspective on technologies and learning is necessary to avoid the pitfalls of technological determinism. He views a critical perspective on technologies as located in a consideration of the 'development and implementation of technological innovations as set within specific social and economic contexts' (Selwyn, 2010, p. 69). In this book, we have thus far focused on technological innovation in cultural-historical terms, considering the role of knowledge and the range of social and economic contexts that have influenced the development of the digital age, including the movement from industrialism to post-industrialism, the influence of the Cold War and the counter-cultural movement of the 1960s on the invention of the internet, and the impact of the dot.com boom on consequent generations or 'versions' of the internet – from Web 1.0 to the semantic web and IoT. The breadth of cultural-historical engagement we have presented thus far is not typically considered in texts regarding technologies in early childhood education. Yet we have consistently argued that it does in fact matter that researchers, teachers and policy-makers have a broad frame of reference for understanding how and why the digital age in which the young learners of today are growing up came about. This is because the circumstances of the present are always preceded by the activities of the past. It is not possible to appreciate why we need to consider young children's learning in a digital age if we do not know and understand how the digital age evolved over time. For example, in Chapter 3 we suggested that understanding the basis of networked technologies is a new learning requirement of the digital age for young children. Understanding how young children's encounters today with social media, such as YouTube Kids, and play with IoT toys, such as Disney Infinity and Skylanders, depend on historic innovations in networked computing allows us to think critically about the implications of these technologies for what and how young children learn and what is needed from adults to support their learning.

Selwyn (2010) argues that a strong grounding in the literature and research beyond that focused solely on educational technology is necessary to inform critical perspectives on technologies and learning. In fact, he argues that a broader perspective enables criticality because it re-focuses attention on what he calls 'state-of-the-actual' questions with respect to technology use. For Selwyn, state-of-the-actual questions move beyond the potential of technologies to wrought changes in learning and consider instead what is actually happening with technologies in different contexts – socially and educationally. In this way, researchers, administrators and educators are able to focus more carefully on the role of technologies in the historically shaped 'everyday' contexts experienced by young children, their families and their teachers. This call to consider how technologies are being used in everyday contexts in order to better understand the social and educational opportunities and challenges of the digital age, is central to the cultural and critical perspective that underpins this book.

In 2015 Edwards, Nuttall, Mantilla, Wood, and Grieshaber applied Selwyn's critical perspective on technology education to a common problem in early childhood education – that of technological integration with traditional approaches to play-based learning. Using the notion of 'state-of-the-actual' questions, they argued that little attention had been paid to *what* early childhood teachers recognised as play in the context of the digital age within the more localised context of their own classroom. Researching closely with three teachers and a group of five male pre-schoolers, they offered children the opportunity to play with representations of 'farm' or 'train' sets along a continuum of traditional to digital play (Marsh, 2010). In the first iteration of activity children were invited to play with a traditional unbranded farm or train set. Children's play with the selected sets was video-recorded. Next children were invited to use a branded play set – including a Peppa Pig and Thomas the Tank Engine set. Again the play was recorded. Finally, children were invited to play with Peppa Pig and Thomas the Tank Engine apps on an iPad. The play was once again recorded. Later, footage of the children at play in each iteration was shown to the teachers individually in a stimulated video recall interview. Further, a focus group interview involving all three teachers was held during which they reflected on their individual responses to each filmed episode of play. The findings suggested that the teachers saw more value for learning in the unbranded farm or train set play than they did in either the branded or iPad play.

The teachers in this study struggled to recognise the branded and digital play as the kind of play they considered viable for learning. While they acknowledged that the children were highly engaged in the latter two activities they nonetheless asked 'but is it play?' In their article, Edwards *et al.* argued that a focus on the state-of-actual meant understanding teachers' perspectives on digital play and what they valued as 'educational play' within their classroom rather than a continued focus on using technology in early childhood education. In contrast to existing research that promoted the potential of technologies to support young children's learning (e.g. Lee & O'Rourke, 2006) or described the failure to achieve this potential from a pedagogical perspective (e.g. Blackwell, Lauricella, & Wartella, 2014), the work of Edwards *et al.* (2015) offered new insights into the nature of the problem – teachers' understanding of what constitutes play for learning when that play involved technologies. In an earlier paper, examining this same theme, Nuttall, Edwards, Mantilla, Grieshaber, and Wood (2015) argued that it would not matter how much professional development teachers participated in regarding technology use in early childhood education – while their ideas about play did not include the digital they were unlikely to successfully incorporate technologies into the curriculum. Nuttall *et al.* (2015) argued that this situation emerged because the teachers were committed to an historical view or definition of play that was no longer serving their purposes in light of the children's new engagements in the digital age. Their pedagogical commitment to a version of play that values active engagement with real-world objects did not easily accommodate what may be seen as 'engaging' games or activities which they considered more suitable for home-based leisure than learning in an educational setting. This distinction is likely to be heightened when digital games or apps include features that teachers associate with cartoons, digital media and particular commercial brands, a reaction which relates to a broader debate about appropriate resources for play in educational settings (Cook, 2014).

Focusing on the everyday context of technology is also described by Caldwell (2000) as central to better understanding technology use in society and education. Caldwell argues that new technologies too often capture attention when they are on the 'pre-curve' of their wave to peak popularity. Researchers and educationalists will typically feature the latest technology (or more contemporarily the latest 'app') with the potential to 'change' educational processes. Caldwell says that it is not the pre-curve or peak curve that should be of interest to researchers and teachers. Instead, Caldwell is interested in the post-curve, or the historical time point when the hype about a technology has died down and we can see how the innovations are 'embedded in the day to day'. Following Caldwell (2000) and Selwyn (2010), we argue in this book that focusing on the 'state of the actual' or the 'everyday' in relation to the cultural-historical evolution of the digital age provides a suitable basis for understanding and critically responding to young children's play and learning in the digital age. One source of knowledge to inform our understanding of the 'state of the actual' with respect to young children's play and learning in the digital age is what is known as the Learning Sciences.

Looking to the Learning Sciences

The Learning Sciences represents the collective body of research, theory and philosophical thought describing contemporary thinking about learning and teaching. Sawyer (2005) argues that the Learning Sciences represent a response to the problem of instructionism as a heritage model of learning relevant to the industrial age and still operating in the new digital age. As we discussed in Chapter 2 of this book, the industrial age was driven by the production of saleable goods on a mass scale. Living and working during this time required adherence to routine-based tasks and chronological time management so that mass production could be achieved. The role of education, rather baldly speaking, was the achievement of a sufficient level of literacy and numeracy to enable participation in the action of production. Mimicking the notion of production, industrialised education tended towards what Kalantzis, Cope, and the Learning by Design Project Group (2005) describe as 'didactism' to 'produce' learning – one teacher, teaching many children of the same age, the same material, at the same time (p. 17). Didactic instructionism arguably reached its pedagogical limits as the digital age evolved. As we discussed in Chapter 2, Masuda's (1980) theory of societal technology described how increments in knowledge production would result in combined technological innovations leading to changed social patterns of communication and economic participation. Bell (1976) called this the 'knowledge society' – arguing that in the future it would be knowledge, and not skills alone that mattered for social and workforce participation. For example, Mills (2011) in an examination of the required literacies practices of contemporary primary school-aged children wrote:

> The existing and emerging social practices in which these students must engage include reading books, resisting advertisements, using machines (scanners, printers, voicemail), interpreting public transport information, writing memos, following directories and maps and conducting internet transactions. Similarly, SMS messaging, word processing, emailing, digital relay chatting, internet navigation, critiquing websites, digital photography, slide-show presentations, computer programming and website design represent some of the diverse forms of literacy.
>
> *(p. 3)*

As researchers became increasingly alert to the changes in social and communicative engagement associated with innovations in technologies, more attention was paid to the complex nature of the evolving learning environment facing children in the digital age. Increasingly, a mono-theoretical reliance on one approach towards learning was viewed as ineffective in tackling this complexity when explanations for how children learned with and from multi-modal technologies and asynchronous forms of communication were needed. Beginning in the literature associated with literacy learning, inter-disciplinarity began to be favoured as an alternative perspective. Inter-disciplinarity is defined as the application of one or more established bodies of knowledge in the search for a solution to an existing problem situation (Choi & Pak, 2008).

Brooker and Edwards (2010) examine this movement to plurality in research and theorisation about young children's play in early childhood education settings. In the introduction to their edited collection about play titled *Engaging Play*, they used the concepts of Mode 1 and Mode 2 knowledge as defined by Nowotny, Scott, and Gibbons (2001) to understand the difference between working from a mono-theoretical perspective of knowledge generation and using inter-disciplinary knowledge. Mode 1 knowledge is the form of knowledge generation Nowotny *et al.* describe as homogeneous and consistently working to build knowledge within a single field. In contrast, Mode 2 knowledge responds to the 'context of application' or the problem situation in which people find themselves located at any given time. Mode 2 knowledge draws on multiple knowledge perspectives to inform how a situation may be interpreted, engaged with and addressed. Mode 1 and Mode 2 knowledge are not necessarily mutually exclusive. Rather, Mode 1 knowledge feeds into how Mode 2 knowledge is used and adapted, and indeed, insights from the application of Mode 2 knowledge can drive forward thinking and innovation in Mode 1 knowledge. In their book, Brooker and Edwards (2010) used the plurality suggested by Mode 2 knowledge as a basis for engaging with different views on play and play-based learning in early childhood education settings against a background of technological change.

The Learning Sciences represents a way of thinking about Mode 2 knowledge. It encapsulates a variety of theoretical and philosophical perspectives and disciplines. These include: constructivism, sociocultural studies, cognitive science, sociology, computer science, neuroscience and psychology (Sawyer, 2005). A highly cited summation of the foundational knowledge to be generated from the Learning Sciences indicates some core ideas about contemporary thinking with respect to learning in the digital age (Bransford, Brown, & Cocking, 2000). These ideas draw on understandings about the social, cultural and historical construction of knowledge by people including the role of pre-existing knowledge in building new knowledge, the significance of community context in framing cultural understandings and expectations of learning and the role of activity in learning. Simply described, the foundational ideas in the Learning Sciences include:

1. Building on the pre-existing knowledge base of learners.
2. Engaging learners in multiple types of learning, including active and observational learning.
3. Ensuring that learning is directed towards the development of understanding.
4. Creating culturally relevant learning through community connectedness.

(Bransford et al., 2000)

Derived from a multidisciplinary perspective on learning, the foundational ideas of the Learning Sciences are not necessarily entirely new to the field of early childhood education. As a discipline, early childhood education has in some respects always been characterised by inter-disciplinarity, drawing as it does in historical terms on the earliest ideas of Plato, through to the work of Rousseau and later the contributions of psychoanalytic theory and developmental psychology (Bergen, 2014). This range of ideas has informed a largely 'active' perspective on young children's learning in the early years. In the introduction to *The SAGE Handbook of Play and Learning*, Brooker, Blaise, and Edwards (2014) wrote of the range of theoretical ideas and inquiry informing early childhood education:

A reader of early childhood research might well encounter ideas and arguments from philosophy, psychology, history, evolutionary biology, anthropology and sociology. Each of these disciplines follows its own traditions and lines of arguments. They hold varying epistemological and ontological positions, which in turn means they understand play and learning in sometimes complementary and at other times entirely contrary ways. To grasp an understanding of play and learning in early childhood is to recognise the breadth and depth of ideas on which the field draws and to which it contributes.

(p. 1)

To take a multidisciplinary perspective means to summarise, understand and apply the insight and knowledge different fields have to offer for understanding a complex 'context of application' (Nowotny *et al.*, 2001) – such as that represented by the digital age. From the perspective of the Learning Sciences, multi-disciplinarity means considering what an extensive body of research and literature suggests for how people learn (Bransford *et al.*, 2000). For early childhood education, this same construct suggests drawing on a multiplicity of theoretical perspectives, research and philosophical orientations to understand the learning of young children. The identification by the Learning Sciences of the four fundamental ideas pertaining to how people learn should not make unfamiliar reading for those involved in the education of young children. The social and active construction of knowledge in community contexts that builds on children's pre-existing knowledge is a long held tenet of early childhood education. This being so, what, if anything, does the Learning Sciences have to offer early childhood education as an informant to young children's play and learning in the digital age?

The answer to this question is located in Kalantzis and Cope's (2014) carefully sustained argument for the role of Learning Sciences in 21st century knowledge contexts. They argue that attention should be paid to the word 'science'. Typically, science is understood as the 'hard' sciences – physics, chemistry and biology. Alternative ways of thinking are attributed to the 'humanities' – the arts, religion, music, literature and language. Kalantzis and Cope (2014) draw attention to the etymology of the word 'science' over the more typical use of the word as a representative of the 'hard' sciences. Science, as they describe the term, derives from the Latin 'sciens' which means 'knowing'. Applied to the Learning Sciences, science does not mean 'hard' science – but a way of knowing. Thus the Learning Sciences focuses on *knowing about learning*:

> The main goal of science we want to propose implies an intensity of focus – science is focused, systematic, premeditated, reflective, purposeful, disciplined and open to scrutiny by a community of experts.
>
> *(Kalantzis & Cope, 2014, p. 105)*

This reflection on the notion of 'science-as-knowing' enables alternative forms of thinking about young children's learning in the digital age. Instead of being governed in our responses to young children's technology use by moral panic or assumptions about the potential of technologies to impact children's learning, we can as Selwyn (2010) and Caldwell (2000) suggest take a more 'critical' or 'embedded' stance. The Learning Sciences reminds us to engage with children's learning in the digital age in a 'reflective and purposeful' way (Kalantzis & Cope, 2014). When thinking about young children's learning in a digital age, recourse to romanticism about the learning of the previous era will not necessarily be helpful for meeting the learning needs of the current generation. Indeed it can result in educators feeling disempowered and unsure of their pedagogical role. Instead, the notion of 'sciens' – or 'knowing' – about learning is productive because it reminds us to balance the technological with the pedagogical. In this way, young children's learning in the digital age is not characterised as a dichotomous situation in which technologies are considered either inherently 'good' or 'bad' for learning. Instead, 'sciens' allows us to shift the balance of our attention back to the pedagogical in relation to the technology in a way that draws on what we know about young children's learning and consider to be valued outcomes.

Alan Kay – the original Learning Scientist?

Now that we are thinking about the balance between learning and technologies we wish to ask yet another question. Alan Kay, the computer scientist we introduced in Chapter 2, produced the conceptual foundation for touchscreen technologies that later led to the invention of the iPad in 2010 via his DynaBook concept. Biographically, Alan Kay is described as a computer scientist. Our question, is: what would happen to understandings about learning in the digital age if, instead of being thought of as a computer scientist, we considered Alan Kay as amongst the most original of Learning Scientists ever to have significantly impacted the field of early learning? We ask this question because his thinking in the design of the DynaBook was not focused per se in the form of 'potential' – his thinking was instead orientated towards the dialectical relationship between learning *and* technologies. As a consequence of this orientation the design of his DynaBook laid the foundations for the range of tablet technologies that have increased the saturation of easily used technologies by very young children into daily life within many post-industrialised societies. This saturation, as we will discover in Chapter 6, has reached countries as diverse as Estonia, South Africa, Thailand and China. Between 2011 and 2013 access to a tablet computer at home for children aged 0–8 years in the USA rose from 8 per cent to 40 per cent (Common Sense Media, 2013). Children are now reported to be using touchscreen technologies while they are 'still in diapers' (Rosin, 2013) and by 2013 38 per cent of under 2s had used a smartphone or tablet in the USA (Common Sense Media, 2013). In the UK in 2016 more than half of three to four year olds made use of a tablet computer at home (Ofcom, 2016). The DynaBook, with its premise that it become a 'personal, portable information manipulator' (Kay, 1972, p. 1) for children, has opened a new relationship between learning and the concept of the digital in a way that was not previously available to very young children.

While Alan Kay is widely cited and known in the computing science literature (Alesso & Smith, 2008), his work is not highly evident in the early childhood research literature pertaining to young children's learning with digital technologies. Yet, his interest in the dawning digital age of the 1970s was firmly focused on the dialectic between learning and technologies. Consistent with the Learning Sciences principles of multidisciplinarity and 'knowing-about-learning' he read widely across many disciplines, including in the areas of learning and creativity, anthropology and psychology, philosophy, art and design, technology and media, science and mathematics, politics, economics and computing. From this reading, he came to hold a specific view of the child-as-learner in relation to their engagements with technologies. Contrary to previously popular notions of transmissionist education, Kay (1972) understood the child: 'as a verb not a noun, an actor rather than an object. He [*sic*] is not a scaled-up pigeon or rat; he is trying to acquire a model of his surrounding environment in order to deal with it' (p. 1). As such, Kay understood that learning and technologies are in relationship with each other. Existing attention on technologies at the time focused on using technologies as 'learning machines'. Typically, learning machines deployed a transmissionist approach towards teaching children 'facts'. Kay (1972) viewed this approach as a waste of technological capacity, describing a learning machine as 'information delivered in a box – well-intentioned but lacking in talent' (p. 1).

Being focused on learning meant that Kay understood technologies as autotelic environments. Influenced by psychologist Omar Khayyam Moore's (1966) work on the role of the environment on children's learning, Kay believed that his Dyna-Book should be an engaging space for *learning in and of itself*. This view contrasts with an emphasis on technological potential in which the technology alone is often considered responsible for the learning (or more probably the 'teaching' of content to children). Understanding the DynaBook as an engaging space meant that Kay was able to consider how the evolving technological landscape of his time related to his view of the child-as-learner. He saw that advances in GUI design would enable symbolic representations to be employed in his DynaBook. Reflecting his reading of Piaget and Inhelder (1969), Piaget (1974) and Bruner (1966, 1971) about young children's symbolic representations, Kay argued that the DynaBook GUI would be designed in: 'a language which uses linguistic concepts not far removed from the owner of the device. The owner will be able to maintain and edit his own files of text and programs when and where he chooses' (Kay, 1972, p. 6). For young children, this meant an accessible GUI based on icons and images which the pre-literate child would be able to operate independently of adult support. In this example, we see how Kay's 'sciens' or 'knowing about learning' integrated with the technological evolutions of the time to create a new dialectical relationship between learning and technologies such that each provided a continually evolving counterpoint for the other. Previously, computers for children had been seen as machines that 'produced' learning. Kay's knowledge about learning meant that he was able to balance the capacity of technologies to digitise information with his understanding about how young children learn.

Alongside Kay's vision for the interface design of the DynaBook was his belief that children should be able to engage with symbolic representations using technologies to build their own knowledge base. Kay was influenced by Papert's (1970) ideas about LOGO computing whereby Papert (1980) had asked 'should the computer program the child or the child the computer?' (p. 19). Once again, the technology was not overly invested with the potential for supporting learning – it was balanced in relation to the child's own learning and activity. A technology, such as the DynaBook should be understood as a type of 'meta-medium' – containing access to all the information and guidance for engaging with that information a learner was likely to need. In this view of technology, Kay was influenced by his reading of Montessori (1972), Vygotsky (1986) and Bruner (1966). He understood learning in terms of discovery, believing a 'meta-medium' would foster children's discovery of ideas and concepts. However, drawing on Vygotsky (1986), Kay was clear that such discovery should be guided by more knowledgeable others. What the child should independently discover was not necessarily the content of a discipline, but the final connections between ideas within a discipline. He wrote:

> It is very difficult for human beings to come up with good ideas from scratch – hence the need for forms of guidance – but that things are learned best if the learner puts the effort to make the final connections themselves – hence the need for the processes of discovery.
>
> *(Kay, 2013, p. 8)*

With this view of learning, technologies could no longer be effectively positioned as learning machines delivering content to children. Nor could the technology alone be viewed as holding the 'potential' to do anything for the child – whether this be positive in terms of learning achievement, or negative in relation to moral panic and romanticised notions of learning from previous generations. In contrast, Kay (2013) began to talk of technologies as *amplifiers* for children's activities. Again, reading widely in the areas of history, technology and media, and psychology he reflected on the history of writing and the invention of the printing press as a new technology in the early part of the 15th century. He argued that writing and the mass publication of printed materials were new forms of technology that rapidly increased or 'amplified' the access people had to information, and therefore contributed a corresponding increase in their opportunities to grow new knowledge. Kay (2013) argued that new technologies (whether writing by hand, the printing press or a computer) should be thought of as 'amplifiers that add or multiply to what we already have rather than replacing them' (p. 1). According to Kay, thinking of technologies as amplifiers had the benefit of increasing the communicative reach of information over time and space. A technology such as the printed word, 'added to' or 'multiplied' the effect of the already existing spoken word because it had increased reach over time and space. Augmented reach over time and space enabled efficiencies in the creation of knowledge amongst people. In this way, all people would have 'more to think about and with' (Kay, 2013, p. 1).

By considering Kay as the original Learning Scientist, we are able to reflect more carefully on what young children's learning in the digital age is likely to mean. A new technology is neither good nor bad for learning – but it is qualitatively different from the technologies that came before. Young children's learning in the digital age is a co-evolving process in which learning influences technological innovation and technological innovation amplifies knowledge possibilities. This idea mirrors a claim made by cultural-historical theory that all cultures create tools and practices that attend to their needs over a period of time (Davydov, 1982). As cultural tools and practices are developed by people over time they create new cultural ecologies or developmental niches for their children. This is important to remember when thinking about learning in the digital age because young children are born into and grow up in communities that are already using a range of historical and more recent technologies to achieve their goals. This idea is succinctly expressed by van Oers (2008), a contemporary cultural-historical theorist, who like Kay also draws on the ideas of Vygotsky to inform his thinking about learning:

> Different cultures and generations will get their children and pupils involved in different types of actions [activities], depending on the educators' worldview, epistemological beliefs, and image of the child and of a future society.
>
> (p. 7)

A dialectical perspective on learning and technologies highlights the process of amplification that contributes to a continuous evolving relationship between learning and technologies. As van Oers (2008) describes 'the process of learning itself' (p. 7) changes. So far in this book we have illustrated how changes in knowledge have contributed to technological innovation, and how technological innovation in turn has created qualitatively new forms of learning and communication opportunities for children. For example, the developing knowledge base in solid state physics we described in Chapter 2 gave rise to the transistor and then the microprocessor that enabled the digitisation of information. As technologies such as the microprocessor were developed the capacity for a massive increase in the storage and retrieval of information via personal computing was realised. The storage of information led to the desire for networked information and so gave rise to the internet. New forms of sharing via the internet generated increased possibilities for communication and promoted the invention of the World Wide Web. Following the World Wide Web we now have advances taking place in cognitive computing, the IoT and semantic web. These advances in technological knowledge have amplified current communication and information sharing practices that change the everyday experiences of adults and children and afford new ways of learning in the digital age. This new learning is commonly described as being multi-modal, communication focused and problem-orientated (Kalantzis & Cope, 2012).

In this book we do not see this 'new' learning as any better or worse than older forms of learning. Instead, as we have argued in Chapter 2, learning is related to the cultural-historical activities of the time in which it is located. Alongside Kay, we understand that technologies do not of themselves replace older forms of learning. The amplification of information sharing and communication made possible by technologies co-evolves with new learning. As digital literacy theorists Lankshear and Knobel (2012) describe it:

> New literacies are best understood in terms of an historical period of social, cultural, institutional, economic, and intellectual change that is likely to span many decades – some of which are already behind us. We associated new literacies with an historical conjecture and an ascending social paradigm. From this perspective we suggest that the kinds of practices we currently identify as new literacies will cease to be new once the social ways characterising the ascending paradigm have become sufficiently established and grounded to be regarded as conventional.
>
> *(pp. 45–46)*

Learning in the digital age therefore requires that we pay attention to where, how and with whom young children use technologies. In Part III of this book we explore further the empirical evidence about the technologies that children engage with, the uses to which they put digital resources and the ways in which their family practices are evolving in the digital age. However, we continue with our discussion in this Part II of the book by examining another key theme in early childhood research, scholarship and practice – that of young children's play in the digital age and the emerging concept of digital play.

References

Alesso, H.P. & Smith, C.F. (2008). Connections: patterns of discovery. John Wiley and Sons. Hoboken, New Jersey.

Barron, B., Cayton-Hodges, G., Bofferding, L., Copple, C., Darling-Hammond, L., & Levine, M. (2011). *Take a giant step: a blueprint for teaching children in a digital age.* The Joan Ganz Cooney Centre at Sesame Workshop and Stanford University.

Bebell, D., & Pedulla, J. (2015). A quantitative investigation into the impacts of 1 : 1 iPads on early learner's ELA and math achievement. *Journal of Information Technology Education: Innovations in Practice, 14,* 191–215. Retrieved from www.jite.org/documents/Vol.14/JITEv14IIPp191-215Bebell1720.pdf.

Beer, D. (2009). Power through the algorithm? Participatory web cultures and the technological unconscious. *New Media & Society, 11,* 985–1002. doi: 10.1177/1461444809336551.

Bell, D. (1976). The coming of the post-industrial society. *The Educational Forum, 40*(4), 574–579.

Bergen, D. (2014). Foundations of play theory. In L. Brooker, M. Blaise, and S. Edwards (Eds.), *The SAGE handbook of play and learning in early childhood* (pp. 9–20). London: SAGE.

Blackwell, C., Lauricella, A., & Wartella, E. (2014). Factors influencing digital technology use in early childhood education. *Computers and Education, 77,* 82–90.

Bolstad, R. (2004). *The role and potential of ICT in early childhood education: a review of New Zealand and international literature*. Wellington: New Zealand Council for Educational Research.

Bransford, J. D., Brown, A. L., & Cocking, R. R. (2000). *How people learn: brain, mind, experience, and school*. Washington, D.C.: National Academy Press.

Brooker, E., & Edwards, S. (2010). *Engaging play*. Maidenhead: Open University Press.

Brooker, L., Blaise, M., & Edwards, S. (2014). Introduction. In L. Brooker, M. Blaise, & S. Edwards (Eds.), *The SAGE handbook of play and learning in early childhood*. London: SAGE.

Bruner, J. S. (1966). *Toward a theory of instruction*. Cambridge, MA: Harvard University Press.

Bruner, J. S. (1971). 'The Process of Education' revisited. *The Phi Delta Kappan, 53*(1), 18–21.

Burnett, C. (2010). Technology and literacy in early childhood educational settings: a review of research. *Journal of Early Childhood Literacy, 10*(3), 247–270.

Caldwell, J. T. (2000). *Electronic media and technoculture*. New Brunswick, NJ: Rutgers University Press.

Choi, B., & Pak, A. (2008). Multidisciplinarity, interdisciplinarity and transdisciplinarity in health research, services, education and policy: discipline, inter-discipline distance and selection of discipline. *Clinical and Investigative Medicine, 31*(1), 41–48.

Common Sense Media (2013). *Zero to eight: children's media use in America 2013*. Retrieved from www.commonsensemedia.org/research/zero-to-eight-childrens-media-use-in-america-2013.

Cook, D. T. (2014). Whose play? Children, play and consumption. In L. Brooker, M. Blaise, & S. Edwards (Eds.), *The SAGE handbook of play and learning in early childhood*. London: SAGE.

Couse, L. J., & Chen, D. W. (2010). A tablet computer for young children? Exploring its viability for early childhood education. *Journal of Research on Technology in Education, 43*(1), 75–96. doi: 10.1080/15391523.2010.10782562.

Cuban, L. (1993). Computers meet classroom: classroom wins. *Teachers College Record, 9*(5), 185–219.

Daugherty, L., Dossani, R., Johnson, E.-E., & Oguz, M. (2014). *Using early childhood education to bridge the digital divide*. Santa Monica, CA: RAND Corporation. Retrieved from www.rand.org/pubs/perspectives/PE119.html.

Davydov, V. (1982). Translated by S. Kerr. The influence of L. S. Vygotsky on education, theory, research and practice. *Educational Researcher, 24*(3), 12–21.

Edwards, S. (2015). New concepts of play and the problem of technology, digital media and popular-culture integration with play-based learning in early childhood education. *Technology, Pedagogy and Education, 25*(4), 513–532.

Edwards, S., Nuttall, J., Mantilla, A., Wood, E., & Grieshaber, S. (2015). Digital play: what do early childhood teachers see? In S. Bulfin, N. F. Johnson, & C. Bigum (Eds.), *Critical perspectives on early childhood education* (pp. 66–84). Palgrave Macmillan's Digital Education and Learning Series. New York, NY: Palgrave Macmillan.

Flewitt, R., Messer, D., & Kucirkova, N. (2015). New directions for early literacy in a digital age: the iPad. *Journal of Early Childhood Literacy, 15*(3), 289–310. doi: 10.1177/1468798414533560.

House, R. (2011). The inappropriateness of ICT in early childhood: arguments from philosophy, pedagogy and developmental research. In S. Suggate & E. Reese (Eds.), *Contemporary debates in childhood education and development* (pp. 105–121). New York, NY: Routledge.

Kalantzis, M., & Cope, B. (2012). *New learning: elements of a science of education*. Cambridge, UK: Cambridge University Press.

Kalantzis, M., & Cope, B. (2014). Education is the new philosophy to make a metadisciplinary claim for the Learning Sciences. In A. D. Reid (Ed.), *A companion to research in education* (pp. 101–115). Dordrecht, Netherlands: Springer.

Kalantzis, M., Cope, B., & the Learning by Design Project Group (2005). *Learning by design.* Melbourne: Victorian Schools Innovation Commission.

Kay, A. C. (1972, August). A personal computer for children of all ages. In *Proceedings of the ACM annual conference – Volume 1* (pp. 1–11). ACM.

Kay, A. (2013). The future of reading depends on the future of learning difficult to learn things. In B. Junge, Z. Berzina, W. Scheiffele, W. Westerveld, & C. Zwick (Eds.), *The digital turn: design in the era of interactive technologies.* Chicago: University of Chicago Press.

Kay, A., & Goldberg, A. (1977). Personal dynamic media. *Computer, 10*(3), 31–41.

Lankshear, C., & Knobel, M. (2012). New literacies: technologies and values. *Revista Teknokultura, 9*(1), 45–69.

Lee, L., & O'Rourke, M. (2006). Information and communication technologies: transforming views of literacies in early childhood settings. *Early Years, 26*(1), 49–62.

Marsh, J. (2010). Young children's play in online virtual worlds. *Journal of Early Childhood Research, 8*(1), 23–39.

Marsh, J., Brooks, G., Hughes, J., Ritchie, L., Roberts, S., & Wright, K. (2005). *Digital beginnings: young children's use of popular culture, media and new technologies.* Sheffield: Literacy Research Centre, University of Sheffield.

Masuda, Y. (1980). *The information society as post-industrial society.* Tokyo: Institute for the Information Society.

Mills, K. A. (2011). *The Multiliteracies Classroom.* New Perspectives on Language and Education, Vol. 21. Multilingual Matters. Bristol: Channel View Publications.

Montessori, M. (1972). *The secret of childhood.* New York, NY: Ballantine Books.

Moore, O. K. (1966). Autotelic responsive environments and exceptional children. In *Experience Structure & Adaptability* (pp. 169–216). Berlin and Heidelberg: Springer.

NAEYC (2012). Technology and interactive media as tools in early childhood programs serving children from birth through age 8. A joint position statement issued by the NAEYC and the Fred Rogers Center for Early Learning and Children's Media at Saint Vincent College. Retrieved from www.naeyc.org/files/naeyc/PS_technology_WEB.pdf.

Nowotny, H., Scott, P., & Gibbons, M. (2001). *Rethinking science: knowledge and the public in an age of uncertainty.* Cambridge, MA: Polity Press.

Nuttall, J., Edwards, S., Mantilla, A., Grieshaber, S., & Wood, E. (2015). The role of motive objects in early childhood teacher development concerning children's digital play and play-based learning in early childhood curricula. *Professional Development in Education, 41*(2), 222–235.

Ofcom (2016, 16 November). Children and parents: media use and attitudes report 2016. Retrieved from www.ofcom.org.uk/__data/assets/pdf_file/0034/93976/Children-Parents-Media-Use-Attitudes-Report-2016.pdf.

Papert, S. (1970). *Logo book notes.* A1 Laboratory: MIT.

Papert, S. (1980). *Mindstorms: children, computers, and powerful ideas* (2nd edn). New York, NY: Basic Books, Inc.

Piaget, J. (1974). *Understanding causality.* (Trans. D. & M. Miles). New York, NY: W. W. Norton.

Piaget, J., & Inhelder, B. (1969). *The psychology of the child* (Vol. 5001). New York, NY: Basic Books.

Rosin, H. (2013, April). The touch-screen generation. *The Atlantic.* Retrieved from www.theatlantic.com/magazine/archive/2013/04/the-touch-screen-generation/309250/.

Sawyer, R. (2005). The new science of learning. In K. Sawyer (Ed.), *The Cambridge handbook of the Learning Sciences* (pp. 1–16). Cambridge, MA: Cambridge University Press.

Selwyn, N. (2010). Looking beyond learning: notes towards the critical study of educational technology. *Journal of Computer Assisted Learning, 26*, 65–73.

Stephen, C., McPake, J., Plowman, L., & Berch-Heyman, S. (2008). Learning from the children: exploring preschool children's encounters with ICT at home. *Journal of Early Childhood Research, 6*(2), 99–117.

Stephen, C., & Plowman, L. (2008). Enhancing learning with information and communication technologies in pre-school. *Early Child Development and Care, 178*(6), 637–654.

Turvey, K., & Pachler, N. (2016). Problem spaces: a framework and questions for critical engagement with learning technologies in formal educational contexts. In N. Rushby & D. W. Surry (Eds.), *Wiley handbook of learning technology* (pp. 113–130). Chichester: Wiley-Blackwell.

van Oers, B. (2008). Learning and learning theory from a cultural-historical point of view. In B. van Oers, W. Wardekker, E. Elbers, & R. van der Veer (Eds.), *The transformation of learning: advances in cultural-historical theory* (pp. 3–15). Cambridge, UK: Cambridge University Press.

Vygotsky, L. (1986). *Thought and language*, Revised Edition. Cambridge, MA: MIT Press.

Yelland, N. (2011). Reconceptualising play and learning in the lives of young children. *Australasian Journal of Early Childhood, 36*(2), 4–12.

5
DIGITAL PLAY

Introduction

Digital play is a burgeoning area of research in early childhood education. Prior to the release of the iPad in 2010 very little attention was paid to the notion of digital play. Researchers were interested instead in the influence of technologies on children's learning and development (e.g. Gee, 2003; Lewin, 2000; Shaffer, 2007). Predominately, this research investigated the relationship between children's cognitive and social development when using technologies such as desktop computers. In the early 1980s there was a very strong focus on the use of developmentally appropriate software with young children (Shade, 1991). This focus emerged from the popularity at the time of the constructivist-based developmentally appropriate practice (DAP) guidelines as a basis for early childhood education (NAEYC, 1986). Abstracted to the use of computers with young children (see for example Donohue, 2015), the DAP guidelines were used to inform the argument that technology use for children was of educational benefit so long as it was used in a way considered 'developmentally appropriate' (Haugland, 1999). From a technological perspective 'developmentally appropriate' involved young children in the use of software that was defined as open-ended and exploratory. Software that tended towards the use of drill and practice activities intended to promote mathematical and literacy learning was typically frowned upon (Davis & Shade, 1999).

It is interesting to note that the emphasis placed on open-ended and exploratory software during this period of time converged with the constructivist orientation to play as embedded in existing views about development. These views defined play from a Piagetian perspective as central to learning, in that it was understood that children would construct knowledge of their world through play (Kamii & Ewing, 1996). Given this constructivist emphasis, a criterion of productive play was that it would consistently involve children in opportunities to solve problems and create

their own representations of the world. The application of constructivist ideas
about play to the promotion of appropriate software for young children represents
what we believe was an early form of thought about 'digital play' – although it was
predominately located in developmental thinking regarding the use of technologies
by young children. In this chapter we consider how evolving understandings about
play in early childhood education led to a new focus on sociocultural descriptions
of play over developmental views. We then consider how sociocultural ideas about
play emphasised the technological aspects of young children's lives in contemporary
society. We argue that this emphasis led to some of the earliest work seeking to
understand digital play by applying existing theories of play to young children's
interactions with technologies. We go on to reflect on the extent to which a critical
perspective on technologies enables theories of play to be seen as co-evolving
alongside technologies, resulting in new ideas positioning digital play as a form of
activity that integrates or blends the traditional and the technological.

Evolving understandings about play

Towards the late 1990s understanding about play and the role of play in early
childhood education began to shift from a cognitive constructivist viewpoint to
the post-developmental perspective (Grieshaber & Cannella, 2001). The post-
developmental perspective challenged accepted universalistic thinking that regarded
stage-based and constructivist ideas of children's play as culturally normative. At
this time a multiplicity of ideas, reflecting the application of Mode 2 or contextually
aware knowledge, was brought to bear on the problem situation of better understanding young children's play in the social and cultural contexts in which it
occurred. The emphasis on 'context' was in response to a rising concern with the
dominance of developmental constructivist theory which was increasingly viewed
as overly and inappropriately universalistic in its assumptions about how and why
young children played. The range of ideas deployed during this period included the
critical reconceptualist (Soto & Swadener, 2002), feminist (Blaise, 2009) and sociocultural (Fleer, 2003).

In the USA, a new reconceptualist theoretical movement was born and critiques
of the validity of DAP for all young children were raised in terms of children's
social, cultural, economic and gendered experiences (Cannella, 2000). Likewise,
the growing pedagogical innovation from Reggio Emilia was also attracting international attention. This work, like the basis of the post-developmental movement,
also emphasised a multiplicity of theoretical thinking, including the work of Bruner,
Vygotsky, Dewey and scholars associated with the sociology of childhood (see for
example James, Jenks, & Prout, 1998 and later Qvortrup, Corsaro, Honig, & Valentine, 2009) to position young children as active and agentic meaning-makers in
their own lives. Within the context of a growing acceptance of multi-theoretical
perspectives on young children's play, sociocultural theory in particular emerged as
a significant theoretical framework for theorising and better understanding the
cultural complexity of young children's lives. In this framework, ideas related to

cultural mediation, learner activity, cultural context, social interactions and young children's play gained traction as a means of explaining how young children's multiple experiences from a social, cultural and economic perspective could be productively understood in relation to learning.

As the digital age progressed with technologies becoming more dialectically situated in social, cultural and economic activity, these aspects of sociocultural theory were increasingly drawn on to inform thinking and theorisation about young children's use of technologies. We now provide a very brief summation of Vygotsky's ideas about play, prior to considering the convergence of theories of play with the use of digital technologies by young children.

Vygotsky on play

Sociocultural views of play hold that play is a leading activity in early childhood. By leading activity Vygotsky did not mean that play was the 'main' activity of the child. Rather play is understood to lead children from one central psychological function to another (Edwards, 2011). Central psychological functions are the dominant means available to children for engaging in their social and cultural worlds. In the early years, the central psychological functions include sensorimotor, perception, emotions and memory. The leading activities for these functions are relating, experimenting and play. For infants and toddlers, the leading activity of 'relating' creates a bridge between the psychological functions of sensorimotor activity and perception. For a slightly older child, experimenting operates as the bridge between perception and emotions. For the preschool and early-school-aged child play is the leading activity that connects emotions and memory. Core to each leading activity is the new psychological function that underpins or informs how the leading activity operates (Kravtsova, 2006). For play, the new psychological function is imagination. From a sociocultural perspective all new psychological functions derive from a child's social situation of development. Play as a leading activity derives from 'imagination in action' as the social situation of development. A very important idea regarding leading activities is that it is mastery of a leading activity that enables a child to enter the new social situation of development (Duncan & Tarulli, 2003). Each new social situation of development is necessary to underpin the new psychological functions that promote the consequent leading activity.

Vygotsky's (2004) ideas about imagination are very interesting. He held that imagination was a new psychological function derived from 'imagination in action' as the child's social situation of development. This means that Vygotsky did not see imagination as a form of fantasy or as akin to imaginative pretend play. Instead, imagination as a psychological function is a way of connecting with the social and cultural world. Imagination therefore operates to connect children with their reality. Vygotsky (2004) identified four main 'ways' in which imagination connects children with reality. In the first way, reality provides children with access to the materials that comprise the building blocks for the imaginative act itself. The second way, connects the imaginative use of a material to the experience of a broader concept. For example, using an old sheet to create a pond. Here, the use of the sheet represents the first way and the creation of the pond the second way. The third way, refers to genuine emotions experienced by the child in the experience of the imaginative act. This may be where the sheet-as-pond gives the child a joyful feeling of actually 'paddling' in the water. The final and fourth way is the contribution of the imaginative act back to the reality from which it first emerged. This could occur when a child invites another child to join her in swimming in the pond. In 'reality' the pond really is a pond and no longer a sheet and thus makes a new contribution to reality for the child herself and for others to enjoy.

What is important about the process of play in early childhood is the extent to which children are able to master it as a leading activity such that it changes their social situation of development beyond a reliance on imagination in action to that of collective theorising (Vygotsky, 2005). Collective theorising supports the new psychological function of attention which is necessary for the psychological function of learning activity. Thus, play is fundamental to learning and simultaneously connected to the life world of the child as it is imagination that funnels 'reality' into the cultural expression and actions of the child's play.

In discussing the role of play in childhood, Vygotsky (1976) also spoke of the role of mature play. Mature play is achieved when a child is able to substitute meaning for object. The classic example Vygotsky (1976) provides of this process is when a child is able to pretend that a stick is now a horse – that is, the meaning of horse substitutes for the object of stick. Mature play is important for children because the capacity to substitute meaning for object is a pre-cursor for conceptual development – particularly as this pertains to literacy and numeracy. For example, understanding that a stick can represent a horse also means understanding that a symbol can represent a spoken word. Vygotsky's theory included a role for play in the Zone of Proximal Development (ZPD). Chaiklin (2003) argues that the ZPD is often typically described as the difference between what a child can achieve alone and what they are able to achieve with adult assistance. However, Vygotsky (1987) also spoke about the ZPD in relation to the child's construction of what he called 'mature concepts'. Mature concepts are the blended results of everyday and scientific concepts. Vygotsky described an everyday concept as something the child experiences in their daily life. For example, a child has an everyday concept of the 'internet' as related to using an iPad to go 'online' to watch a video on YouTube Kids. The corresponding scientific concept is that the internet comprises a series of networked technologies on which data, such as video data, is hosted. The child constructs a mature concept when she understands that watching a video on YouTube occurs via a series of interconnected technologies hosting digital data. Vygotsky (1987) believed that the ZPD could represent the difference between the child's everyday and scientific concepts. He argued that adults needed to be involved with children to bridge either end of the proximal or 'nearest' zone of the child's understanding, a key pedagogic action. In this space, play was also considered of value because children could experience or do within play what they were not yet necessarily able to achieve outside of play. For example, in play a child could use the imaginative process to create a pretend network of technologies or computers sharing 'data' amongst each other. Thus, the child experiences a scientific concept of the internet that is not achievable outside of her play.

Digital play

In the introduction to this book we described how research and thinking about young children in a digital age was for a long time a 'niche' area of early childhood education. This is because the early use of technologies in society more broadly were still debated according to their relevance or potential for young children's learning – indeed, it can be argued that technologies were only valued or thought worthy of investment because of their apparent positive value for learning, not because they were part of children's everyday cultural and social experiences. This niche area of research therefore focused on the developmental aspects of using technologies, such as desktop computers and software, and the role of early forms of programming on young children's development. For example, a comprehensive review of the literature by Clements (1987), a leading proponent of technologies in the early years, covered the following topics: gender equity, age of computer use, developmental appropriateness, social and emotional development, cognitive interaction, attitudes, language development, writing, mathematics and problem solving. Play and the relationship of play to young children's engagement with digital technologies did not feature. Thus, during the early part of the digital age (remembering that the digital age is defined as beginning with the invention of the transistor in 1952), post-developmentalism and the works of Vygotsky were not strong informants to thinking at the time regarding young children's technology use. Rather the notion of digital play was somewhat implicitly related to descriptions of the type of technological activity that was thought most likely to benefit young children's learning. For example, Haugland and Shade (1988) in what was to become a highly cited paper drew on constructivist ideas about the role of exploration and experimentation in children's play to define appropriate technological activities as those that were open-ended and likely to involve children in experimentation. Child-centredness, represented as child-control of the technological activity was highlighted as important (p. 37).

However, as we also discussed in the introduction chapter to this book, the launch of the iPad in 2010 was a significant game changer for early childhood thinking about technology. With the limitations of input devices such as the mouse and keyboard removed for children by the use of a touchscreen device, the engagement by children with technologies increased rapidly in a very short period of time (this increase is discussed in more detail in Chapter 6). It was about this time that a noted convergence between theories of play and the concept of the digital began to occur in the published literature and research about young children's technology use (e.g. Verenikina & Kervin, 2011). This is because as technology, from a substantive viewpoint, was increasingly integrated with the daily life experiences of young children, researchers and teachers scrambled to understand how children were using and making meaning of these digital engagements and the consequent role of such engagement in the early childhood setting. As this process of understanding developed, the notion of 'digital play' gradually took hold in the early childhood nomenclature.

One of the earliest uses of the term 'digital play' occurred in the field of game studies. Kline, Dyer-Witheford and De Peuter (2003) defined the notion of digital play in relation to the interaction occurring between technology, culture and marketing in the early part of the 21st century, suggesting that digital play 'comes into being at the convergence of technologies, cultural and marketing forces in the mediatized global marketplace' (Kline *et al.*, 2003, p. 23). They argued that the interactive game industry, comprising video and computer games, was increasingly networked with the marketing of culture via movies and associated paraphernalia. Against a background argument describing technological advancement as promoting the birth of the 'infosphere', they argued that digital play was a new form of social and cultural interaction via which people of all ages would participate and engage in the digital age. Kline *et al.*'s (2003) description of digital play found a wide audience in research about gaming and literacy in particular, but was not as widely adopted in the field of early childhood.

Early childhood research associated with the concept of digital play first appeared to focus on the changing social and cultural context in which young children of the digital age were growing up. During the late 1990s and early 2000s, in the years prior to the release of the iPad, there was increased emphasis on the need for technologies to be made available to young children in early childhood education settings (Burnett, 2010). Much of this research justified the inclusion of technologies to young children in their educational settings based on a social-contextual perspective in which technologies were increasingly noted as an accepted part of daily life for young children. It is interesting to note here, that while the psychological theory informing these justifications was sociocultural in nature, such research infrequently provided a stated theoretical stance on technology. As we noted in the introductory chapter to this book, theory of technology is not strongly evident in much of the early childhood located technology and digital play research (a notable exception being the work of Gibbons, 2010). We noted, too, that we ourselves have not always positioned our own research according to a stated theoretical position on technology. Reading much of the available research of the time, in which socio-contextual and/or sociocultural perspectives are taken, there is evidence of a strongly technological determinist orientation in which technologies are understood to be changing society and therefore having an increased role in young children's lives. In consequence, the inclusion of technologies in early learning settings was increasingly argued for by researchers (see for example: Parette, Quesenberry, & Blum, 2010).

Regardless, of the theoretical stance taken in terms of technologies, research in the early 2000s began to show that children's engagement with technologies in the family home typically reflected well-known principles of learning, such as those evident in the Learning Sciences and particularly as derived from a sociocultural perspective. For example, Plowman, McPake, and Stephen (2008) found that rather than children simply 'picking up' technological skills in the family home, these skills were in fact co-built and supported between young children, adult family members and siblings. This included through the use of processes such as direct instruction, modelling, experimentation, observation and play with technological artefacts.

Another important paper indicate a movement towards the notion of 'digital play' was that by Zevenbergen (2007). Using Bourdieu's concept of habitus she presented an essentially technologically determinist argument whereby the increased use of technologies by young children was considered an unavoidable reality of daily life. She suggested that this new daily life created a new 'habitus' for young children in which children were described as 'digital natives'. The use of technologies by digital natives in their homes meant that early childhood educational settings should be required to reconsider the provision of technologies beyond those deemed to promote particular developmental outcomes. Instead, Zevenbergen (2007) argued for a 'reconceptualised' perspective on play to better inform the use of technologies in early childhood education settings (p. 20). In 2010, Jackie Marsh a leading researcher in the area of digital technologies, popular-culture, literacy and young children's play in the 21st century, was writing of play in terms of virtual world participation. Marsh (2010) defined play as contextually relevant, citing scholars such as Sutton-Smith (1997) and Pellegrini (1991). She went on to identify the range of play-types she saw evidenced in her study of young children's play in virtual worlds. These included: 'fantasy play, socio-dramatic play, ritualised play, games with rules, and rough and tumble play' (p. 30). The convergence of existing theories and descriptions of play against a predominately social-contextual description of the role of technologies in young children's lives was beginning to gain traction.

Verenikina and Kervin (2011) were amongst the first researchers to use the term 'digital play' in relation to young children's engagement with iPads. This paper continued the use of existing theories of play and used these to create a definition of play that was then applied to children's engagement with apps. Drawing on Vygotsky (1976), Singer and Singer (1990) and Piaget (1953), Verenikina and Kervin (2011) defined play as 'a spontaneous, self-initiated and self-regulated activity of young children, which is not necessarily goal-oriented' (p. 6). Digital play was consequently understood as any form of engagement or participation by children with apps on an iPad that could be categorised according to this definition. While early contributions to the concept of digital play were therefore of significance to the field, a limitation of much of this early work and thinking was the extent to which traditional theories of play were applicable to the digital. This limitation may in fact be derived from the lack of attention paid to theories of technology with respect to young children's technology use. As we pointed out earlier, a reliance on existing theories of play against a socio-contextual description for technology use tended to result in technological determinist justifications for understanding young children's play with technology. Here, given technology was frequently described as 'rapidly advancing' and children as natural 'digital natives' of its application, attention was paid to best describing children's interactions with digital technologies using historical and pre-existing understanding of play. This approach has been continued in attempts to categorise forms of digital play. For instance, Marsh, Plowman, Yamada-Rice, Bishop and Scott (2016) argue that a taxonomy of play originally devised without recourse to digital play can be an effective tool for analysing play with technologies if a category they label as 'transgressive play' is added.

However, a more critical perspective on technology seeks to understand the historical evolution of technologies and the human purposes and social needs to which these are put – what Selwyn (2010) describes as an examination of the state of the actual. Paying attention to the state of the actual from a critical perspective means that historical ideas about play do not need to be viewed as a 'limitation' when applied to thinking about children's digital engagements. Research we reported in Chapter 4 by Edwards, Nuttall, Mantilla, Wood, and Grieshaber (2015) suggested that for early childhood teachers, existing theories of play are in fact part of the state of the actual (Selwyn, 2010) when it comes to their thinking about how and why young children play with technologies. Because there is not necessarily an alternative theory of digital play available to teachers (or researchers for that matter), it is unsurprising that it is existing theories of play to which people turn when trying to understand children's play with digital technologies. For example, Verenikina and Kervin (2011) applied existing theories of play to their analysis of children's digital play with apps. Likewise, Marsh's (2010) consideration of the range of play-types observed during children's participation in virtual worlds used existing ideas about play.

However, as we also reported in Chapter 4, a cultural perspective on young children playing and learning in the digital age highlights the dialectical relationship between tools and knowledge – as technological tools are created and deployed, so too does knowledge evolve. As knowledge evolves, technological tools are recreated. We have showed this dialectical relationship throughout this book by illustrating the relationship between Einstein's (1907) ideas about quantum mechanics and the invention of the microprocessor; and later, by describing the influence of Vygotsky, Piaget and Montessori's ideas about young children's learning on Alan Kay's (1972) DynaBook and the consequent creation of the iPad. Given this dialectical stance, there is in fact no reason for ideas about play to remain static and historically embedded in the times from which they came. Like knowledge in other areas, knowledge about play is capable of evolution, meaning that new ideas about digital play are becoming increasingly possible.

New ideas about digital play

Prior to the digital age, there was of course no need for a digital perspective on play. Play was variously described as 'freely chosen and non-literal' (Rubin, Fein, & Vandenberg, 1983) and in terms of different types, such as role play, pretend play or gross motor play. Traditional play had no connection to the truly digital, because prior to the invention of the transistor television, radio and online digital content did not exist. However, research shows that young children's play begins to reference the digital as their participation with different forms of technologies evolves over time. Marsh and Bishop (2014) have illustrated this in their research into young children's popular-culture interests. They have shown that radio and later television influenced the play narratives of children. New ideas about digital play are beginning to evolve beyond the initial approaches in which existing theories of play were applied to digital contexts. This shift towards newer ideas about digital play is related to a stronger focus on the 'state of the actual' – asking what is actually happening for young children and their play within the digital age. One answer to this question appears to be that play is no longer experienced as a strictly real or virtual activity. Rather, research points to an increasing blurring of the boundaries between the digital and the non-digital.

Marsh (2010) argued that in the context of increased use of digital activities by young children it was no longer useful nor valid to continue distinguishing between traditional and digital forms of play. She argued that more productive was the notion of a continuum of activity with digital play at one end and non-digital play at the other. Likewise, Plowman, McPake, and Stephen (2010) reported on a study in which they examined young children's technology use in the home. In this study, they reported little distinction by the children regarding their traditional and digital play. They also found that children frequently used digital activity to support non-digital play. One example they provided was of a boy playing with some Star Wars figurines. He did not have a sufficient range of characters available to progress his play. His solution was to go online and search for some images of the characters he required. He then printed these characters, cut them out and physically pasted them onto some cardboard. His cardboard cut-out figures then joined his figurines and he continued with his role play. It is difficult to see at which point in this play the activity would be labelled 'traditional' or 'digital'. Is it only the play with the figurines that is traditional? If so, how does this account for the view of some scholars that figurines manifest the digital as a representation of digital media (Wohlwend & Lewis, 2011), such as that indicated by movies such as Star Wars? Is it only searching for the images that is digital? If so, how is the fact the child was searching for the images with the intention of printing, cutting and pasting them to create 'real' artefacts accounted for as being solely digital play? Unlike the play of the post-industrial era, play in the digital age is neither entirely non-digital nor fully 'digital' – it is somewhat blended.

Edwards (2014) adapted Marsh's (2010) continuum concept to plot a series of possible digital and non-digital activities experienced by children interested in the popular-culture character Peppa Pig. She illustrated that it was possible to 'play' with some form of Peppa Pig across this entire continuum according to an episode in the series in which Peppa Pig, the main character enjoys jumping in muddy puddles outdoors with her brother George. The forms of play along this continuum included, using an app to 'jump' Peppa in and out of puddles, watching the 'Muddy

Puddles' episode on television, as streamed content or on YouTube, physically jumping in a muddy puddle at Peppa Pig World, or purchasing a pair of welling-tons (gumboots) to jump in one's own puddle at home. While this plotting of digital to non-digital activities showed how children were able to engage in dif-ferent forms of activity, it did not necessarily fully encompass the blurring boundary between traditional and digital play as expressed by Plowman *et al.* (2010).

In response to this problem Edwards (2013) generated the concept of web-mapping. Web-mapping followed her research with young children and families in a suburban area of Melbourne, Australia. In this research Edwards (2013) invited parents and children to talk about their play. What she found was that traditional play was still present in the family home. This included outdoor play, construction play, fine motor play and pretend play. However, this traditional play almost always integrated with a form of digital participation by children. For example, role play would draw on children's knowledge of their favourite movies or television games. Outdoor play saw children use characterised toys, such as Bob the Builder diggers in the sandpit. Conversely, any digital play described by the parents and children related to traditional activities. This might include using drawing and painting apps on an iPad for craft. Fine motor or construction play involved building blocks tied in with movies (e.g. Harry Potter Lego). Interestingly, the parents in this study described how their children used digital and traditional play to create meaning about experiences in their lives. One parent described a child role playing a scenario in which he was a character from the Octonauts. The scenario was a repeat of a recent family experience in which their car had had a puncture. As an Octonaut, he was coming to rescue someone in his play with a new tyre. Stephen (2017) reports an observation in which a five-year-old girl decided to make a laptop com-puter when she wanted to pretend to go to work. She folded a piece of card then drew a screen on the upright portion and keys and a mouse pad on the horizontal and went on to make use of the 'computer' with apparent satisfaction in her pretend role. These descriptions of personalised meaning-making were connected by Edwards (2013) to Geertz's (1973) claim that people spin or create their own webs of meaning from their culture situation. Edwards created a 'web' in which digital forms of activity integrated directly with the traditional. In this web, the digital formed the sectors, while the traditional play was represented by the radial rings (Figure 5.1). Edwards argued that the individual meaning-making of a child's integ-rated digital and traditional play could be 'mapped' into such a web, thus creating the new concept of 'web-mapping'.

Research in the use of web-mapping with teachers of young children con-sequently showed that this new representation of 'digital play' provided a powerful framework for early childhood teachers to incorporate digital experiences into the early childhood curriculum (Edwards, 2015). This includes the observation, plan-ning and implementation of experiences for children that integrated both the tradi-tional and digital. Thus, rather than applying existing theories of play to a digital activity, the concept of web-mapping evolves historical ideas about play into a new representation for the digital age.

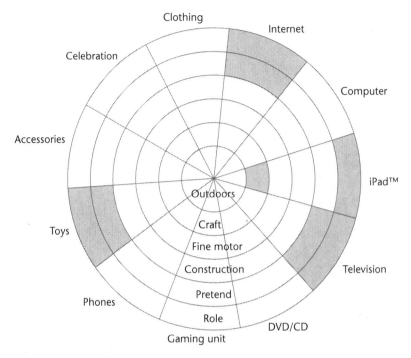

FIGURE 5.1 An example of web-mapping in which digital and traditional activities are integrated to represent young children's meaning-making (Edwards, 2013, p. 21).

Source: Reprinted with permission from Peter Lang International Academic Publishers.

Conclusion

Digital play is a rapidly developing area of research in early childhood education. Early understandings about digital play used constructivist notions of developmentally appropriate practice to define what was considered useful software for young children's learning. Later, as digital technologies were increasingly dialogically related with the daily life experiences of young children, existing theories of play began to converge with the actual use of technologies by young children. The application of 'theories of play' to young children's technology use resulted in descriptions of technological activity by children that could be described in terms of traditional types of play, such as pretend play, games with rules and fantasy play. A critical, rather than technological determinist and even substantive perspective on technologies highlights a focus on the state of the actual with respect to children's play in the digital age. This means that instead of theories of play being limited in their application to technologies, existing theories of play are considered in terms of their evolutionary potential to contribute to newer ideas about digital play within the digital age. In this chapter, we have considered how research has noted the presence of both traditional and digital play in the contemporary activities of young children. We have also described how these forms of play have been said to be increasingly blurred in that it is no longer possible to indicate where one begins and another ends. Drawing on the work of Edwards (2013, 2015) we have presented the concept of web-mapping as a new description for digital play that highlights the cultural meaning-making concept of traditional and more technological play as an integrated process. We propose that future research be directed towards the continual evolution of new concepts of play for the digital age.

References

Blaise, M. (2009). 'What a girl wants, what a girl needs': responding to sex, gender, and sexuality in the early childhood classroom. *Journal of Research in Childhood Education*, *23*(4), 450–460.

Burnett, C. (2010). Technology and literacy in early childhood educational settings: a review of research. *Journal of Early Childhood Literacy*, *10*(3), 247–270.

Cannella, G. S. (2000). Critical and feminist reconstructions of early childhood education: continuing the conversations. *Contemporary Issues in Early Childhood*, *1*(2), 215–221.

Chaiklin, S. (2003). The zone of proximal development in Vygotsky's analysis of learning and instruction. *Vygotsky's educational theory in cultural context*, *1*, 39–64.

Clements, D. H. (1987). Computers and young children: a review of research. *Young Children*, *43*(1), 34–44.

Davis, B. C., & Shade, D. D. (1999). Integrating technology into the early childhood classroom: the case of literacy learning. *Information Technology in Childhood Education* (pp. 221–254). Retrieved from www.learntechlib.org/index.cfm/files/paper_8857.pdf?fuseaction=Reader.DownloadFullText&paper_id=8857.

Donohue, C. (2015). *Technology and digital media in the early years*. New York: Routledge.

Duncan, R., & Tarulli, D. (2003). Play as the leading activity of the preschool period: insights from Vygotsky, Leont'ev and Bakhtin. *Early Education and Development*, *14*(3), 271–292.

Edwards, S. (2011). Lessons from 'a really useful engine'™: using Thomas the Tank Engine™ to examine the relationship between play as a leading activity, imagination and reality in children's contemporary play worlds. *Cambridge Journal of Education*, *41*(2), 195–210.

Edwards, S. (2013). Post-industrial play: understanding the relationship between traditional and converged forms of play in the early years. In J. Marsh & A. Burke (Eds.), *Children's virtual play worlds: culture, learning, and participation* (pp. 10–26). New York: Peter Lang.

Edwards, S. (2014). Towards contemporary play: sociocultural theory and the digital-consumerist context. *Journal of Early Childhood Research*, *12*(3), 219–233.

Edwards, S. (2015). New concepts of play and the problem of technology, digital media and popular-culture integration with play-based learning in early childhood education. *Technology, Pedagogy and Education*, *25*(4), 513–532.

Edwards, S., Nuttall, J., Mantilla, A., Wood, E., & Grieshaber, S. (2015). Digital play: what do early childhood teachers see? In S. Bulfin, N. F. Johnson, & C. Bigum (Eds.), *Critical perspectives on early childhood education* (pp. 66–84). Palgrave Macmillan's Digital Education and Learning Series. New York, NY: Palgrave Macmillan.

Einstein, A. (1907). "Theorie der Strahlung und die Theorie der Spezifischen Wärme" [Planck's theory of radiation and the theory of specific heat]. *Annalen der Physik*, *4*(22), 180–190. doi: 10.1002/andp.19063270110.

Fleer, M. (2003). Early childhood education as an evolving 'community of practice' or as lived 'social reproduction': researching the 'taken-for-granted'. *Contemporary Issues in Early Childhood*, *4*(1), 64–79.

Gee, J. (2003). What Video Games Have to Teach Us About Learning and Literacy. ACM *Computers in Entertainment, 1*(1), 1–4.

Geertz, C. (1973). *The interpretation of cultures* (Vol. 5019). New York, NY: Basic Books.

Gibbons, A. (2010). Reflections concerning technology: a case for the philosophy of technology in early childhood teacher education and professional development programs. In S. Izumi-Taylor & S. Blake (Eds.), *Technology for early childhood education and socialization: developmental applications and methodologies* (pp. 1–19). Hershey, NY: IGI Global.

Grieshaber, S., & Cannella, G. (2001). From identity to identities: Increasing possibilities in early childhood education. In S. Grieshaber & G. Cannella (Eds.), *Embracing identities in early childhood education: diversity and possibilities* (pp. 3–23). New York, NY: Teachers College Press.

Haugland, S. W. (1999). What role should technology play in young children's learning? Part 1. *Young Children, 54*(6), 26–31.

Haugland, S., & Shade, D. D. (1988). Developmentally appropriate software for young children. *Young Children, 43*(4), 37–43.

James, A., Jenks, C., & Prout, A. (1998). *Theorizing childhood*. Cambridge, MA: Polity Press.

Kamii, C., & Ewing, J. K. (1996). Basing teaching on Piaget's constructivism. *Childhood Education, 72*(5), 260–264.

Kay, A. C. (1972, August). A personal computer for children of all ages. In *Proceedings of the ACM annual conference – Volume 1* (p. 1). ACM.

Kline, S., Dyer-Witheford, N., & De Peuter, G. (2003). *Digital play: the interaction of technology, culture and marketing*. Montreal: McGill-Queen's University Press.

Kravtsova, E. E. (2006). The concept of age-specific new psychological formations in contemporary developmental psychology. *Journal of Russian & East European Psychology, 44*(6), 6–18.

Lewin, C. (2000). Exploring the effects of talking book software in UK primary classrooms. *Journal of Research in Reading, 23*(2), 149–157.

Marsh, J. (2010). Young children's play in online virtual worlds. *Journal of Early Childhood Research, 8*(1), 23–39.

Marsh, J., & Bishop, J. (2014). *Changing play: play, media and commercial culture from the 1950s to the present day*. New York: Open University Press.

Marsh, J., Plowman, L., Yamada-Rice, D., Bishop, J., & Scott, F. (2016). Digital play: a new classification. *Early Years, 36*(3), 242–253.

NAEYC (1986). Position statement on developmentally appropriate practice in programs for 4–5-year-olds. *Young Children, 41*(6), 20–29.

Parette, H. P., Quesenberry, A. C., & Blum, C. (2010). Missing the boat with technology usage in early childhood settings: a 21st century view of developmentally appropriate practice. *Early Childhood Education Journal, 37*(5), 335–343.

Pellegrini, A. D. (1991). *Applied child study: a developmental approach*. Hillsdale, NJ: Erlbaum.

Piaget, J. (1953). *The origin of intelligence in the child*. London: Routledge and Kegan Paul.

Plowman, L., McPake, J., & Stephen, C. (2008). Just picking it up? Young children learning with technology at home. *Cambridge Journal of Education, 38*(3), 303–319.

Plowman, L., McPake, J., & Stephen, C. (2010). The technologisation of childhood? Young children and technology in the home. *Children & Society, 24*(1), 63–74.

Qvortrup, J., Corsaro, W. A., Honig, M. S., & Valentine, G. (2009). *The Palgrave handbook of childhood studies*. Basingstoke: Palgrave Macmillan.

Rubin, K. H., Fein, G. G., & Vandenberg, B. (1983). Play. In E. M. Hetherington (Ed.), *Handbook of child psychology, Vol. 4, Socialization, personality, and social development* (4th edn). New York: Wiley.

Selwyn, N. (2010). Looking beyond learning: notes towards the critical study of educational technology. *Journal of Computer Assisted Learning, 26*, 65–73.

Shade, D. D. (1991). Developmentally appropriate software. *Early Childhood Education Journal, 18*(4), 34–36.

Shaffer, D. (2007). *How computer games help children learn.* New York: Palgrave Macmillan.

Singer, D. G., & Singer, J. L. (1990). *The house of make-believe.* Cambridge, MA: Harvard University Press.

Soto, L. D., & Swadener, B. B. (2002). Toward liberatory early childhood theory, research and praxis: decolonizing a field. *Contemporary Issues in Early Childhood, 3*(1), 38–66. doi: 10.2304/ciec.2002.3.1.8.

Stephen, C. (2017). ICT made playful. In G. Walsh, D. McMillan, & C. McGuiness (Eds.), *Playful teaching and learning* (pp. 133–147). London: SAGE.

Sutton-Smith, B. (1997). *The ambiguity of play.* Cambridge, MA: Harvard University Press.

Verenikina, I., & Kervin, L. (2011). iPads, digital play and preschoolers. *He Kupu, 2*(5). Retrieved from www.hekupu.ac.nz/Journal%20files/Issue5%20October%202011/ iPads%20Digital%20Play%20and%20Preschoolers.pdf.

Vygotsky, L. (1976). Play and its role in the mental development of the child. In J. Bruner, A. Jolly, & K. Sylva (Eds.), *Play and its role in development and evolution* (pp. 537–555). New York, NY: Basic Books.

Vygotsky, L. S. (1987). Problems of general psychology. In R. Rieber, A. Carton, & N. Minick (Eds.), *The collected works of L. S. Vygotsky* (Vol. 1). New York, NY: Plenum Press.

Vygotsky, L. (2004). Imagination and creativity in childhood. *Journal of Russian and East European Psychology, 42*(1), 7–97.

Vygotsky, L. (2005). Appendix. From the notes of L. S. Vygotsky for lectures on the psychology of preschool children. *Journal of Russian and East European Psychology, 43*(2), 90–97.

Wohlwend, K. E., & Lewis, C. (2011). Critical literacy, critical engagement, and digital technology. In D. Lapp & D. Fisher (Eds.), *Handbook of teaching and researching the English language arts* (pp. 188–195). New York: Routledge.

Zevenbergen, R. (2007). Digital natives come to preschool: implications for early childhood practice. *Contemporary Issues in Early Childhood, 8*(1), 19–29.

PART III

Children and technologies

In previous sections of this book we have examined the cultural-historical evolution of the digital age, looking first at technological change and what Masuda (1980) described as the amplification of mental labour through the new relationships between people and knowledge that innovations in technology facilitated, and then second, at the evolution of our understanding of playing and learning in the digital age from a predominately critical perspective. In this final section of the book we turn our attention to exploring young children's experience of life in the digital age – the everyday culture of their time. Young children spend much of their lives at home or with members of their nuclear or extended family (Plowman, 2014; Tudge *et al.*, 2006). Working from the 'state of the actual' as a means of understanding the cultural-historical implications of technological innovation, our focus in this section is predominantly on young children's experience of the digital at home and with their families. This is not to deny that children also encounter digital technologies in their educational settings and in the places where they live, shop and spend leisure time. Indeed, later in this section we turn to evidence from centre-based educational settings in order to examine the ways in which preschool children interact with their peers and digital technologies. Nevertheless, as we shall see, it is within their home experiences that children most often engage with an extensive range of digital technologies, including the purposes and expectations associated with these technologies within their local culture.

The twin strands of our central argument are continued here. We are concerned with contemporary culture – the ordinary and everyday experience of growing up at this point in time in the digital age. Our cultural-historical perspective leads us to view behaviours, actions and learning as a function of the relationship between individuals and their historically derived social, economic, political and cultural circumstances. We continue too with our advocacy for a critical perspective on our relationship with digital technologies as an empowering way to respond to life and educational decision-making in the digital age. The first chapter in this section (Chapter 6) is concerned with empirical evidence about the ways in which young children are engaged with technologies and the features which contribute to differentiated experiences with technology or digital divides across a society. In Chapter 7 we consider contemporary reactions to what are perceived as novel developments in children's lives associated with the evolving digital age. This section concludes with an exploration of the perspectives and choices of families and individuals that make a difference to the everyday experience young children have of growing up in the digital age (Chapter 8).

Following this section we draw this book to a conclusion in Chapter 9 where we will consider the implications for early childhood teachers and researchers of children's familiarity with digital technologies such that Williams' (1958) contention that 'culture is ordinary' (p. 93) becomes a pedagogical starting point for understanding and responding to young children's play and learning in the digital age.

References

Masuda, Y. (1980). *The information society as post-industrial society.* Tokyo: Institute for the Information Society.

Plowman, L. (2014). Researching young children's everyday uses of technology in the family home. *Interacting with Computers, 27*(1), 36–46.

Tudge, J. R., Doucet, F., Odero, D., Sperb, T. M., Piccinini, C. A., & Lopes, R. S. (2006). A window into different cultural worlds: young children's everyday activities in the United States, Brazil, and Kenya. *Child Development, 77*(5), 1446–1469.

Williams, R. (1958). Culture is ordinary. In J. Higgins (Ed.) (2001), *The Raymond Williams reader* (pp. 10–25). Oxford: Blackwell.

6

DIGITAL TECHNOLOGY USE AND UPTAKE BY YOUNG CHILDREN

Introduction

That there have been worldwide increases in the uptake of digital technologies by young children is made clear in evidence from a range of sources: the growth of manufacturing and sales of targeted technological resources intended for young children (e.g. Euromonitor International, 2015; Juniper Research, 2015); widespread reporting about and observation of children's use of technologies owned by their household (e.g. Cowan, 2016; Prigg, 2014); and the burgeoning market of apps for preschoolers which facilitate direct access to age-appropriate games, stories and activities created to support learning (e.g. Gill, 2015; Vaala, Ly, & Levine, 2015). Terms such as 'explosion' and 'proliferation' characterise descriptions of the uptake of digital technologies amongst young children and the extent of their everyday engagement with visible technologies. The nature of their less visible encounters with digital interactivity through the Internet of Things is not yet a matter of widespread public comment but it seems likely that similar terms will be used in time to describe these more recent features of life in the digital age. Such hyperbole is understandable during the early stages of a new era, particularly at the point when, as Masuda's (1985) theory of societal technological change suggests, many innovations create a new complex system of technology which extends across society to create new ways of doing things and challenge established practices and expectations.

The digital age is less than 100 years old and it is obvious that technological innovative in this age will continue to grow. Nevertheless, it seems important to attempt to explore what is known about the extent and nature of young children's encounters with digital technologies as we develop our thinking in this book. In this chapter we look at the evidence about the kinds of technologies that children are engaging with, at the length of time that they spend interacting with digital resources and what they are doing during these periods of engagement. The chapter closes with an examination of the evidence about what have come to be known as digital divides – the differential access and use of digital technologies by groups within society, specifically looking at gender and socio-economic differences.

Young children's engagement with digital technologies: which technologies?

Among the headlines drawing attention to the increase in children's use of digital technologies two trends stand out: the widely (and sometimes negatively) reported tendency to begin using digital resources at an ever younger age (Prigg, 2015) and the growing preference across all age groups for mobile smart devices (Common Sense Media, 2013; Ofcom, 2016). Globally, the number of families who own smartphones and tablet computers continues to rise and the proportion of children who access digital media on portable devices is growing. However, while such broad generalisations suggest trends in digital technology use at home which may be greeted with alarm or enthusiasm by policy-makers, educators, manufacturers and commentators on social trends, such statements must be qualified by the limitations of the studies from which they are drawn, the kinds of questions asked and people included in surveys. They cannot be taken as indications of the everyday experiences of individual families and children.

There are two sources of evidence about young children's contemporary experience of growing up in the digital age: qualitative studies, often focused on case studies of particular families or settings, and quantitative studies typically using survey methods. We will return to the evidence from qualitative studies below but begin our look at the digital resources that young children are making use of in the digital age with an examination of data from quantitative research.

Quantitative studies present a general picture through descriptive statistics of the resources that families own and through parental accounts of their children's use of each technology. Some surveys also gather evidence on the views that parents hold about the benefits or risks associated with young children engaging with digital technologies (e.g. Broadcasting Standards Authority, 2015). When conducted a national level, with clearly specified sampling techniques, surveys can collect data that allow for correlations between socio-economic factors and digital experiences. Such studies can provide a rigorous account of changes over specific time periods at population level and suggest findings or trends that should be further explored. However, the findings are limited by the assumptions that underpin the survey method, the particular characteristics of the families who are invited to participate and the forms of digital media about which the researchers choose to ask questions. Large-scale surveys are often further limited by their dependence on the de-contextualised recall of parents and their lack of data on the perspectives on digital technologies held by the children themselves, about their other activities and the aspects of their lives that give pleasure, offer opportunities for learning or create dissatisfaction. Furthermore, using survey data to look for global trends or international comparisons must take account of particular national contexts and the specific interests of those funding the survey work. In this chapter we will draw heavily on an annual survey of media use carried out in the UK and a national survey carried out in the USA in 2013. Our reasons for this dependency on these two surveys is largely pragmatic. They offer readily accessible, robust data carried out by agencies without vested interests and address the kinds of questions we want to consider in this chapter. Nevertheless, we offer this review as indicative rather than definitive. The range of digital technologies explored in these surveys limits some comparisons, as does the age of children about whom questions are posed. In our review here we will necessarily be drawn to paying more attention to data about children older than three years of age rather than from birth because that constitutes the bulk of the available evidence in more recent surveys. Indeed, the most detailed and extensive evidence is only available for children over eight years of age.

The annual media use and attitude survey carried out in the UK by Ofcom is an example of a national quantitative study based on a representative sample of the population. The figures given here relate to the survey data published in 2016 (Ofcom, 2016). Although the survey is primarily concerned with the media use and attitudes of children aged 5–15 it includes some data on the digital experiences of 3–4 year olds and, for some questions, presents data for 5–7 year olds separately. Parents of children aged 3–4 years old were asked about their family's ownership of different forms of digital media, the digital resources which the target child used at home, the length of time they spend engaged with these technologies and the content of the material which their child was engaging with during these encounters. In the data published in 2016 responses from the parents of 3–4 year olds revealed that 81 per cent of surveyed households owned a tablet computer, although only 16 per cent of three and four year olds had their own tablet. Among the households with 3–4 year olds 74 per cent owned a desktop or laptop connected to the internet and 50 per cent owned a games console connected to a television. In households in which these children were growing up 85 per cent owned a standard TV, 50 per cent a smart TV and 96 per cent a mobile phone (including smartphones). Comparable data in this survey suggested that 5–7 year olds were more likely than 3–4 year olds to be growing up in a home which contained a tablet computer (83 per cent), a desktop computer or laptop (82 per cent) and a games console (75 per cent).

But the presence of a device in the household did not necessarily mean that preschool children made use of the resource. For example, where there was a smart TV at home 43 per cent of 3–4 year olds made use of it and 24 per cent made use of the desktop or laptop computer in their home. There was little change or a slight decline in the numbers of 3–4 year olds using hand-held games players, games consoles connected to the TV or educational games systems in the years 2013–16. In contrast, there was a notable increase in children's access to their family's tablet computer in the same time period: the proportion of 3–4 year olds using a tablet at home increased from 20 per cent in 2013 to 53 per cent in 2015 and 55 per cent in 2016. However, Ofcom point out that while the proportion of 3–4 year olds using tablets at home had increased, this figure lagged behind the increase in the proportion of households with children in this age range owning a tablet in 2016, suggesting that not all youngsters are given access to a newly acquired tablet. The proportion of 5–7 year olds using the tablet in their home was 67 per cent in 2016.

The UK trend towards greater access to and use of tablets by children before they begin primary school is replicated internationally. A similar trend is clear in survey evidence from the USA, although the age range of children surveyed for *Zero to Eight: Children's Media Use in America* (Common Sense Media, 2013) is wider and the devices differently clustered in the analysis. Their survey of media use among children aged 0–8 years reported that 75 per cent of all the children had access to a mobile device (smartphone or tablet) at home and that tablet ownership had increased from 8 per cent in 2011 to 40 per cent in 2013. Amongst under two year olds in the USA (a group not included in the UK Ofcom survey) 38 per cent made use of a mobile device in 2013. In Estonia 50 per cent of parents responding to an online survey in 2014 confirmed that they allowed their 0–3 year olds to make use of their smart devices, both phones and tablets (Nevski & Siibak, 2016). Among that (non-representative) sample children under three years old were more likely to make daily use of a smartphone (39 per cent) than a tablet (25 per cent). In Singapore too children under seven years old were found to have daily access to smart devices (Ebbeck, Yim, Chan, & Goh, 2016). In New Zealand 2–5 year olds seem less likely than their peers elsewhere to make use of a smartphone to access internet content (18 per cent, reported in 2015) and tablet use increased with age. On average 2–5 year olds in New Zealand were just as likely to use a tablet as a desktop computer or laptop for internet access (about 30 per cent in each case) but by five years old 50 per cent used a laptop or desktop to access internet content and 44 per cent made use of a tablet for this (Broadcasting Standards Authority, 2015).

To explore the digital encounters of children under three years old further we must turn first to the large-scale survey conducted in the USA by Vanderwater *et al.* (2007) as this is one of the few in which survey data about access to and use of digital technologies are differentiated throughout by age. That they found televisions and VCR/DVD players to be almost universal was not a surprise to the researchers but they did not expect to find that even among 0–2 year olds 18 per cent had televisions in their bedrooms. Almost half of 0–2 year olds were living in a household with access to a video games console, 80 per cent had a computer with internet access in their home and 45 per cent had high-speed internet at home. Moving to 2013 and the evidence from the Zero to Eight survey we find that 66 per cent of children under two years of age watched television daily, a figure very similar to the 63 per cent found by Vanderwater *et al.* in 2007. However, the number of under 2s with a TV in their bedroom had almost halved in 2013 compared with the previous Zero to Eight survey in 2011. Watching DVDs had become a more frequent occurrence for the youngest children over time, rising from 33 per cent in 2007 to 52 per cent in 2011 before declining to 46 per cent in 2013. Some of these changes may be related to the trend towards more under 2s making daily use of a computer (rising from 4 per cent in both the 2007 and 2011 datasets to 10 per cent in 2013). By 2013 the arrival of mobile devices (smartphones and tablets) had added an even more substantial new area of activity to the lives of the youngest children as well as their older siblings; 38 per cent of under 2s in the USA were then making regular use of a mobile device (either a smartphone or tablet).

Young children's engagement with digital technologies: what are they doing and how long for?

Preschool children were more likely than older or younger children to have some educational apps (e.g. about phonics or counting) provided by their parents (Marsh *et al.*, 2015). However, that research team found that the top priority for parents when selecting an app for their child was that it should be experienced as fun, with having some educational features a close second priority. Among the 3–5 year olds whose families participated in the survey conducted by Marsh *et al.* the five most popular apps were YouTube, CBeebies (Playtime and Storytime), Angry Birds, Peppa's Paintbox and Talking Tom. The Ofcom survey conducted in 2016 (Ofcom, 2016) pointed to YouTube as an important source of media content for children from three to 15 years old. Thirty seven per cent of 3–4 year olds and 57 per cent of 5–7 year olds included in the survey made use of YouTube mostly to view what they describe as '"TV-like" content' (Ofcom, 2016, p. 2). These activities with apps may typically be considered as 'entertainment orientated', to varying degrees but, following Kay (1972, 2013) and Kay and Goldberg (1977), we understand their potential as engaging spaces where learning can happen rather than employing software that directly results in learning.

Among young children in the USA in 2013 the most popular activity on a tablet was playing games (63 per cent), closely followed by using apps (50 per cent) and watching videos (47 per cent) (Common Sense Media, 2013). In the UK (Ofcom, 2016) tablets were the device most likely to be used by 3–4 year olds to play games; 28 per cent of children in that age group made use of a tablet to play games compared with 15 per cent playing games on a mobile phone or 17 per cent using a hand-held or 'through TV' games console. As tablets rose in popularity and ease of access, the use of laptops or desktops to play games almost halved between 2015 and 2016, falling from 9 per cent to 5 per cent. Mobile devices were also competing successfully with products specifically designed and marketed to support young children's learning, for example, Leapster Explorer or hand-held or video game players. By 2016, with the exception of television sets, mobile devices were the only digital device being used by the majority of children across the age range 3–15.

The rising popularity of playing games on a mobile phone or tablet has been accompanied by a huge increase in the range of apps available. Introducing their study to create a framework to enable assessment of the educational potential of publically available apps Hirsh-Pasek *et al.* (2015) referred to the 80,000 apps categorised as 'educational' (Apple, 2015, p. 4) which were then available at the Apple App Store. The Zero to Eight study suggested that just over 40 per cent of the apps used by children in the USA gave access to educational games while a similar proportion provided games described as 'just for fun'. Thirty eight per cent of the apps used were described as being associated with creative activities such as drawing, music making or creating video. Most recently there has been interest among games producers, such as those responsible for Angry Birds, in creating cartoon stories using characters from their games and launching educational programmes associated with their games but involving a range of media. This development is an interesting blending of 'old' and 'new' era technologies by which to engage young children in characters, stories and games and one which reflects the blended nature of children's play we discussed in Chapter 5.

Further evidence specifically about children's engagement with apps (via tablet computers) is available from the Technology and Play (TAP) study conducted by Marsh *et al.* (2015) in the UK. This investigation began with a survey of 2000 parents/caregivers of children from birth to five years old, representative of socioeconomic, geographical and ethnic diversity across the UK. The findings from this survey element of the study suggest that children have access to multiple digital technologies at home, with only 9 per cent having three or fewer digital technologies such as televisions, smartphones and tablets available to them. Half of the families surveyed had access to between four and 10 devices. The 0–5 year olds who had access to tablets in their own home or through their extended family or friends made use of them for a wide range of activities and were more likely to access an app on a tablet than on a smartphone. They used tablets to watch videos and listen to audio and popular music, often through YouTube. The youngsters used drawing and colouring tools, took photos and made videos, created storyboards and added text or audio. They played games, including dressing up characters, taking care of virtual pets and construction activities such as building a car. Around 60 per cent of parents reported downloading apps for their child to 'support their learning' or to 'encourage play and creativity'. Some parents also offered a new app as a reward (37 per cent of parents of 3–5 year olds) or as another way to enjoy a character encountered through an alternative medium, for example, TV programme or book.

Although there had been an increase in the numbers of young children making use of tablets watching television continued to dominate total screen time among those reported in the USA Zero to Eight study in 2013. Among the children surveyed, half of their screen time was spent watching television sets and 38 per cent also watched television on their mobile device. As to the content of the television programmes the children were watching, educational TV was highest among 2–4 year olds while watching children's entertainment shows was more common among 5–8 year olds. In the UK the 2016 UK Ofcom survey found that while the television set was the most usual way for young children to watch broadcast or on-demand television some were turning to alternative devices to watch TV or video. In the UK, 34 per cent of 3–4 year olds sometimes watched television programmes on a device that was not a television set, with 32 per cent using a tablet to watch on-demand television and 11 per cent using a mobile phone for this. Both of these national surveys pointed to a further trend – the move to watching television on demand rather than through scheduled programming.

So far we have examined the quantitative evidence about the technologies with which young children are engaging and the kind of activities in which they are involved with those resources. However, it is necessary to add in one further dimension of children's experience if we are to portray their home-based digital activities. The missing dimension so far is time spent with visible digital technologies, and it is one which can modify perceptions. For example, one of the headline findings in the 2013 Zero to Eight study is that the number of children who have used a mobile device almost doubled in the two years from 2011 to 2013 and the average length of time spent each day on mobile devices trebled in that period. However, the scale of the change is qualified when we understand that this means that, on average children moved from using mobile devices for five minutes to 15 minutes per day. At the same time as mobile screen time in the USA increased by 10 minutes per day 'traditional' screen time reduced by an average of 31 minutes. The average 0–8 year old in the USA watched television for one hour 55 minutes each day in 2013.

The UK media survey carried out annually by Ofcom posed questions about the time that children spend watching television in a different way, considering total time in one hour bands. In 2016 they found that 41 per cent of children watched television at home or elsewhere for up to one hour and 33 per cent for up to two hours on a typical school day. A minority watched for longer on a weekday, 13 per cent for up to three hours and 6 per cent for up to four hours. At weekends the distribution moved towards more television watching with only 27 per cent watching for up to one hour, 30 per cent up to two hours, 18 per cent up to three hours and 13 per cent up to four hours. Like the 2013 figures for the USA there is a suggestion in the UK 2016 data of a trend towards children spending slightly less time watching a television set than in previous years. The TAP survey (Marsh *et al.*, 2015) about the media habits of 0–5 year olds in the UK suggested that, on average, children in that age range in the UK spent one hour 19 minutes per day engaged with a tablet and one hour 23 minutes on a typical weekend day. The youngest children (0–2 years old) spent slightly more time engaging with tablets each day than 3–5 year olds, a finding that may be influenced by the older children spending more time out of their homes in educational settings each day. As Marsh *et al.* report, the convergence of access to media sources through one device means that children were watching television and playing games on the tablet and no further breakdown of the time spent on either activity is given. However, this study was able to investigate patterns of tablet use across the day. Tablets were used most between 4pm and 6pm on weekdays but at weekends use was more evenly spread across the day. The portability of these devices is evident in the data too: tablets were most likely to be used in the living room but before 9am they were more evident in kitchens and after 6pm in bedrooms.

Like their older siblings the very youngest children's screen time is dominated by television watching. They typically spend much less time playing games on a mobile device or a computer than watching television programmes or DVDs. The 2013 Zero to Eight survey in the USA found that under 2s watched television for an average of 44 minutes each day and children 2–4 years old just over one hour. In contrast, the average time in any one day that children under one year old spent playing games on either a computer or a mobile device was less than one minute and even 2–4 year olds spent only three minutes playing games on a computer in a typical day and seven minutes with games on a mobile device. A look at the figures on frequency of use explains some of these low daily average time figures. For instance, although 38 per cent of under two year olds have used a mobile device, only 6 per cent do so daily and 8 per cent weekly. Even across the whole 0–8 age range only 17 per cent used a mobile device daily and 28 per cent weekly. Such figures suggest the more general conclusion that while the youngest children do interact with the full range of digital devices available they typically only do so for short periods of time, particularly when compared to time spent watching television, other forms of play and activity and attending educational settings.

The second source of contemporary evidence about what children are doing with digital technologies comes from qualitative studies, often case studies or smaller-scale investigations, sometimes targeted at addressing particular theoretically informed or practice-driven questions. Such qualitative explorations do not make any claims about generalisability or applicability but seek to provide rich, contextualised findings about the everyday activities and perspectives of parents and children by methods that allow for emerging themes to be explored through an iterative process of data collection and analysis. Examples of such studies include the seven-country exploratory study managed by the European Union (EU) Joint Research Centre (JRC) published in 2015 (Chaudron, 2015). This study set out to find out more about how children aged 6–7 years old in Belgium, the Czech Republic, Finland, Germany, Italy, Russia and the UK engaged with digital technology and how their parents were involved in the children's digital activities. The TAP study conducted by Marsh et al. (2015) followed the initial large-scale survey of tablet and apps use drawn on above with a second qualitative phase. In that phase case studies of six families explored the use that children ranging in age from six months to four years made of augmented reality apps at home. The qualitative methods used included interviews with parents and children, parent- and researcher-recorded video and photographs and video from body cameras worn by two of the children as they engaged with the selected apps.

Across the seven countries included in the EU report it was clear that the children were growing up in what were described as 'media-rich' homes (Chaudron, 2015, p. 7). Many were keen users of digital technologies, particularly playing app games on tablets and watching videos but it was also evident that not all children engaged frequently with the digital resources in their homes, and that even those who did also made extensive use of other traditional, non-digital play resources and took part in other physical and creative activities. For instance, children in Belgium talked about enjoying riding bikes, going swimming and reading books. In Russia seven-year-old Anton and his younger brother enjoyed watching Lego cartoons on the family tablet but then went on to make their own similar constructions. In the Czech Republic children in one family mentioned football training and painting as activities they chose after school while the favourite activity of the two sisters in another family was horse riding.

The JRC study conducted by Chaudron (2015) concluded, as we have suggested in our discussion about digital play in Chapter 5, that there was a reciprocal relationship between children's 'offline' interests and their digital activities. For instance, children went online to gather information about a special interest, to seek out favourite characters or topics on YouTube. They followed a favourite character across a number of digital mediums and read stories and coloured in pictures of these characters offline. The earlier survey phase of the TAP study reported on the way in which children's interests drove choices about which app to download. Nearly one third of parents of 3–5 year olds reported that they downloaded apps to satisfy their child's 'interest or passion' and the case studies provided instances of on- and offline engagement with particular topics. For example, one girl shared her father's interest in dinosaurs, an enthusiasm that she engaged with through computer games and apps, television programmes, cuddly toys, figurines and print magazines.

The case studies in the JRC and TAP reports suggest a further finding that is less visible in the quantitative studies that rely on parents' accounts; young children favour individual rather than shared or social digital games and activities. The case study evidence shows that when children engaged with apps their parents typically reported their own involvement in terms of offering initial support as their child became familiar with an app and then maintaining a largely supervisory role. In turn the children involved preferred to interact independently to have fun with a game or other digital activity and were noted as having 'actively resisted' their parents' attempts to participate. The children's desire for independence extended to aspirations to own high-status digital technologies such as a tablet or smartphone and some parents made use of the attractiveness of access to digital resources as part of their reward or punishment regimes. Activities done together as a family were typically offline such as watching television together or taking part in outdoor or cultural events, with the exception of shared communication with distant families using tools such as Skype and Facetime.

Digital divides

In the discussion above we have considered generalised findings from representative samples of a population and some examples of particular instances from the qualitative investigations of case study families. In this section we will look again at the quantitative evidence to consider whether there are significant differences between the digital age experiences of groups in a population, differentiated by specific characteristics. Our intention is not to define children or families as in deficit or to suggest that particular features determine outcomes. Rather, we introduce this discussion here in the light of our argument that the cultural context in which children develop and in which technological innovation occurs makes a difference to the ways in which new possibilities become part of everyday experiences and familiar practices. Our attention will focus on two dimensions which can be expected to influence the experience of individual children: gender and socio-economic status. However, as we explained above, the data available and the questions posed in the studies reported constrain our discussion.

The Zero to Eight survey data from the USA (Common Sense Media, 2013) does not report gender differences but both the TAP study (Marsh *et al.*, 2015) and the UK media survey (Ofcom, 2016) attend to data for boys and girls separately for some questions at least. The 2015 TAP study found that more boys owned tablets than girls and that boys were more likely than girls to have access to a higher number of digital resources in their household. There were gender differences too in the kind of apps with which children engaged. For example, parents reported that girls were more likely to engage with apps that involve 'colouring in' a scene or characters than boys were; 9 per cent of parents of boys named Peppa's Paintbox among their son's favourite apps compared with 13 per cent of parents of girls including this as a favourite. The UK Ofcom 2016 survey also presents evidence of some gender differences. For example, in 2016 boys had significantly more access to games consoles connected to a TV than girls, on average boys aged 3–4 years watched significantly more television than girls and girls were somewhat more likely than boys to be subject to family rules which restricted their television viewing to particular programmes or times of day.

Reporting on qualitative case study evidence Stephen (2011) found that while there was no gender difference in the proportion of children's toys that were digital or traditional there were differences in the nature of the digital resources given to boys and girls and in the items with which they chose to play. Girls favoured digital games which featured princesses, dressing up, caring for pets and Barbie or other 'girl' characters while boys played games featuring vehicles, obstacle races, male characters from children's television programmes and videos, sports and construction activities. When offered a choice by the research team the girls participating in the case studies focused on interactions with specific resources were more likely to choose a technological pet while both boys expressed a preference for games consoles (Stephen, Stevenson, & Adey, 2013). The studies of everyday engagement with technologies by Marsh *et al.* (2015) and Livingstone, Marsh, Plowman, Ottovordemgentschenfelde, and Fletcher-Watson (2015) report a similar form and degree of gender differentiation. The gendered marketing and uptake of digital resources and playthings appears little different from gender influences on the use and desirability of traditional play objects and activities, particularly when the toys are linked to multi-media characters and tie-in products. It seems that growing up in the digital age may have extended rather than challenged the areas in which gender stereotypes can influence children's preferences and behaviour.

In the UK both the Ofcom survey (Ofcom, 2016) and the TAP study (Marsh *et al.*, 2015) found many more statistically significant differences in digital practices associated with socio-economic circumstances than with gender. Better-off families were significantly more likely to have a smart TV, desktop or laptop and tablet than those categorised as less well off. In 2016 only 9 per cent of better-off families did not have any kind of tablet but this proportion rose to 28 per cent for poorer families. There were differences in brand ownership suggested too. The TAP study of the families of 0–5 year olds found that those who were better off were more likely to own an iPad while less-well-off families tended to own cheaper brands of tablets. Poorer households were less likely to own a radio or DVD recorder, hand-held games player, educational games system designed for young children (e.g. VTech or Leapster) or an e-book reader. As the authors of the TAP study point out, parents made little mention of their children engaging with digital technologies at their educational setting, suggesting that an opportunity to enrich the technology experiences of children from less-well-off homes may be being neglected. The UK studies also found that children growing up in better-off households were more likely to have access to satellite TV and to be able to make use of TV on-demand services while those in less-well-off homes were more likely to make use of Freeview services.

Lower family income does then seem to be related to having experience of a more restricted range of technologies or to what might be considered to be cheaper forms of digital resources but it does not appear to be associated with less engagement with the most popular form of media – television. The Ofcom 2016 data suggests that children in less-well-off families are more likely to be among those watching television for three hours or more each weekday, while those living in better-off households are more likely to watch for less than one hour per day. Although all children are reported to watch television for longer at the weekend, a similar trend occurs with those watching least being more likely to be from better-off families and those watching for longest belonging to less-well-off households. Both surveys also found that better-off parents express more concern about the length of time that their children spend watching television and the UK Ofcom survey reported that better-off families were more likely to set a time at which their 3–4 year olds had to cease watching television.

Similar patterns of access to technologies associated with family income were found in the USA by the Zero to Eight survey (Common Sense Media, 2013). Children from poorer families were much less likely to have access to tablet computers or smartphones than their peers growing up in more affluent circumstances, although the gap in ownership of smartphones was reported to be narrowing. There were differences in the accessibility of high-speed internet reported in the USA too. Less than half of lower-income families had access to high-speed internet in 2013 compared to 86 per cent of better-off households. This survey identified what the researchers labelled an 'app gap' as well as the digital divide in access to technological hardware. They found that only 35 per cent of lower-income parents had downloaded an educational app for their child compared with 49 per cent of middle-income families and 75 per cent of higher-income households. Furthermore, even when lower-income families did have access to a mobile device they did not take the opportunity to download educational apps to the same extent as better-off families.

In some cases ethnicity was found to interact with socio-economic status. In the USA data no clear pattern emerges but it does appear that African-American families are more likely than others to have the television playing throughout the day and that among the least-well-off families Black and Latino children watch more TV each day than White children. Children from middle-income Black families were more likely to experience television as a constant presence in their home but the figures for the amount of time that children spend actually watching television daily show no differences across ethnic groups. Among the UK respondents in the TAP survey Black and Minority Ethnic (BME) families typically owned more technological resources than others but children in these families were less likely to engage with educational apps. On the other hand, BME households were more likely than others to use apps for social reasons and to use tablets for their children to view magazines. BME parents in the UK reported experiencing a further divide – the lack of new media attention to the characters and stories which were particularly attractive to their children.

Conclusion

Survey evidence suggests that young children throughout the early years have access to a broad and growing range of digital technologies in their homes but the biggest growth is in their access to tablet computers. This is unsurprising given the development of the iPad as connected with Alan Kay's thinking about young children's engagement with technologies. Although the devices that children typically engage with have changed since 2010, watching television remains the dominant screen-time activity for young children, whether on a mobile device or traditional television screen. Increases in the portability of digital devices have been accompanied by moves to on-demand media and app-mediated activities. There is evidence too of the blending of digital and non-digital activities as children engage with technologies. These general trends and population level findings conceal digital divides between the ways that boys and girls engage with technologies and the impact that socio-economic status has on young children's experience of the digital age at home.

References

Apple (2015). iPad in education [website]. Retrieved from www.apple.com/education/ipad/apps-books-andmore/.

Broadcasting Standards Authority (2015). *Children's media use study: how and why children engage with media today.* Broadcasting Standards Authority NZ. Retrieved from https://bsa.govt.nz/images/assets/Research/Childrens_Media_Report_2015_FINAL_for_publishing_2.pdf.

Chaudron, S. (2015). Young children (0–8) and digital technology: a qualitative exploratory study across seven countries. Luxembourg: Publications Office of the European Union. Retrieved from http://publications.jrc.ec.europa.eu/repository/handle/JRC93239.

Common Sense Media (2013). *Zero to eight: children's media use in America 2013.* Retrieved from www.commonsensemedia.org/research/zero-to-eight-childrens-media-use-in-america-2013.

Cowan, J. (2016, 20 July). High tech family life. *The Parenting Place.* Retrieved from www.theparentingplace.com/technology/high-tech-family-life/.

Ebbeck, M., Yim, H. Y. B., Chan, Y., & Goh, M. (2016). Singaporean parents' views of their young children's access and use of technological devices. *Early Childhood Education Journal, 44*(2), 127–134.

Euromonitor International (2015). Hong Kong toys fair: the rise of technology in toys. *Euromonitor Research.* Retrieved from http://blog.euromonitor.com/2015/02/hong-kong-toys-fair-the-rise-of-technology-in-toys.html.

Gill, L. (2015). Playtime or learning time, the potential of children's apps. *Entrepreneur Country Global.* Retrieved from www.entrepreneurcountryglobal.com/zoo/item/playtime-or-learning-time-the-potential-of-children-s-apps.

Hirsh-Pasek, K., Zosh, J. M., Golinkoff, R. M., Gray, J. H., Robb, M. B., & Kaufman, J. (2015). Putting education in 'educational' apps: lessons from the science of learning. *Psychological Science in the Public Interest, 16*(1), 3–34.

Juniper Research (2015). Smart toy revenues to hit $2.8bn this year, driven by Black Friday and Christmas holiday sales. *Juniper Research.* Retrieved from www.juniperresearch.com/press/press-releases/smart-toy-revenues-to-hit-$2-8bn-this-year.

Kay, A. C. (1972, August). A personal computer for children of all ages. In *Proceedings of the ACM annual conference – Volume 1* (p. 1). ACM.

Kay, A. (2013). The future of reading depends on the future of learning difficult to learn things. In B. Junge, Z. Berzina, W. Scheiffele, W. Westerveld, & C. Zwick (Eds.), *The digital turn: design in the era of interactive technologies.* Chicago: University of Chicago Press.

Kay, A., & Goldberg, A. (1977). Personal dynamic media. *Computer, 10*(3), 31–41.

Livingstone, S., Marsh, J., Plowman, L., Ottovordemgentschenfelde, S., & Fletcher-Watson, B. (2015). *Young children (0–8) and digital technology: a qualitative exploratory study – national report-UK.* LSE Research Online. Retrieved from http://eprints.lse.ac.uk/60799/1/__lse.ac.uk_storage_LIBRARY_Secondary_libfile_shared_repository_Content_Livingstone,%20S_Young%20children%200-8_Livingstone_Young%20children%200-8_2015.pdf.

Marsh, J., Plowman, L., Yamada-Rice, D., Bishop, J. C., Lahmar, J., Scott, F., Davenport, A., Davis, S., French, K., Piras, M., Thornhill, S., Robinson, P., & Winter, P. (2015). Exploring play and creativity in pre-schoolers' use of apps: final project report. *TAP: Technology and Play.* Retrieved from www.techandplay.org/TAP_Final%20Report.pdf.

Masuda, Y. (1985). Three great social revolutions: agricultural, industrial, and informational. *Prometheus, 3*(2), 269–274.

Nevski, E., & Siibak, A. (2016). The role of parents and parental mediation on 0–3-year old's digital play with smart devices: Estonian parents' attitudes and practices. *Early Years, 36*(3), 227–241.

Ofcom (2016, 16 November). *Children and parents: media use and attitudes report 2016.* Retrieved from www.ofcom.org.uk/__data/assets/pdf_file/0034/93976/Children-Parents-Media-Use-Attitudes-Report-2016.pdf.

Prigg, M. (2014, 21 February). How the iPad replaced the toy chest: researchers find children play with touchscreens more than traditional toys. *Mail Online.* Retrieved from www.dailymail.co.uk/sciencetech/article-2565061/How-iPad-replaced-toy-chest-Researchers-children-play-touchscreens-traditional-toys.html.

Prigg, M. (2015, 4 July). The iPad really IS child's play: more than half of toddlers can use Apple's tablet when they are just ONE researchers say. *Mail Online.* Retrieved from www.dailymail.co.uk/sciencetech/article-3149025/The-iPad-really-child-s-play-half-toddlers-use-Apple-s-tablet-just-ONE-researchers-say.html.

Stephen, C. (2011). Playing and learning with technologies. Scottish Universities Insight Institute. *Research Briefing, 2.* Retrieved from www.stir.ac.uk/research/hub/publication/13566.

Stephen, C., Stevenson, O., & Adey, C. (2013). Young children engaging with technologies at home: the influence of family context. *Journal of Early Childhood Research*, *11*(2), 149–164.

Vaala, S., Ly, A., & Levine, M. H. (2015). Getting a read on the app stores: a market scan and analysis of children's literacy apps. Full Report. In *Joan Ganz Cooney Center at Sesame Workshop*. Joan Ganz Cooney Center at Sesame Workshop. 1900 Broadway, New York, NY 10023.

Vanderwater, E. A., Rideout, V. J., Wartella, E. A., Huang, X., Lee, J. H., & Shim, M. (2007). Digital childhood: electronic media and technology use among infants, toddlers, and preschoolers. *Pediatrics*, *119*(5), 1006–1015.

7

MORAL PANIC – SOCIAL AND CULTURAL VALUES

Introduction

As we have outlined in the first two chapters of this book digital technologies have a history of evolution located in the knowledge practices and cultural determinants of their time. Technological change is not a new phenomenon. Digital technology has evolved to its present state through a process of knowledge application about solid state physics through to the invention of the internet and World Wide Web to the ready availability of internet-enabled touchscreen technologies. Most recently tablet and mobile technologies have made digital resources ubiquitous in daily life, including the everyday experiences of young children. But the ubiquity of digital technologies and the continuing evolution of knowledge applications does not mean that the digital age is welcomed by everyone, and especially in so far as it relates to the experiences of younger children. Reactions to technological innovations appear to be shaped by the three theories of technology we outlined in Chapter 4: technological determinism, substantive and critical. While for many people the substantive contribution of digital technologies to everyday life is welcomed or even taken for granted, for others these technological innovations are associated with new play and learning practices which they view more negatively. From a critical perspective it is the degree of coherence between values and expectations and the purposes, behaviours and practices around technological innovation that influence the ways in which individuals and social groups react. When there is a mismatch between values and expectations and changing practices, accompanied by an assumption of technological determinism, then concerns, such as the possible social isolation of children or stunted social development, are likely to be more keenly expressed.

Reporting on the digital era

Newspaper articles and blogs across the world frequently raise alarms about young children spending many hours each week playing games online and being more familiar with virtual worlds than they are with face-to-face communications and relationships. For example, in the UK one headline referred to giving 'babies' an iPad as like playing Russian roulette with their developmental prospects (Harris, 2015). In the previous year an article reporting the un-evidenced claims made on behalf of a teachers' union was headlined 'Infants unable to use toy building blocks due to iPad addiction' (Paton, 2014). In Australia a headline linked screen time and the risk of harm to oral language development (Forwood, 2014). *Huffington Post* (2014) too linked use of digital technologies to negative outcomes for children's development and in Kenya and Singapore newspapers reported potential dangers ranging from obesity, damage to eyesight, challenges to social and emotional development, cyber-bullying and online abuse (Ondieki, 2016; Teng, 2013).

Concern with the digital experiences of infants and children appears to reflect a continuing surprise (or alarm) that they wish to and are able to make use of digital technologies. This interest in age per se suggests an implicit expectation that such resources might be considered to be the preserve of adults or adolescents. Whether this sentiment arises from assumptions that adults and children inhabit different worlds or that new technologies should be first adopted by adults is unclear. However, what is clear is that the ways in which digital technologies have spread through all aspects of contemporary life (especially with the evolution of the IoT and the semantic web) mean that adults and children are routine participants in the digital age.

An example of the kind of moral panic to be found among social commentators and in the traditional press around the digital experiences of preschool-age children in particular is to be found in an article which followed the publication of the UK Ofcom media use survey data for 2016. The article in the *Daily Mail* (Lambert, 2016) began with the headline 'The under-5s glued to screens for four hours each day', before going on to explain that the latest survey data revealed that more than half of three and four year olds now 'used' a tablet and that they now spent 13 minutes more online daily than in 2015. These headline points were followed in the article by statements from groups and individuals campaigning on a range of issues such as 'better parenting', spending time in nature and 'values in education'. In their expressions of concern about the extent of children's engagement with technologies these campaigners employed such terms as 'digital addiction' and 'catastrophic consequences'. That parents reported satisfaction with the balance between technological and other activities in their children's lives, and that they continue with traditional practices such as reading stories at bedtime and watching family television programmes together was mentioned but was heavily outweighed by the reporting of negative reactions. The article does not suggest that adults should forego the use of tablets or that they may be at risk. The focus of attention is on the apparent tension between particular expectations about how young children should spend their time and how adults should parent and the assumed 'power' of technological resources to impact children's health and wellbeing.

Some press reports raise alarm from the findings of single studies, suggesting direct associations between technology use and socially or developmentally undesirable (or occasionally desirable) behaviours, often without taking account of the age of the users or the context or any apparent awareness of alternatives to their position of technological determinism. An example from an article in a UK newspaper illustrates this tendency. The article was headlined 'How digital technology and TV can inhibit children socially' (*Telegraph Reporter*, 2014). The details of the article revealed that this headline was based on a comparison of 11 and 12 year olds who had no access to digital technologies for five days while at a nature and science camp and others who accessed the media as usual. The findings suggested that the children who had been at the camp and denied access to digital technologies were better able to identify emotions expressed in photographs of faces than the other participants. It is of course a considerable jump from this contextually specific and narrowly defined evidence to the generalised headline claim that spending time with digital resources inhibits the social development of all children. The tendency to over-claim from individual studies is particularly problematic when attending to the implications for young children because, as we described in Chapter 6, they are the least likely age to be represented in the research. Only 20 per cent of research studies about the outcomes of engaging with digital technologies include any children under nine years old. Strikingly, despite children now being born into a digital age, only 4 per cent of research studies look specifically at the effects on children up to four years old (Holloway, Green, & Livingstone, 2013).

Research publications are not immune either from expressions of concern that appear to be based on an untheorised position on technology. For instance, Dinleyici, Carman, Ozturk, and Sahin-Dagli, (2016) surveyed children's use of specific forms of digital media by parents' report and explored parents' perspectives on their children's digital activities. The researchers went on to conclude that their findings suggest that parents were ill informed about what was appropriate access to digital media 'especially in the age group where electronic media use should be discouraged' and that 'Therefore, physicians, especially paediatricians, should make parents and teachers media-literate' (online publication – no page numbers, see Conclusion). It is important to ask if reflections of this type on children's engagement with digital technologies can be seen as a contemporary manifestation of an anxious reaction to change that has occurred over many innovations which have followed since the invention of the transistor, through microprocessors, computing, the internet, World Wide Web and the advent of tablet computing. Wartella and Jennings (2000) point out that research about new forms of media typically begins by examining who is engaging with the innovations and in what circumstances, then moves to focus on the implications of exposure to the novel technology. They conclude that debates about children's use of computers 'echo those surrounding the introduction of other new media throughout the past century' (p. 32). It seems that researchers too may have a tendency to focus on potential negative outcomes.

Reactions to innovations in media

Early studies on children and radio listening attended to questions about what children were listening to and how much time they spent listening to the radio. By the 1940s this had shifted to examining the effects of listening to radio on children's lives and behaviours, such as their performance in school, emotional reactions and ability to distinguish between fantasy and reality. Listening to radio was found to be a 'powerful force' on children's development, but was considered one mediated by other elements of the ecology of children's lives such as stage of development and family background (Wartella & Jennings, 2000). Later in the 20th century television was widely written about as a threat to book reading and to social life. This valorising of book reading seems commonplace now, however, at the time when technological developments began to reduce the cost of printing and make books accessible to more of the population, this was not greeted by all as a positive development. Pearson (1999) suggests that in the mid-18th to mid-19th centuries reading was considered as a potentially 'dangerous recreation' by some members of society who were concerned about the impact that ready access to novels could have on young women who may begin to develop new ambitions and neglect their domestic duties. Even earlier writing by Plato (2005) suggested that writing was challenging memory skills as it removed the need to memorise.

During the period of predominately broadcast media (the 1960s and into the 1990s) there is an extensive research literature on the impact of young children watching television that echoes forward into 21st-century reactions to digital technology use by young children in both the popular media and research literature. For example, Singer and Singer (1984) argued:

> The television set has become so intrinsic a feature of the American household that studies of the development and socialization of children must consider it as much a potential source of influence as the home environment, the parents' behavioural style and their socioeconomic milieu.
>
> *(p. 73)*

Nevertheless, much of the potential influence that was studied focused on the ways in which television watching could have negative outcomes on children's development and behaviour rather than the ways in which engagement with this particular technology might enhance children's participation in the world, support their learning or enhance their capacity to participate in the culture or practice of broadcast media in which they were growing up (see for instance Zuckerman & Zuckerman, 1985). There were, and indeed continue to be, concerns expressed about the influence of television on the amount of time children spend sleeping, exposure to social stereotypes, advertising and inappropriate sexual behaviour, and attitudes to alcohol and substance abuse. For example, each of these topics, along with concerns about children becoming inactive, and consequentially obese, as a result of the time they spend watching television is listed on a current website giving advice to parents on children's development and behaviour (University of Michigan, 2017). The title of an investigation by Dietz Jr and Gortmaker (1985) gives a clear flavour of the direction of their work – 'Do we fatten our children at the television set?' They present findings headlined as showing that there were significant associations between the time children spent watching television and obesity but the authors go on to temper this by concluding that their analysis shows a less definitive picture of television viewing as an activity which may cause obesity in some children.

Perhaps the most researched potential impact was the relationship between watching television programmes that contained images of violent actions and subsequent measurement of aggressive behaviour by the young viewer. However, it is important to note the age of the children involved in the studies, the nuanced nature of the findings and that the conclusions are often based on correlations not causal associations. For instance, Eron, Hussman, Lefkowitz and Walder (1972) found that male and female 3rd grade children in the USA who preferred watching violent television programmes were rated by their peers as more aggressive in school. Following up both male and female participants 10 years later the researchers found that among boys (but not girls) a preference for violent television in 3rd grade was related to aggression in later years. The authors go on to suggest that, while it was not the only cause of aggressive behaviour, watching violent television in the early years was a probable causal influence.

Josephson (1987) offers data that presents an even more confounded picture. This study focused on boys in 2nd and 3rd grade. The children watched violent and non-violent television programmes together in groups and their teachers rated each participant on an aggression scale before and after watching the television programmes. Josephson found that boys rated as typically aggressive behaved more aggressively during a follow-up activity when they had watched a violent programme rather than a non-violent programme. For typically aggressive children aggression in the follow-up activity was heightened by being given a violence-related cue at the beginning of that phase. However, for boys rated as typically low in aggressiveness the findings were different. The evidence suggested that for these participants watching a violent programme and experiencing a violence-related cue suppressed aggression in the follow-up activity.

These historically presented research findings alert us to over-simplified claims about cause and effect when considering the impact of new technologies on young children's play and learning in a digital age, based on technological determinist expectations that innovations in technology will in themselves shape specific outcomes. Such over-simplified claims can be found in studies that appear to herald the end of childhood due to the increasing presence of digital technologies in family life through to the plethora of recent research about the implications for children's learning from the use of iPads in early childhood education settings. Yet gender, personality factors and the priming effect of the behaviour of others are all suggested by these historical studies alone as factors which intervene to make a difference to outcomes in a way that is not yet evidenced in all contemporary discussions about young children's engagement with digital technologies. As Wartella and

Jennings (2000) pointed out, 'the relationship is always between a kind of television and a kind of child in a kind of situation' (p. 36).

Furthermore, it is noteworthy that such 'effects' studies do not typically compare the influence of television with other activities, such as playing outside or imaginative play, likely to be experienced by children in the relevant age group. Such activities appear to be taken for granted as appropriate and supportive of development and historically it is what is seen as the 'innovation', particularly when it is a technological innovation, that is the subject of study when monitoring effects. However, when researchers do examine children's contemporary play experiences from a more holistic perspective, digital technologies appear to augment rather than replace more traditional forms of play and learning. For example, using the American Academy of Pediatrics guidelines as a measure of the extent of engagement with digital resources, Vanderwater et al. (2007) found no differences in the length of time that children spent being read to or in outdoor play, regardless of whether they spent only the length of time recommended for digital activities or exceeded the guideline figure. Research in Australia by Moore (2015) attests to the cultural adaptiveness of play rather than the power of technological innovations to shape play. Moore (2015) investigated the imaginative play practices of children over four generations. She found that seven play practices (e.g. playing in trees, bedrooms and with popular-culture) remained stable over 40 years with three new play practices (e.g. accessibility to private play places and using toys in private and public play) emerging in the last 10 years.

Proper childhood – proper parenting

Just as television in the 20th century was seen by some social commentators as a threat to their understanding of traditional constructions of a 'good childhood', in the early 21st century technological innovations may once again be being treated as epitomising the threats and opportunities of contemporary society, especially for children and their families. Among writers concerned primarily with current and past parenting practices and the behaviour and educational outcomes of children and young people, digital technologies and online activities can be perceived as a symptom or driver of change for the worse, or at least a change that challenges their expectations about appropriate childhood activities (e.g. Goddard Blythe, 2011; House, 2011; Louv, 2010). Such commentators have an historically based understanding of the values and culture that they see as central to the macrosystem of their society and therefore representative of the 'correct' or 'normal' experiences supporting children's development. As such, digital technologies and engagement with the World Wide Web can be characterised as a site of tension in which a society's culture is being recreated and disputed. In this context, attention is often focused on the apparently singular relationship between technology and/or outcomes or behaviours that are or have been highly valued in a society such as outdoor play or reading books. Such an essentially conservative and deterministic perspective contrasts with a more critically aware approach concerned with the play and learning of young children growing up during the digital age and now with the reach of the IoT and the semantic web in young children's knowledge economy.

In *Toxic Childhood* Palmer (2006) places children's engagement with digital technologies alongside other apparent ills of contemporary life, writing about the damaging potential for children of a 'competitive, consumer-driven, screen-based lifestyle' (p. xiii) and placing encounters with technology alongside chapters on the decline in outdoor play, family mealtimes and other societal changes in family practices. She expresses concern about the amount of time that children spend on screen-based activities and contrasts that with what she describes as interacting with real people in real play rather than in junk or screen-based play. Elsewhere, Palmer (2010) argues that what she sees as children's screen-saturated lives are linked to the reported rise in attention deficit hyperactivity syndrome, dyslexia and autism. In his writing advocating 'slow parenting' Honoré (2008) too includes time spent on computers as one of the negative characteristics of contemporary life. Other areas of concern for Honoré include a lack of time and opportunity for outdoor play, an excess of extracurricular activities, and parental efforts to ensure that their child makes ideal developmental and educational progress. However, unlike Palmer who advocates limiting digital technology experiences, Honoré suggests that there are 'no one size fits all' rules about the right number of hours to spend on the computer. His approach is concerned with what feels right for individual families, while also ensuring that children spend time outdoors and have opportunities to explore and take risks.

Beyond a concern with lifestyle changes and the use of particular resources for play and learning the content of digital media and its impact on young children raises anxieties for some commentators and policy-makers. Although we can agree that what children see, experience or hear will affect their development, it seems that it is the potential negative influences that attract more attention in terms of guidance for parenting and education. In 2013, the American Academy of Pediatrics (AAP) argued that children under two years of age should not be exposed to screen time in any medium but went on to advise that children older than two years can engage with 'entertainment media' with 'high quality content' for one to two hours per day. By 2016, the updated AAP guidelines recognised the pervasiveness of digital technologies in young children's lives. The new recommendations place an emphasis on high-quality programming and avoiding 'fast-paced' or 'distracting' content. High-quality content is a phrase which raises questions about the definition of 'quality' and the kind of debate we are already familiar with around high culture and popular-culture in music, films and art (e.g. Gans, 1999). Furthermore, the substantive content of a story or game will be important regardless of the medium. Stories can be moral, aggressive, instructive, fun, scary and educative whether told, read, played in a game or accessed via digital media.

Kaufman (2013) argues that it is what children do when interacting with screen-based technologies that is influential for learning. He points out that on-screen time can be used to learn science, communicate with grandparents, watch educational videos or create works of art. On the other hand, children may spend time playing inappropriate traditional games or passively watching entertainment videos. Given these nuanced possibilities, Holloway *et al.* (2013) argue for more understanding about the impact of different screen-based activities rather than quantifying time on-screen or imposing a total ban on encounters with digital technologies. Interestingly, in its revised advice in 2016 even the AAP (2016) has set aside their strong position on screen-avoidance for the youngest children in the case of video-chatting. Writing about the AAP's review of evidence about children's encounters with digital media, Brown, Shifrin, and Hill (2015) point out that research and the policy statements that are derived from empirical studies 'lag behind' digital innovation and that the Academy's previous position statements pre-dated the proliferation of iPads and apps. They go on to suggest that the ubiquity of digital encounters in contemporary life means that 'screen time' is 'becoming simply time' (p. 1, online).

Conclusion

Moral panic is a barometer for adult perceptions of what childhood should be like in any given age and is not necessarily an effective response to the developmental niche in which children are growing up. With social media and IoT digital mediation sinking into daily life moral panic can be seen as an even less appropriate or constructive response for equipping children for life in the 21st century. How can teachers, researchers, administrators, policy-makers respond? We have begun to answer this question already by identifying the transformative developments in knowledge that have contributed to changing patterns of communication in the digital age. We have shown how the shift from point-to-point telephony engendered new ways of thinking about communication and how new forms of communication have embedded digitalised forms of knowledge and practices into daily activity. So far in this book we have tried to illustrate how the transformative capacity of cultural knowledge continuously shapes and reshapes the developmental niche for each generation of children – necessitating new respondent forms of play and learning. In the next chapter we turn our attention to exploring the digital age from the perspectives and experiences of children and their families.

References

AAP Council on Communications and Media (2013). Children, adolescents, and the media: policy statement. *Pediatrics*, *132*(5), 958–961. doi: 10.1542/peds.2013-2656.

AAP Council on Communications and Media (2016). Media and young minds. *Pediatrics*, *138*(5), 1–6. doi: 10.1542/peds.2016-2591.

Brown, A., Shifrin, D. L., & Hill, D. L. (2015). Beyond 'turn it off': how to advise families on media use. *AAP News*, *36*(10). Retrieved from www.yaldatuhls.com/wp-content/uploads/2016/03/AAP-Publication.pdf.

Dietz, W. H., Jr, & Gortmaker, S. L. (1985). Do we fatten our children at the television set? Obesity and television viewing in children and adolescents. *Pediatrics*, *75*(5), 807–812.

Dinleyici, M., Carman, K. B., Ozturk, E., & Sahin-Dagli, F. (2016). Media use by children, and parents' views on children's media usage. *Interact Journal of Medical Research, 5*(2), e18. doi: 10.2196/ijmr.5668.

Eron, L. D., Hussman, L. R., Lefkowitz, M. M., & Walder, L. O. (1972). Does television violence cause aggression? *American Psychologist, 27*(4), 253–263.

Forwood, C. (2014, 1 December). Too much screen time may harm children's oral skills, research suggests. *Sydney Morning Herald*. Retrieved from www.smh.com.au/national/education/too-much-screen-time-may-harm-childrens-oral-skills-research-suggests-20141114-11mvo1.html.

Gans, H. (1999). *Popular culture and high culture: an analysis and evaluation of taste*. New York: Basic Books.

Goddard Blythe, S. (2011). *The genius of natural childhood: secrets of thriving children*. Stroud: Hawthorn Press.

Harris, S. (2015, 22 September). Giving babies iPads is playing 'Russian roulette with their development', says leading psychologist. *Daily Mail*. Retrieved from www.dailymail.co.uk/news/article-3244062/Giving-babies-iPads-playing-Russian-roulette-development-says-leading-psychologist.html.

Holloway, D., Green, L., & Livingstone, S. (2013). Zero to eight: young children and their internet use. LSE, London: EU Kids Online. Retrieved from http://eprints.lse.ac.uk/52630/.

Honoré, C. (2008). *Under pressure: rescuing our children from the culture of hyper-parenting*. London: Orion.

House, R. (2011). The inappropriateness of ICT in early childhood: arguments from philosophy, pedagogy and developmental research. In S. Suggate and E. Reese (Eds.), *Contemporary debates in childhood education and development* (pp. 105–121). New York, NY: Routledge.

Huffington Post (2014, 15 September). How technology is having a serious impact on your child's development. *Huffington Post*. Retrieved from www.huffingtonpost.co.uk/2014/09/15/children-technology-impact-addiction_n_5821492.html.

Josephson, W. L. (1987). Television violence and children's aggression: testing the priming, social script and disinhibition predictions. *Journal of Personality and Social Psychology, 53*(5), 882–896.

Kaufman, J. (2013, 24 April). Touch-screen technology and children. *Child*. Retrieved from www.childmags.com.au/child/development/5453-touch-screen-technology-and-children.

Lambert, L. (2016, 16 November). The under-5s glued to screens for four hours each day: fears 'very worrying' figures are showing that children are becoming online addicts. *Daily Mail*. Retrieved from www.dailymail.co.uk/news/article-3940134/The-5s-glued-screens-four-hours-day-Fears-worrying-figures-showing-children-online-addicts.html.

Louv, R. (2010). *Last child in the woods: saving our children from nature-deficit disorder*. London: Atlantic Books.

Moore, D. (2015). *A place within a place: toward new understandings on the enactment of contemporary imaginative play practices and places* (Doctoral dissertation). Australian Catholic University. Retrieved from http://researchbank.acu.edu.au/theses/538/.

Ondieki, E. (2016, 9 October). Rise of the digital kids and what that means for parents. *Daily Nation*. Retrieved from www.nation.co.ke/lifestyle/lifestyle/Rise-of-the-digital-kids-and-what-that-means-for-parents/1214-3409652-mdm31xz/.

Palmer, S. (2006). *Toxic childhood: how the modern world is damaging our children and what we can do about it*. London: Orion.

Palmer, S. (2010). Modern childhood. *SuePalmer.co.uk*. Retrieved from www.suepalmer.co.uk/modern_childhood_info_the_effects.php.

Paton, G. (2014, 15 April). Infants 'unable to use toy building blocks' due to iPad addiction. *Telegraph*. Retrieved from www.telegraph.co.uk/education/educationnews/10767878/Infants-unable-to-use-toy-building-blocks-due-to-iPad-addiction.html.

Pearson, J. (1999). *Women's reading in Britain, 1750–1835: a dangerous recreation*. Cambridge, MA: Cambridge University Press.

Plato (2005). Translated by C. J. Rowe. *Phaedrus*. London, UK: Penguin Classics.

Singer, J. L., & Singer, D. G. (1984). Family patterns and television viewing as predictors of children's beliefs and aggression. *Journal of Communication, 34*(2), 73–89.

Telegraph Reporter (2014, 25 August). How digital technology and TV can inhibit children socially. *Telegraph*. Retrieved from www.telegraph.co.uk/news/science/science-news/11054305/How-digital-technology-and-TV-can-inhibit-children-socially.html.

Teng, A. (2013, 5 June). Kids 'using gadgets at earlier age being exposed to risks': study. *Strait Times*. Retrieved from www.straitstimes.com/singapore/kids-using-gadgets-at-earlier-age-being-exposed-to-risks-study.

University of Michigan (2017). Your child development and behavior resources – television and children (last updated 2010). Retrieved from www.med.umich.edu/yourchild/topics/tv.htm.

Vanderwater, E. A., Rideout, V. J., Wartella, E. A., Huang, X., Lee, J. H., & Shim, M. (2007). Digital childhood: electronic media and technology use among infants, toddlers, and preschoolers. *Pediatrics, 119*(5), 1006–1015.

Wartella, E. A., & Jennings, N. (2000). Children and computers: new technology old concerns. *Future of Children, 10*(2), 31–43.

Zuckerman, D. M., & Zuckerman, B. S. (1985). Television's impact on children. *Pediatrics, 75*(2), 233–240.

8

CHILDREN, FAMILIES AND TECHNOLOGIES

Introduction

In this chapter we turn to the everyday experiences of children and their families in the digital age. We will consider research findings about the ways in which children's experiences are shaped by family values and attitudes and their family's cultural practices. We explore the social and cultural context in which young children are growing up and encountering digital technologies and new media, including the ways in which their relationships with siblings and peers make a difference to their experiences. We look too at the evidence about children's own perspectives on their digital encounters. A cultural-historical theoretical framework, along with a critical perspective on the roles and purposes of digital technologies helps us to conceptualise children's experiences in the digital age. We acknowledge the agency of young children and their purposeful engagement in digital activities that amplify the ways in which they can act to pursue their interests and enhance their development as members of a family and peer culture.

At home in the digital age

The homes in which children are growing up in the digital age offer an array of opportunities for entertainment, fun, creating, learning and communicating that were not available to previous generations and which continue to evolve with technological knowledge innovations. The early 21st-century dependence on desktop computers with games loaded on to the hardware and hand-held games consoles (see Plowman & Stephen, 2005) has been widely replaced within 10 years by the use of laptops, tablets, smartphones and activities accessed via apps, downloaded from the internet or played online (Marsh *et al.*, 2015). Tablet computers have made a difference to young children's encounters with digital technologies.

Their physical scale, portability and capacity to be used in different locations and the direct relationship between screen and user action they offer has overcome the restrictions previously imposed by the size of devices and the forms of connectivity they offered. Tablets remove some of the difficulties which desktop computers and laptops could present for the youngest users who sometimes struggled to manage cursor, mouse and keypad interface options via traditional GUIs. Instead tablets operate via touchable icons via a new form of user interface known as Natural User Interface (NUIs) (Jayemanne & Nansen, 2016). Kay's understanding of how children learn and make use of knowledge has become embedded in the everyday digital life of preschool children and their families.

As our review of the data about young children's access to digital technologies in Chapter 6 made clear, contemporary homes in post-industrial countries typically offer a rich array of digital technologies. However, beyond the kind of educational resources such as those marketed by VTech or Leapster, most children in their early years are not autonomous owners of the range of technologies to which they have access at home or in preschool (Marsh et al., 2015; Ofcom, 2016). Livingstone, Marsh, Plowman, Ottovordemgentschenfelde, and Fletcher-Watson (2015) found that parents were widely considered by children to be the owners of the smartphones in their homes, although when children asked to make use of a parent's smartphone it was typically made available to them. Laptops and tablets were thought of as shared household or family resources, part of the material culture of everyday life in the digital age. The objects that make up that material culture reflect the cultural evolution of technologies over time. For instance, Livingstone et al. (2015) argue that the shift among young children to playing games on a tablet computer has been responsible for the decline in use of games consoles. They also associate the use of portable devices to watch television and video with the reduction noted in the number of young children who have television in their bedrooms, a trend also noted in the USA Zero to Eight survey in 2013 (Common Sense Media, 2013).

Not only are parents influential as providers of physical digital resources at home, survey evidence from across Europe suggests that they are important mediators of engagement with these resources. Although there was some evidence of children around six years old browsing for and downloading free apps, deciding on which apps to acquire is more typically the role of parents (Livingstone et al., 2015). The TAP survey (Marsh et al., 2015) found that on most occasions (62 per cent) when young children engaged with a tablet it was because their parent had suggested this activity. Only 16 per cent of tablet use was considered to be at the sole request of a child. Both Marsh et al. and Livingstone et al. reported that parents' reasons for suggesting that their child make use of a tablet or for agreeing to a request were often a pragmatic response to social circumstances. Engaging with a tablet computer was seen as an agreeable way of passing the time, perhaps if the child had woken early, parents were busy with domestic activities or children needed to be occupied during a journey or while they waited in a queue. Among the respondents to a survey carried out in Estonia with parents who make their tablets and smartphones available to their 0–3 year olds, 97 per cent reported using their portable devices with their child at home and 29 per cent during car journeys (Nevski & Siibak, 2016). This survey found a more even balance between adult- and child-initiated engagement with portable devices (47 per cent, and 44 per cent respectively), perhaps reflecting the different ways in which the youngest children spend their time.

Despite their dependence on others to make digital resources available to them, young children are keen to claim ownership or assert rights of access, giving us insights into their enthusiasm for the activities ownership can confer and, perhaps more importantly, the desirable practical status which they associate with possession of a tablet or a smartphone in daily life. This characterisation of new technologies as desirable objects, typically owned by parents or older siblings, has been an ongoing feature of young children's everyday experience with technologies for some time. Research by Stephen, McPake, Plowman, and Berch-Heyman (2008) in which home technology tours were conducted with children, established that children were keen to claim ownership, or at least shared access, to resources such as hand-held games consoles that were used by their older siblings but which the researchers' observations (and the children's comments) suggested they were not yet able to use effectively. The JRC report (Chaudron, 2015) also suggests that children express a preference for technological devices which they do not own but would like to possess. They concluded that the device then takes on the 'magical' character of an object of high desire, conferring digital technologies with positive cultural value in their social setting.

Family values and attitudes

Throughout this book we have considered the evolution and enactment of the digital age as a cultural phenomenon. Young children experience the digital age first through the immediate social and cultural environment of their family, the perspectives and expectations that their parents and siblings hold about digital technologies and the ways in which technologies are embedded in the 'ordinary' culture of family life (Williams, 1958). Livingstone *et al.* (2015) argue that their data suggests that, although digital technologies have a significant presence in the everyday lives of most of the families who participated in their study, 'aspects of family philosophy or style' (p. 28) made a difference to the particular ways in which family members engaged with digital resources and activities.

Starting from a sociocultural theoretical position, Hedegaard (2009) argues that the social context of learning also includes the cultural values of the institutions with which individuals interact, including their families. The attitude of parents towards the relative value or otherwise of engaging with technologies is then a critical influence on early digital experiences. It makes a difference to parents' purchasing decisions, the ways in which young children are encouraged to learn, experience leisure, and the ways in which parents model life in the digital age. The three theories about the relationship between people and technology that we outlined first in Chapter 1 can be seen to be present at the micro-level in families. Parents may take a technological determinist view, seeing the technology as driving change, which they either accept or resist. Others will focus on the substantive position, being concerned only with what technology can help them to achieve and some may adopt a more critical perspective, questioning the purposes of technological advances and evaluating the outcomes of encounters with digital devices and programmes.

These perspectives on technology interact with socio-economic factors and expectations about 'good' or 'proper' parenting and appropriate or beneficial activities for young children to create the local culture of the digital age that is experienced in the family. These ethnotheories (Plowman, McPake, & Stephen, 2008; Plowman, Stevenson, McPake, Stephen, & Adey, 2011) shape children's access to specific digital devices and to the particular content with which they interact. Every family will have its own definition of suitable content for books and films and this judgement can be extended to the content of digital games, DVDs and apps. Parents have a preference for free apps but make decisions about which ones to download on three main criteria: a judgement about how much fun the activity will give their child, how easy an app is for a young child to use, and the presence of educational features, declared educational outcomes or the inclusion of educational topics such as healthy eating or caring for the environment (Marsh *et al.*, 2015). Livingstone *et al.* (2015) also found that parents talked about selecting apps that they viewed as educational, particularly for preschool children but the activities they talked about when they described 'good parenting' typically did not involve digital resources or were based on broadcast media such as shared television watching.

As we discussed in Chapter 7, social commentary and media reporting raises doubts and criticisms about the benefits to children of engaging with digital technologies and often presents arguments that seem to suggest that children should be 'protected' from the digital age and that good parenting attends to traditional or non-digital pastimes at home. However, research findings suggest that children are growing up in homes where parents have more varied or nuanced perspectives. A survey of US parents with children aged from two to seven years old revealed 'very positive' attitudes towards the role that technologies played in the lives of young children, leading the authors of this study to suggest that the scepticism about the potential benefits present in earlier studies (e.g. Rideout, Vanderwater, & Wartella, 2003) may be in decline as digital devices become an integral part of the lives of parents (Vittrup, Snider, Rose, & Rippy, 2016). Vittrup *et al.* (2016) also found that parents disagreed with the American Academy of Pediatrics' guidance that children under the age of two should not be exposed to any screen time. Only 11 per cent of participating parents believed claims that computers were associated with long-term physical, emotional or intellectual damage. On the contrary, the majority agreed with a statement suggesting that familiarity with digital devices at a young age was important for future success in the workplace. These parents were relaxed about making use of technologies to 'occupy' a child while adults attended to important tasks and the majority reported doing this at home. In Estonia, Nevski, and Siibak (2016) found that among those parents who allowed their child under three years of age to have access to smart technologies digital activities (particularly for watching videos and cartoons), they valued the potential of these devices to entertain their child as well as the apparent educational potential opportunities involved.

A recent study across six European countries and Russia found that parents of children under eight years old were alert to anxieties about the dangers of physical inactivity and passivity but expressed less concern about risks associated with access to the internet (Chaudron, 2015). Drawing on European research, Holloway, Green, and Livingstone (2013) suggest that parents are less concerned about young children's access to the internet than older children's potentially worrying encounters with inappropriate content. Evidence from Scotland suggested that parents were aware of negative ideas about children's engagement with technologies through their exposure to the media and their interactions with family and friends (Plowman et al., 2008). This longitudinal qualitative study of 24 case study families carried out by Plowman et al. found that parents' responses to statements about the benefits or drawbacks of young children's engagement with technologies were typically characterised by ambiguity and indecision. Only one quarter of the case study parents agreed with the statement 'Using some kinds of technology can be damaging to children's health and development'. The remaining three quarters of parents responded by referring to things which they had read or heard about the possible negative outcomes of time spent with digital devices. They mentioned concerns about the impact on physical development if children's gross motor activity was reduced in favour of time with technologies and were concerned too about the consequences of the lack of social interaction if technologies were used over extended periods and the danger of access to inappropriate content.

Nevertheless, Plowman et al. (2008) concluded that engaging with technologies was not perceived by parents to be the threat that some commentators, researchers and advisors claim. Parents' awareness of questions about the outcome of time spent with digital technologies did not deter the families participating in the Plowman et al. (2008) study from offering children some access to technologies at home. The research team found that while parents had concerns about children's use of technology in general, each family was confident that their decisions about which technologies were available and under what circumstances in their home mitigated any negative outcomes. With only one exception, participants agreed with the statement 'I think that we have got the use of new technologies right for our child'. This judgement seemed to be based on the decisions they made about how to regulate their child's use of technologies and their efforts to ensure that their youngsters engaged in a varied range of play opportunities at home to achieve a balanced diet of indoor and outdoor pursuits, individual and shared activities. Some families restricted the length of time each day that their young child could spend using a computer or games console. Time spent watching television was monitored too, often limited to times of day when the content was considered to be appropriate or when this activity was a good fit with family schedules.

The picture which emerges from the Plowman *et al.* (2008) study is one in which parents are aware of the debate in the popular media (see Chapter 7) about the potential negative outcomes of engagement with sustained use of digital technologies at home but are also confident that they have arranged their family time and access to activities and resources in a way which they feel minimises the risks. In Estonia too there was evidence of parents taking a hands-on approach to mediating their young child's use of the family's smart technologies by restricting use, co-using and supervision (Nevski & Siibak, 2016). The JRC study (Chaudron, 2015) found that parents across six European countries and Russia attempted to balance the benefits and risks of digital technologies by establishing family rules that restrict the time that can be spent on screen-based activities, limit the games and videos available and enforce passwords.

However, the evidence gathered by Marsh *et al.* (2015) suggests parents' claims about safeguarding their child by sharing their digital activities may be illusory. They argue that while the parents of young children surveyed said that they used apps along with their child, their case study evidence from children aged six months to four years old suggests that co-use was largely restricted to periods when a child was being introduced to a new app and in response to specific requests. They found that in practice children 'actively resisted' parental involvement and that close supervision was a more appropriate description of parents' activities than co-use. The pan-European study reported by JRC (Chaudron, 2015) also found that children's practice is to use digital technologies alone rather than with others. However, they point to an interesting difference in Finland where digital activities are more often shared with family and friends. Activities perceived as family or social pursuits are more likely to be traditional such as shared viewing of specific television programmes, playing board games or going on outings.

Research evidence suggests then that for most parents engaging with technologies is a part of everyday living for themselves and their children and they approach this element of contemporary life as they do other elements such as travel and health, with a concern to minimise the risks and maximise the opportunities, especially in this case the opportunities to support their children's learning with technologies. When parents perceive digital technologies as embedded in everyday life they view them and act towards them as part of the cultural process of learning, neither inherently good or bad, but as cultural tools that they teach their children to use safely and appropriately just as they themselves learned to use older technologies such as phones and televisions.

Family practices

A key finding of the qualitative exploration of the experiences of children and families with digital technologies across seven countries reported by the JRC (Chaudron, 2015) was that '[d]igital technologies are an important (but not dominant) part of children's lives' (p. 7). The researchers point out that children enjoy non-digital activities as well as playing games on smartphones, tablets and computers and watching videos. This finding endorses the conclusion of an earlier study entitled 'Young Children Learning with Toys and Technology' (2008–2011) and reported in a series of articles by Plowman and Stephen (e.g. Plowman *et al.*, 2011; Stephen, Stevenson, & Adey, 2013). In that project the researchers drew on the Vygotskian cultural-historical tradition which sees learning and development as mediated through interactions with others and the social and cultural circumstances in which a child is growing up (Hedegaard, 2009; Rogoff, 2003; Schaffer, 2004). In order to explore the cultural context of family homes the project was designed to attend to the typical activities and practices at home, along with the resources, relationships and local and temporal circumstances which constitute a family's cultural setting (Tudge, Freitas, & Doucet, 2009; Weisner, 2002). Focusing on the everyday experiences with digital technologies of three to five year olds, the researchers examined: 1. the resources available in each home; and 2. the family practices around the use of these resources – most notably the ways in which children were introduced to the technologies and were supported to use them at home.

In order to explore digital resources and associated family practices the study employed a variety of methods over the 15 months that case study families participated in the study (Stephen *et al.*, 2013). An audit of the toys and technologies was completed in the home of each of the 14 participating families, a series of interviews was conducted with parents, structured conversations held with children and mobile phone diaries kept to illustrate 'typical' days. The data collected revealed plentiful supplies of traditional resources for indoor and outdoor activities, individual and group games, props for pretend play and materials for creative endeavours, as well as a range of technologies for leisure, work and education for all the family members (Stephen, 2011). Perhaps the most remarkable finding from the toy audits was the sheer quantity of traditional toys and playthings available to children in these family homes. This finding was evident regardless of the socioeconomic circumstances of the families taking part.

In these homes, digital technologies had not 'taken over' traditional activities. While the technology was evident in the form of games consoles, access to apps, laptops, interactive televisions, mobile phones and interactive educational toys, these did not supplant traditional toys and activities such as cars, construction sets, dolls and dolls houses, soft toys, farm sets, train sets, board games, balls, climbing frames, tents, dressing up clothes, crayons and paints and craft resources and much more. In most households in that study traditional toys outnumbered those with technological features by three to one. Typically, about 10 per cent of any family's toys and playthings could be categorised as technological, although this rose to 33 per cent in one family. In line with the thinking we examined in Chapter 4 (e.g. Kay, 2013; Lankshear & Knobel, 2012) there was a mix of technological and traditional resources in each home. This mix of resources suggests that children in these homes were well placed to blend the digital and non-digital in their play. These empirical findings complement the arguments of scholars such as Caldwell (2000) that new technologies sink into the everyday over time. As this occurs, new forms of play and learning become possible and co-evolve as children and their families engage with digital devices.

Stephen *et al.*'s (2013) investigation of family practices when engaging with technologies, in particular the detailed videos recorded by four case study families, established that parents engaged in the same range of supportive practices as the researchers had previously observed employed by practitioners in preschool playrooms. They found that as parents introduced their child to a new technology or supervised the use of one already present in their home they employed multiple practices for supporting children's learning. Parents demonstrated and modelled how to use the technologies, explained and instructed, offered feedback and monitored progress, prompted responses and actions and shared children's pleasure and success in the games and activities in which they were engaged. More recent survey evidence reaffirmed that young children do not engage with digital technologies in a social vacuum. Parents and siblings engaged with them in these activities supporting the development of their operational skills, joining in games and searching for appropriate sources or activities, for instance, finding rhymes to learn together or creating a tune or video via an app (Marsh *et al.*, 2015). Indeed, over 60 per cent of parents said that using the tablet was their decision rather than their child's.

Stephen *et al.* (2013) went on to argue that while their analysis of the video and interview data suggests that technology use by young children was supported by parents employing practices from a common repertoire, each child's experience was different because of the particular nature of the cultural and social context of each family. They suggested that key elements of the family practices depended on parents' perspectives on technology as an educative tool, parents' preferred ways of supporting their child's learning and the nature of family relationships and interactions. For instance, the extent to which parents chose to be directly involved in their child's learning activities, whether digital or involving more traditional resources, made a difference to family practices with technology. In two households parents felt that children learn and develop their competencies through solo exploration. The boys growing up in each of these households were only offered help if they became very frustrated or unhappy with their technological encounters. In contrast, the girl growing up in another of the case study homes was only given access to a new technological or a traditional resource when her mother was satisfied that she was cognitively ready for it and after they had been through a careful introduction to the functions of the resource or the way to play a game. In a family keen to introduce their preschool child to reading, a commercial interactive device marketed as enhancing early reading skills was a welcome resource incorporated into family practices to support literacy. However, for those parents who thought that reading was the responsibility of the school or best left to the expertise of teachers, devices to support early reading offered by the researchers were less valued and little used.

Everyday family practices, for example, about pre-bedtime activities, the ways in which parents use the time available to them after work, at weekends or between domestic tasks, and the age range of the children in the family all influenced the experiences offered to the young children who were the focus of the case studies in the Plowman *et al.* (2008) project. Growing up in a single parent household with a mother who worked as a teacher and was studying for a further degree meant that one girl was familiar with a computer as a work tool and the Wii as a resource for family fun when she and her mother and brother developed their football skills during the time set aside each day for the family to do things together. On the other hand, with two younger siblings, one four year old was used to having to wait until his brother and sister were asleep before he could use the games console and other technologies in his home and understood these resources had to be protected from potential damage from inappropriate handling.

Competitive interactions were encouraged in some families while collaboration was favoured in other case study households. Playing a game on the computer or Wii, watching a DVD or playing with a technological pet might be suggested in some of the participating families but in others children were more likely to be encouraged to paint, create, ride a bike or offered ideas for pretend play. Across the qualitative studies describing children's experiences with technologies in particular contexts we have discussed in this book there were examples of digital devices being used when children had to wait or parents were occupied by other tasks. Even in the avowedly 'low tech' family participating in the study reported by Livingstone et al. (2015) the children were allowed to make use of their limited digital technologies when they were bored or unable to go outside. Marsh et al. (2015) found that the most popular time of day for children 0 to eight years old to engage in digital activities was between 4 pm and 6 pm on weekdays, a time when parents are likely to be cooking or busy with chores.

The findings from the 'Young Children Growing Up With Toys and Technology at Home' project (Plowman, Stevenson, Stephen, & McPake, 2012; Stephen et al., 2013) discussed here make clear the highly contextual nature of each child's play and learning experiences with the technologies to which they have access at home. Livingstone et al.'s (2015) study offers further evidence that family context matters; they concluded that the resources owned and their locations in the home, along with 'family dynamics, habits and rules' (p. 24) influenced the encounters that children have with digital technologies. Selwyn's (2010) notion of the 'state of the actual' – conducted from a critical perspective on technologies, is informative here as it points to understanding how and why young children are using technologies within the family. Parental views about the educative potential of digital resources, the range of practices supporting children learning to use technologies in the family, and the routine practices through which family life is enacted in the home all contribute to young children's learning with technologies in the digital age.

Sibling influences

While we have thus far concentrated on the parental aspect of the family in comprising young children's engagements with digital technologies, we now pay some attention to the role of siblings in technology use by young children. As Holloway et al. (2013) argue, young children's digital experiences can only be understood by paying holistic attention to the family sociocultural practices, and that must include the behaviours of siblings. Brothers and sisters influence young children's encounters with digital technologies, as with many other aspects of family life. This influence was evident in the Plowman *et al.* (2008) study which established, for example, that one five year old's intense interest in online sports games was sparked by watching his older siblings viewing sports news on a dedicated website. Livingstone *et al.* (2015) also relate the particular digital experiences of younger children to the interests and activities of older siblings. Among the examples of sibling influences in their data were two six-year-old girls whose television watching and music listening was shaped by the choices of their older brother and sister. The twins showed little interest in a football game which their brother played on a games console but were keen on some games which their sister played with them, though they lost interest in these when their sister stopped using the games console.

Younger siblings inherit digital and traditional toys and resources from older siblings as well as receiving new technologies, toys and games as gifts given to them personally and in some instances the youngest children are offered non-functioning versions of the kind of resources they see their older brothers and sisters engaging with. Younger siblings typically have access to (or are at least aware of) more sophisticated technologies or resources intended for older children at a younger age than first-born children. Livingstone *et al.* (2015) give the example of a six-year-old girl who enjoyed games found for her by her 13-year-old sister but who found the games which her 16-year-old brother chose for himself scary. A six year old in another of their case study families was described as spending 'a lot of time' engaging with her brother's Facebook page, facilitated by him. There are further examples of sibling influences in the cases included in the cross-Europe study published by JRC (Chaudron, 2015). These include younger siblings beginning to watch television earlier than first-born children and watching or participating in digital games designed for older children, sometimes to the consternation of their parents. Of course the corollary of this is that the digital experiences of first-born children can be limited by the presence of younger children in the family if parents restrict access to what are perceived to be expensive or fragile resources to times when the youngest children are absent or asleep (Stephen *et al.*, 2013).

Such evidence suggests that not only do older brothers and sisters offer younger siblings the advantage of growing up in a family where the technological resources are often in advance of what might be considered age appropriate, they identify games likely to be of interest, facilitate access to the internet, share their own tastes and interests and are also a source of knowledge about the attractions and pitfalls of past and cutting-edge forms of digital engagement. Verenikina and Kervin (2011) describe older siblings, along with parents, as 'technical expert[s]' and argue that data from their study of three and four year olds engaging with iPads suggests that, even if fleeting, this technical support can shape and extend young children's imaginative play with tablet computers. The EU Joint Research Centre report (Chaudron, 2015) argues that older siblings are a source of protection from the risks associated with the internet for younger family members, although Livingstone *et al.* (2015), in the UK contribution to this report, also include examples of parents expressing some anxiety about the content of games or websites which their younger children become aware of through the activities of older siblings. However, it is worthy of note that some older siblings would have begun their engagement with digital technologies before the introduction of the iPad in 2010. The implications of this 'generational leap' are not evident in the research literature but are ripe for further research. What is clear is that a 'state of the actual' perspective reveals siblings sharing experiences around digital encounters as they do in other areas of life.

Stevens, Satwicz, and McCarthy's (2008) ethnographic study of older (9–15 years) siblings playing video games together describes learning and teaching each other as they play as a 'natural part' of this shared cultural activity which is 'quite tangled up with other cultural practices, which include relations with siblings and parents' (p. 43). In the Plowman et al. (2008) study, older siblings were observed attuning software to the needs of their brothers or sisters, for instance setting an appropriate level of difficulty for a game, advising on ways of improving a score, navigating around a set of options or manipulating controls and quietly correcting mistakes. But this study also showed less positive interactions between siblings taking place when they were in competition in digital activities such as sports on the Wii. Younger children are most likely to be at a disadvantage when competing at 'playing tennis' or 'bowling' on the Wii just as they would be on a tennis court or bowling alley. As digital technologies are embedded in everyday family life, or 'hunkered down' to use Stevens et al.'s (2008) phrase to describe the place of gaming devices in the lives of older children, so they are involved in the pleasures and benefits, tensions and conflicts of family life. This is not to suggest that it is the technologies that 'determine' these positive or negative outcomes. Rather it is the result of the dynamics of family life, of the physical, social and emotional results of interactions between siblings in the cultural practices of their homes (e.g. about bed-times, eating habits or material possessions). Family life in the digital era involves sibling relationships about digital and non-digital activities and opportunities.

Peers and digital technologies

In the preceding sections of this chapter, we have considered young children's engagement with digital technologies in the immediate environment of their family. We have presented evidence to support our argument that within the family context, digital technological engagement is influenced by parental values and attitudes towards technologies, family resources and practices pertaining to technologies in the home and the consequent access and forms of social negotiation involved in technology use between siblings. In this section, we now turn our attention to children's relationships with their peers and how, within the contexts of these relationships, children experience their engagements with technologies. We begin from the position that digital technologies and the kinds of new media forms which they afford are an integral feature of the peer culture of young children. As Marsh (2005) argues, evidence from studies considering a range of forms of engagement with the products of the digital age makes clear the potency and value of digital engagement with the social and cultural lives of children.

Published studies of children engaging with peers in digital activities are typically carried out in group educational settings rather than in family homes so to explore this form of social and cultural behaviour we turn now to research in early education environments. A number of studies in the late 1990s and early years of the 21st century described children as collaborating on tasks and engaged in positive, constructive peer relationships around desktop computers (e.g. Clements, Nastasi, & Swaminathan, 1993; Siraj-Blatchford & Siraj-Blatchford, 2002). The benefits that new technologies offer for developing collaboration and shared learning opportunities have become part of the familiar justification for their use in early education settings (e.g. Kankaanranta & Kangalasso, 2003; Ljung-Djärf, 2008; Siraj-Blatchford & Siraj-Blatchford, 2006). However, the evidence for the impact of encounters with digital technologies on children's behaviours appears to be more mixed.

In 2002 Brooker and Siraj-Blatchford identified a variety of constructive and collaborative interactions between children aged from three to four years old as they engaged with a computer, and with one program in particular in a nursery setting. These interactions included support for language development through shared talk and vocabulary; pro-social behaviour, assisted performance (in which a more competent child helped another); collaboration (with children tutoring each other); and off-screen play behaviour prompted by on-screen action. A change in social behaviour patterns over time, moving from independent user to a more integrated way of working with a computer and other children was also identified by Chung and Walsh (2006). On the other hand, Stephen and Plowman (2003) in an observational study of seven varied preschool settings found no clear evidence of collaboration occurring between young children as they used technologies together in their preschool settings. They found that although children would gather around a desktop computer it was the child who was seated in front of the screen who dominated the play while others came to and went from the group of observers. Their observations suggested that when a child asked a peer for help it was just as likely that the more competent player would take over the mouse and begin to play for themselves as it was that two or more children would solve the problem together. Turning to digital activities at home, Holloway et al. (2013) point to the kind of negative personal encounters that can occur when young children engage with others online and to the distress that they can experience when friends exclude them from a game, interfere with their online profile, or the actions of other players results in lost rewards or a spoilt game.

It is our contention that these studies should be seen not as presenting conflicting findings about the ways in which technologies promote or determine behavioural outcomes (collaboration and shared support for exploration and learning in this case) but as instances which illustrate how the contexts in which children engage with digital activities make a difference to the nature of their experiences. That friends sometimes support each other in play but on other occasions compete for access to a resource, can explore excitedly together or seek to maintain solo use of a plaything or activity will be no surprise to adults familiar with the social behaviours of children in the early years. The evidence about ways in which children engage with digital technologies in social situations suggests that they respond to this kind of resource as they would to traditional artefacts and activities. Some material resources afford more social engagement. For example, Brooker and Siraj-Blatchford (2002) found that it was only one of the four computer games available in the playroom which supported the kind of collaborative behaviours which they report. Kutnick, Brighi, and Colwell (2016) draw attention to the ways in which the different social contexts for learning are created in educational settings and how these contexts influence who is involved in an activity and the kind of activity with which groups of children engage. They found that groups which were practitioner-orientated were more likely to be inclusive, be made up of boys and girls and be engaged in more cognitively challenging activities. Child-orientated groups are typically more gendered and exclusive and, in the case of boys in particular, engaged in activities that are less cognitively demanding. Such contextual differences reinforce the need for a critical perspective on encounters with digital technologies, suggesting again that attention be paid to the 'state of the actual' to best understanding what and how children are playing and learning with technologies in the digital age.

Ljung-Djärf's (2008) exploration of the nature of social interactions occurring between peers when using digital technologies mirrors the critical perspective advocated by Selwyn (2010). Ljung-Djärf was concerned by studies that identified collaborative behaviour between children without paying attention to the details of the circumstances in which this collaboration occurred. She set out to explore the forms of interaction that could be observed around computer activity in preschool settings. Starting from a theoretical position which sees episodes of social interaction as dynamic processes in which individuals are given or adopt positions (Harré & van Langenhove, 1999), she argued that peers gathered around a desktop computer or other device take up roles that are relational and intentional. Her analysis of 13 hours of video recordings of the behaviour of three to six year olds engaging with the computer in their preschool setting found that they adopted three kinds of positions: the owner (in charge of the mouse and keyboard); the participant (allowed to make suggestions and support the owner) and the spectator (having no active part in the activity and kept on the edge of the group). This is an important contribution to our understanding which does not deny that collaboration may be possible between young children as they engage with digital technologies but which, starting from a concern with the 'state of the actual' 'provide[s] a contrast to the sometimes unproblematic picture of children's cooperation around the computer as something more or less obvious' (Ljung-Djärf, 2008, p. 69).

Likewise, a more recent study conducted by Arnott (2016) identified the nature of children's social engagements during technology use. She argued that children in an early learning setting with access to technologies formed evolving 'clusters' into which children readily moved in and out. Clusters comprised three main types of social engagement, including: 1) pro-social peer-driven; 2) anti-social, and, 3) task driven engagement. Like Ljung-Djärf (2008), Arnott's findings suggest that technologies neither promote nor restrict particular forms of social interaction amongst peers. Instead, in common with the line of argument we have taken in this book, technologies themselves are not invested with the potential to cause any type of particular relationship between children in a social setting. Rather, the relationships interact with the dynamics of the technological activity. As children engage in digital activities they participate in a range of social behaviours that will be commonly seen in other areas of the curriculum – sometimes they engage in pro-social sharing behaviours and sometimes they are task orientated and at other times they are less interested in being socially helpful.

These findings remind us that children's experiences with digital technologies will be influenced by their social relationships and the positions which they are given or choose to adopt with regard to peers and to the technologies. Furthermore, as Ljung-Djärf (2008) points out, our current understanding about the role of social relationships is derived largely from engagement with resources that were designed for one user, had one input device and which addressed instructions and feedback to one, undifferentiated player. Given recent transformations in cultural knowledge informing current technological innovations (such as touchscreens, IoT and semantic web) it seems increased social differentiation may be afforded – especially as NUIs come more and more to define human relationships with technologies for young children. A more nuanced understanding of contemporary engagement with digital technologies is already hinted at by the conclusion of the JRC cross-Europe study (Chaudron, 2015) which found that children up to eight years old engaged with digital resources in an individual manner, whether gaming, gathering information or involved in creative digital activities. Some instances of playing digital games within the family were reported but for the most part collaborative engagement was through online communication such as Skype. Further critically positioned research is required on the nature of social behaviours and actions when children engage with peers at home as well as in educational settings – while making use of technologies designed to be used simultaneously, by multiple players and/or as a specifically group activity (for instance, working with roamers, problem-solving tasks or information gathering projects).

Children's perspectives on digital technologies

Children's perspectives on technologies intersect with their social engagement in any given developmental niche. Thus far we have considered technologies in family life and the role of social interactions with peers around using technologies. Children themselves within these social contexts are also actively involved in their own play and learning. They make choices about their activities and act to achieve their own desires (Corsaro, 2014; James & James, 2004).

Writing at the beginning of the 21st century, Prensky (2001) used the term 'digital natives' to distinguish between those children who have grown up with digital technologies and those adults who have experienced technologies later in life

– the so called 'digital immigrants'. Digital natives has become a recurring trope in early childhood education. It is frequently drawn upon in accounts of young children's engagement with newer technologies. For example, in an article posted to the popular parenting website *Essential Kids* Hawkins and Schmidt (2008) deploy the digital native description to suggest that young children have an apparently natural affinity with the internet as a source of information. In some respects the digital natives concept can be appealing. It appears that young children are growing up in households in the digital era where technologies are a feature of daily life. However, as we have consistently argued in this book, a cultural and critical perspective suggests that young children's encounters with digital technologies are culturally historically derived and consistently shaped by social practices. Furthermore, as we will discuss below, not all children are confident users of new technologies. Some children approach encounters with computer games, the Wii or interactive toys with timidity while other children choose to spend their time on other forms of activity. In these circumstances any universal application of the term digital native to young children seems ineffective for engaging teachers and researchers in how best to understand young children's play and learning in the digital age.

The 2008 study by Plowman, McPake, and Stephen was the first of its kind to examine young children's perspectives on the nature of their engagement with digital technologies. In this study it was reported that the four and five year olds saw their everyday digital activities at home as leisure, fun or play activity rather than 'educational work'; something they engaged in 'because of' rather than 'in order to' (Maddock, 2006). Just under a decade later, in 2015 Chaudron's JRC report on children's digital activities across seven countries concluded that 'Children love digital technologies' but went on to note with apparent surprise 'the little use of digital technology made [*sic*] to support explicitly learning or education' (p. 18). This expectation that technology will be employed for learning (though confounded by the state of the actual observed), suggests a presumption of technological potential on the part of the researchers. This is a standpoint we have considered unhelpful in promoting new thinking about what and how children are playing and learning with technologies because it places the responsibility for an outcome from the technology use onto the technology rather than explicitly considering human relationships with technology as enacted in the culturally historical derived situation in which it occurs. For example, the older children in the sample engaged in Chaudron's (2015) JRC study (seven and eight year olds) talked explicitly about engaging with tablets as leisure time. Across all ages the most popular practices afforded by digital technologies, included watching television and videos, listening to music, playing games and creating virtual worlds. If the children understand their technological engagement as leisure time it should not really be surprising that evidence in the JRC report (Chaudron, 2015) did not point to explicit learning or education. An adult engaged in leisure time is likewise not assumed to always be involved in education. Interestingly, references to digital leisure point to the notion of 'engagement for the sake of engagement' first promoted by Alan Kay (1972) in the initial design of his DynaBook. It was succinctly described by a teenage participant in the study of gaming by Stevens *et al.* (2008) as '[i]t's what we do' (p. 63) – an expression of autotelic cultural activity.

Stephen *et al.* (2008) found that four and five year olds did not see making use of digital resources as something they will grow out of in time, but rather as something with which they would make progress over time to adult levels of proficiency and independent use. This suggests that gaining independent access or ownership of highly used technologies will be as much an expectation for children in the digital age as growing up was once characterised by previous generations as owning a television or telephone. Young children in the Stephen *et al.* (2008) study expressed a sense of developmental progression through activities associated with digital technologies in the same way as they anticipated other milestones such as moving from preschool to primary school, riding a bicycle without stabilisers [training wheels] or being able to read independently. They talked about growing too old for some games and had age-related expectations about the capacity to make use of some technologies, although it was not possible to tell if these judgements are the result of 'received wisdom' or personal experience. For instance, one child was clear that a five year old should be able to use a mobile phone. Another child in the same study, talking about using a remote control car, told the researchers that 'at his age he is able to do that'. On the other hand, a third child suggested that a five year old would become able to write texts and take photographs on a phone when he was older but could make use of it to play games now following a demonstration (Stephen *et al.*, 2008). Although the children were reluctant to admit to 'getting stuck' with digital activities when they mentioned learning how to use digital resources they referred to their parents, a response that seems to locate technology use as part of the shared, everyday family practices of four and five year olds. Here, the children did not view themselves as digital natives, instead describing a gradual enculturation with their use of technologies over time and in relationships with adults.

The ways in which parents view the digital activities of young children endorses this understanding of technologies as part of the cultural practices of home and family life. Plowman *et al.* (2012) report that parents noted and were able to describe new features of their child's engagement with technologies at home, but did not perceive these as explicit examples of learning with technology. For instance, parents talked about noticing that their child could now navigate an on-screen guide to find a favourite television programme, pause or slow down the playing of a DVD or use appropriate technical terms. An analysis of parents' responses to a series of statements about the use of new technologies at home revealed that most parents did not explicitly set out to introduce their three or four year olds to digital devices (Plowman *et al.*, 2008). Children became familiar with and able to engage with the devices in their home, just as they did 'older' technology such as switching on lights or plugging in and switching on appliances. Plowman *et al.* (2008) suggest that children learned how to operate digital technologies through a combination of culturally acquired practices including observation and copying, trial and error and demonstration and instruction. These combinations were frequently referred to by parents as children 'just picking it up'.

Plowman *et al.* (2012) suggest a four-part framework for understanding the kinds of learning associated with digital technologies which includes a change in participation in family life, although they are careful to stress that they are not suggesting any direct or exclusive relationship between engaging with a specific technology and a learning outcome. Their argument is that experiences with interactive technologies can support or provide opportunities for learning. The first three forms of learning were originally identified in studies of young children's experiences with digital technologies in the playroom (Stephen & Plowman, 2008): acquiring operational skills, extending knowledge and understanding of the world (e.g. about people, places and living things as well as literacy and mathematics), and developing dispositions to learn (including building self-confidence and persistence). However, when the research team turned to the evidence from their investigations about young children's encounters with digital technologies at home it became clear that a fourth form of learning should be added to the framework to encompass the children's developing understanding of the use of these devices for social and cultural purposes e.g. sharing photographs on a mobile phone, talking to relatives on Skype, shopping online. Furthermore, as Plowman *et al.* (2012) point out, these social and cultural uses were not necessarily those that might be thought of as of particular interest to preschool children but they were forms of engagement that were part of their everyday home life and valued by their family. The understanding about how children learn which underpinned Kay's thinking as he developed his prototype DynaBook (see Chapter 4) is echoed in Plowman *et al.*'s (2012) conclusion that young children learn to engage with digital devices by watching what others around them do, trying things out and 'by wanting to do the things that technologies make possible' (p. 36).

Individual interests, preferences and evaluations

Some children's digital practices with technologies reflect already-established interests they have in particular topics or activities. This could involve following an individual interest, or a shared family enthusiasm, perhaps for a particular kind of sport or hobby. Typically, it involves children blending a mix of digital and non-digital activities such as playing online games featuring the child's interest, watching appropriate videos, taking part in hands-on physical experiences and attending events, exploring and seeking out information via the World Wide Web, collecting models, taking and curating digital photographs and reading books featuring appropriate contexts, plots or characters. Marsh *et al.* (2015) illustrate the influence of individual and family interests and the blending of digital and non-digital activities with the example of a four-year-old girl whose father was fascinated by and knowledgeable about dinosaurs. The child was introduced to, and enjoyed using a range of dinosaur-related apps, games and children's television, as well as looking at books and owning some model dinosaurs. Livingstone *et al.* (2015) report how a seven year old was described by her father as continuing her interest in viewing natural history programmes on television by focusing on taking photographs of 'natural objects and wildlife' (p. 25).

Further examples come from Stephen *et al.* (2008). For instance, four-year-old Kenneth's interest in cars influenced the television he chose to watch and the outings to car shows selected for him by his parents. He was keen to talk about cars and show the researchers his collection of toy cars and made use of the family's digital resources for games involving cars and taking and storing photographs of cars. Another child, Colin, also aged four years, experienced a family trip to Australia from Scotland. Colin engaged in digital communication with his Australian relatives which consequently shaped the range of digital practices with which he engaged, such as taking photographs, using the webcam and adding emoticons to family emails. In these examples, the concept of amplification evident in the work of both Kay (1972) and Masuda (1980) suggests the use of technologies for the extension of processes and practices beyond what would not typically be available without the digital. Digital experiences extended the range of opportunities available for young children to communicate, learn about the world, curate memories and information and develop confidence in their own knowledge and their ability to share this with others. Notably, as we considered in Chapter 5 with respect to digital play, such amplification did not necessarily preclude the children's engagement in other available activities and/or resources.

While research suggests that young children engage in multiple practices using digital technologies, it is important to remember that these practices reflect the use of technologies by children participating in culturally historically derived social context. As Lankshear and Knobel (2012) explain, practices become embedded over time as new technologies move beyond the 'peak curve' of interest (Caldwell, 2000). This suggests that not all practices will be of interest to all children at all times. For example, as children grow, the kind of apps with which they engage change. Perhaps influenced by parental choice, educational apps are used more by preschool children than those in the 6–7 age range who favour apps that assist with creative activities and online factual and instructional videos accessed via YouTube (Marsh *et al.*, 2015). Some children are more enthusiastic users of technologies over others (just as some children have always enjoyed traditional art and craft activities over active outdoor play). Stephen *et al.* (2013) described one participant in their study as a digital enthusiast. This four-year-old boy was frequently and intensely involved in games on the Wii and on a games console. Another four-year-old participant enjoyed digital games when these were made available to him but a third participant, four-year-old Kelly, was not really interested in the overt use of technologies, despite growing up in a home where there were several computers, a Wii and a games console. Her father worked in the computer industry and her brother was a keen digital games player but Kelly had to be persuaded to join in family time with the Wii or other digital games. Kelly's preference was for imaginative play with dolls and soft toys. When the research team supplied a technological toy 'puppy' and invited Kelly to engage with it as she wished, the video evidence showed that when she did make use of the 'puppy' she incorporated it into her imaginative play with its 'voice' switched off so that it functioned as a traditional soft toy.

So far we have discussed children's practices with digital technologies as positive experiences, a rewarding feature of their participation in the culture of their family and as experiences which amplify their ways of engaging with the world and provide opportunities for learning. However, encounters with both traditional toys and new technologies can be a source of displeasure when the activity is experienced by the child as too difficult or they associate negative emotions with a particular plaything or resource. Stephen *et al.* (2008) found that children growing up in the digital age were able to distinguish between toys, playthings and activities they enjoyed using and others that they liked less and that they extended this discriminating evaluation to technological resources as well as more traditional equipment and activities. For example, they found that a fall from a bicycle or swing, controls on a digital resource that were difficult to manage, struggling with reading and a digital game that took too long to complete were all negatively evaluated by the four and five year olds participating in their longitudinal study. Some traditional activities (e.g. swimming and reading) were described by the young participants as 'too hard' but they were more likely to apply this label to technological activities which gave them displeasure. In some instances the source of dissatisfaction lay with operational difficulties such as managing a remote control or manipulating two forms of control at once (circumstances alleviated in some cases by the advent of tablet computing), but in other cases the problem arose from the substantive activity involved. Some children could not interpret the implications of their score, did not understand the audio instructions or did not know enough about a sport they were playing on the Wii to make sense of the competitive process or make improvements in their skills.

Marsh *et al.* (2015) also found evidence that the content of games was not always appropriate and productive for young children and suggested that 'there are many examples of ways in which apps could be improved to enhance the experience for young children' (p. 44). They described children's encounters with an app that they could not use in the way intended by the designers as reducing the child's engagement to random movements of the objects on the screen. In another example they give an account of an observation during which a young boy failed to complete a jigsaw on screen because the fit of the virtual pieces made no allowance for even a minimal margin of error. Frustrated and unable to continue, the child they observed abandoned the game. Among the UK children in the study by Livingstone *et al.* (2015) young players reported waiting for a game to load as a source of dissatisfaction. One child, who the researchers characterised as 'highly reward-driven', rapidly became bored with games that took what appeared to him to be a long time to complete and with others that did not provide sufficiently rewarding feedback. Games marketed as 'educational' were not always well received by the children for whom they were purchased. Livingstone *et al.* (2015) give an example of a six-year-old girl who quickly became bored with the educational games her mother tried to play with her on the laptop. She favoured what the researchers describe as more 'entertainment-focused' digital activities such as accessing her older sibling's Facebook page and discovering photographs of herself on Facebook.

This evidence suggests that young children are discriminating users of digital technologies, sometimes to the surprise of their parents who claim that their child enjoys and is a capable user of any appropriate resource and, on some occasions, even users of digital devices that might be expected to make demands beyond their current competencies. Stephen *et al.* (2008) found that four and five year olds extended their willingness to discriminate between digital technologies and activities beyond evaluating the resource to considering their own level of competency. In the course of structured conversations with a researcher with whom they had become familiar, the participants were invited to indicate which technologies they were good at using by placing star stickers on a visual array of digital resources (at a time before the widespread uptake of iPads and other forms of tablet computing). The children indicated that they were good at using games consoles, computers, LeapPads, televisions and remote control cars. However, their judgements about their competency with computers suggested that the children were less confident in their encounters with this resource than the more positive evaluations by their parents would suggest. The children's discriminating comments extended beyond particular technologies to specific games and they were not afraid to criticise the games that were available to them. Marsh's (2010) study of six and seven year olds playing in online virtual worlds also found children making distinct choices about the kinds of activities they wished to engage with in the virtual world and willing to point to negative features of the programming. For instance, she described one child's frustration with a requirement that the game designers had built into the program in order to encourage children to return frequently to the game site and with the restrictions built in to the options available to her for dressing an avatar.

In this discussion of young children's perspectives on digital technologies we have suggested that the digital natives trope is not entirely helpful for forwarding thinking about what and how young children are playing and learning with technologies in the digital age. Rather, research indicates that children are discriminating and aware users of technologies and that their decisions about technology use are shaped by the cultural tools (e.g. physical limitations of hardware and/or frustrations with software) to which they have access. Digital technologies are an everyday feature of family life and children are supported by parents and other family members to become participants in these practices. Through imitation, demonstration and sometimes direct instruction and trial and error, young children learn to do what it is they want to do with technologies.

Conclusion

In this chapter we have argued that for children growing up in the digital age engagement with digital technologies is a ubiquitous feature of everyday family life, happening in the particular sociocultural context of their home and their relationships with their parents, siblings and peers. A state of the actual perspective suggests that children are supported in their engagement with digital technologies through interactions with parents, siblings and peers, although neither these encounters nor any changes in behaviours and actions that follow are necessarily thought of as educational. Rather, children are seen as becoming increasingly competent participants in digital aspects of family life, learning to do what they want to be able to do, in the same way as their developing competence with non-digital features of family life is noted with satisfaction by family members. Just as we have argued that encounters with digital technologies do not determine particular outcomes, so too the presence of digital technologies in everyday life does not determine a child's interest in or feeling of confidence with these resources.

References

Arnott, L. (2016). An ecological exploration of young children's digital play: framing young children's social experiences with technologies in early childhood. *Early Years, 36*(3), 271–288.

Brooker, E., & Siraj-Blatchford, J. (2002). 'Click on Miaow': how children of three and four experience the nursery computer. *Contemporary Issues in Early Childhood, 3*(2), 251–270.

Caldwell, J. T. (2000). *Electronic media and technoculture*. Rutgers University Press.

Chaudron, S. (2015). Young Children (0–8) and digital technology: a qualitative exploratory study across seven countries. Luxembourg: Publications Office of the European Union. Retrieved from http://publications.jrc.ec.europa.eu/repository/handle/JRC93239.

Chung, Y., & Walsh, D. J. (2006). Constructing a joint story-writing space: the dynamics of young children's collaboration at computers. *Early Education and Development, 17*(3), 373–420. doi: 10.1207/s15566935eed1703_4.

Clements, D. H., Nastasi, B. K., & Swaminathan, S. (1993). Young children and computers: crossroads and directions from research. *Young Children, 48*(2), 56–64.

Common Sense Media (2013). *Zero to eight: children's media use in America 2013*. Retrieved from www.commonsensemedia.org/research/zero-to-eight-childrens-media-use-in-america-2013.

Corsaro, W. (2014). *The sociology of childhood* (4th edn). Thousand Oaks, CA: Sage.

Harré, R., & van Langenhove, L. (1999). *Positioning theory: moral context of intentional action*. Oxford: Basil Blackwell.

Hawkins, P., & Schmidt, L. (2008). Gen z: digital natives. *Essential Kids*. Retrieved from www.essentialkids.com.au/life/technology/gen-z-digital-natives-20080716-3g5p.

Hedegaard, M. (2009). Children's development from a Cultural-Historical approach: children's activity in everyday local settings as foundations for their development. *Mind, Culture and Activity, 16*(1), 64–82.

Holloway, D., Green, L., & Livingstone, S. (2013). Zero to eight: young children and their internet use. LSE, London: EU Kids Online. Retrieved from http://eprints.lse.ac.uk/52630/.

James, A., & James, A. L. (2004). *Constructing childhood theory, policy and social practice*. Houndsmill, Basingstoke: Palgrave Macmillan.

Jayemanne, D., & Nansen, B. (2016). Parental mediation, YouTube's networked public, and the 'Baby-iPad Encounter': mobilizing digital dexterity. *Jeunesse: Young People, Texts, Cultures, 8*(1), 133–153.

Kankaanranta, M., & Kangalasso, M. (2003). Information and communication technologies in Finnish early childhood. *Childhood Education, 79*(5), 287–293.

Kay, A. C. (1972, August). A personal computer for children of all ages. In *Proceedings of the ACM annual conference – Volume 1* (p. 1). ACM.

Kay, A. (2013). The future of reading depends on the future of learning difficult to learn things. In B. Junge, Z. Berzina, W. Scheiffele, W. Westerveld, & C. Zwick (Eds.), *The digital turn: design in the era of interactive technologies*. Chicago: University of Chicago Press.

Kutnick, P., Brighi, A., & Colwell, J. (2016). Interactive and socially inclusive pedagogy: a comparison of practitioner- and child-orientated cognitive/learning activities involving four-year-old children in preschools in England. *European Early Childhood Education Research Journal, 24*(2), 265–286. doi: 10.1080/1350293X.2016.1143266.

Lankshear, C., & Knobel, M. (2012). New literacies: technologies and values. *Revista Teknokultura, 9*(1), 45–69.

Livingstone, S., Marsh, J., Plowman, L., Ottovordemgentschenfelde, S., & Fletcher-Watson, B. (2015). *Young children (0–8) and digital technology: a qualitative exploratory study – national report-UK*. LSE Research Online. Retrieved from http://eprints.lse.ac.uk/60799/1/__lse.ac.uk_storage_LIBRARY_Secondary_libfile_shared_repository_Content_Livingstone,%20S_Young%20children%200-8_Livingstone_Young%20children%200-8_2015.pdf.

Ljung-Djärf, A. (2008). The owner, the participant and the spectator: positions and positioning in peer activity around the computer in pre-school. *Early Years, 28*, 61–72.

Maddock, M. (2006). Children's personal learning agendas at home. *Cambridge Journal of Education, 36*(2), 153–169.

Marsh, J. (2005). Introduction: children of the digital age. In J. Marsh (Ed.), *Popular-culture, new media and digital literacy in early childhood* (pp. 1–10). London: Routledge Falmer.

Marsh, J. (2010). Young children's play in online virtual worlds. *Journal of Early Childhood Research, 8*(1), 23–39.

Marsh, J., Plowman, L., Yamada-Rice, D., Bishop, J. C., Lahmar, J., Scott, F., Davenport, A., Davis, S., French, K., Piras, M., Thornhill, S., Robinson, P., & Winter, P. (2015). Exploring play and creativity in pre-schoolers' use of apps: final project report. *TAP: Technology and Play*. Retrieved from www.techandplay.org/TAP_Final%20Report.pdf.

Masuda, Y. (1980). *The information society as post-industrial society*. Tokyo: Institute for the Information Society.

Nevski, E., & Siibak, A. (2016). The role of parents and parental mediation on 0–3-year old's digital play with smart devices: Estonian parents' attitudes and practices. *Early Years, 36*(3), 227–241.

Ofcom (2016, 16 November). *Children and parents: media use and attitudes report 2016*. Retrieved from www.ofcom.org.uk/__data/assets/pdf_file/0034/93976/Children-Parents-Media-Use-Attitudes-Report-2016.pdf.

Plowman, L., McPake, J., & Stephen, C. (2008). Just picking it up? Young children learning with technology at home. *Cambridge Journal of Education, 38*(3), 303–319.

Plowman, L., & Stephen, C. (2005). Children, play and computers in pre-school settings. *British Journal of Educational Technology, 36*(2), 145–157.

Plowman, L., Stevenson, O., McPake, J., Stephen, C., & Adey, C. (2011). Parents, pre-schoolers and learning with technology at home: some implications for policy. *Journal of Computer Assisted Learning, 27*(4), 361–371.

Plowman, L., Stevenson, O., Stephen, C., & McPake, J. (2012). Preschool children's learning with technology at home. *Computers in Education, 59*, 30–37.

Prensky, M. (2001). Digital natives, digital immigrants. *On the Horizon, 9*(5), 1–6.

Rideout, V., Vanderwater, E., & Wartella, E. (2003). *Zero to six: electronic media in the lives of infants, toddlers and pre-schoolers*. Mento Park, CA: Kaiser Family Foundation.

Rogoff, B. (2003). *The cultural nature of human development.* New York: Oxford University Press.

Schaffer, H. R. (2004). *Introducing child psychology.* Oxford: Blackwell Publishing.

Selwyn, N. (2010). Looking beyond learning: notes towards the critical study of educational technology. *Journal of Computer Assisted Learning, 26,* 65–73.

Siraj-Blatchford, I., & Siraj-Blatchford, J. (2006). *A guide to developing the ICT curriculum for early childhood education.* Stoke on Trent: Trentham.

Siraj-Blatchford, J., & Siraj-Blatchford, I. (2002). *IBM KidSmart early learning programme: UK Evaluation Report – Phase 1 (2000–2001), IBM White Paper.* London: IBM.

Stephen, C. (2011). Playing and learning with technologies. Scottish Universities Insight Institute. *Research Briefing, 2.* Retrieved from www.stir.ac.uk/research/hub/publica tion/13566.

Stephen, C., McPake, J., Plowman, L., & Berch-Heyman, S. (2008). Learning from the children: exploring preschool children's encounters with ICT at home. *Journal of Early Childhood Research, 6*(2), 99–117.

Stephen, C., & Plowman, L. (2003). Information and communication technologies in pre-school settings: a review of the literature. *International Journal of Early Years Education, 11*(3), 223–234.

Stephen, C., & Plowman, L. (2008). Enhancing learning with information and communication technologies in pre-school. *Early Child Development and Care, 178*(6), 637–654.

Stephen, C., Stevenson, O., & Adey, C. (2013). Young children engaging with technologies at home: the influence of family context. *Journal of Early Childhood Research, 11*(2), 149–164.

Stevens, R., Satwicz, T., & McCarthy, L. (2008). In-game, in-room, in-world: reconnecting video game play to the rest of the kids' lives. In K. Salen (Ed.), *The ecology of games: connecting youth, games and learning: The John and Catherine MacArthur Foundation Series on Digital Media and Learning* (pp. 41–66). Cambridge, MA: MIT Press.

Tudge, J. R. H., Freitas, L. B. L., & Doucet, F. (2009). The transition to school: reflections from a contextualist perspective. In H. Daniels, H. Lauder, & J. Porter (Eds.), *Educational theories, cultures and learning: a critical perspective* (pp. 117–133). London: Routledge.

Verenikina, I., & Kervin, L. (2011). iPads, digital play and preschoolers. *He Kupu, 2*(5). Retrieved from www.hekupu.ac.nz/index.php?type=journal&issue=15&journal=262.

Vittrup, B., Snider, S., Rose, K. K., & Rippy, J. (2016). Parental perception of the role of media and technology in their young children's lives. *Journal of Early Childhood Research, 14*(1), 43–54.

Weisner, T. (2002). Ecocultural understanding of children's developmental pathways. *Human Development, 45,* 275–281.

Williams, R. (1958). Culture is ordinary. In J. Higgins (Ed.) (2001), *The Raymond Williams reader* (pp. 10–25). Oxford: Blackwell.

9
TOWARDS A CULTURAL AND CRITICAL PERSPECTIVE ON PLAYING AND LEARNING IN THE DIGITAL AGE

Introduction

In this book we have explored how technological innovation derives from the historical sociocultural environment in which it develops and how this legacy influences the contemporary experience of playing and learning in the digital age. Throughout this book we have argued that culture is formative for understanding the relationship between knowledge, technologies, societies and people. Taking a cultural and critical perspective on technological innovation reveals a much more substantial picture of historical change than obvious when focusing attention on local circumstances regarding technology use by young children and/or reacting to particular innovations in technology use. We have suggested that since the early 20th century there has been a process of knowledge evolution which transcends individual inventions or the application of new technology to particular tasks. Now, with the evolution of the Internet of Things, the semantic web, tablet computing and artificial intelligence, it is possible to argue that the process of technological change has reached the position outlined by Masuda's (1980) theory of societal change where different systems evolve and join forces to create one new complex system of technology, which spreads throughout society and precipitates a new age – what we described in Chapter 2 as the 'digital age'. Masuda (1980) argues that each new age is characterised by a new type of productive power which transforms society and results in the establishing of new cultural norms and values. In the digital age such productive power is derived from new ways of creating, sharing and applying knowledge resulting in the amplification of mental labour (Masuda, 1980). From a cultural-historical perspective, this amplification of mental labour generates social change that in turn creates new conditions for learning (Davydov, 1982).

In Part I we traced the evolution of the digital age from advances in the understanding of matter making possible the invention of the transistor and in turn the microprocessor. We considered the influence of the microprocessor on the digitalisation of information and all the capacity for storing, manipulating and communicating information that the development of computing afforded. This was followed early in the 21st century with developments in interface design between users and their computers manifest as Graphical User Interfaces (GUIs). Understanding about touchscreen technologies was informed by the work of Alan Kay (1972) and aligned with the ideas of Steve Jobs in the development of the iPad, with resultant implications for the move from GUIs to what are now described as Natural User Interfaces (NUIs). We completed our discussion of the evolution of the digital age with an examination of the development of interconnected computing technologies 'sinking' into everyday life (Beer, 2009) in the creation of new normal cultural practices. We drew particular attention to the role of algorithms in shaping young children's engagement with digital media and suggested an increased need in early childhood education for the pedagogical development of young children's concepts of networked technologies.

In Part II we moved on to a discussion of learning in the digital age, beginning with a critical look at the notion of 'technological potential'. We advanced our culturally informed critical perspective on learning with technologies and the contribution of the Learning Sciences to our understanding of learning in the digital era. We paid special attention to the work of Alan Kay (1972) in the creation of his DynaBook as a key influence on the evolution of the iPad. In the second chapter in Part II we considered existing understandings of play and the emerging concept of 'digital play' in early childhood. Here we considered how traditional ideas about discrete forms of traditional play are challenged by the blurring of boundaries between what might be thought of as 'digital' and 'non-digital' play. Part III we turned our attention to empirical evidence about the ways in which young children are engaging with digital technologies in their everyday lives, mediated by families, peers and children's own interests and preferences. In considering this experience of everyday life in the digital age we included a review of reactions to technological changes across the 20th century, considering the role of moral panic in informing discourse about young children's technology use.

In this final chapter we seek to develop further the implications of adopting a cultural and critical perspective on play and learning in the digital age for those engaged in the care and education of young children. We argue that working from within this perspective enables those engaged in the early childhood sector to consider the educative implications of digitalisation such that teacher 'tips' for using technologies and a reliance on techno-tales as the basis for curriculum formation are challenged. We suggest that, just as knowledge is culturally transformed for technological innovation, so too should the knowledge on which we base our policy, provision and practices in the early years be culturally adaptive for the digital age.

A cultural and critical perspective on young children's play and learning in the digital age

It is not easy to live through a period of new societal change. In the reality of daily life – such as that facing the teachers of the very young, change can be experienced as frustrating and perhaps more revolutionary in practice than truly evolutionary. Learning new ways of using technologies, being challenged in our expectations of what constitutes 'childhood' and observing the cultural adaption of traditional play to a blurred form of integrated digital play can be difficult. For teachers, but also for researchers, policy-makers and administrators, this difficulty is accentuated when the early childhood sector itself offers little in the way of new knowledge perspectives for engaging with the reality of digitalisation in the lives of the very young. In this situation, the experience of being in a digital revolution can seem very real. It can feel as if the iPad 'suddenly' arrived into the lives of young children. However, throughout this book we have drawn on the Vygotskian (1997) notion of cultural mediation to understand that both theory and tools are always culturally derived and generationally transformative. This position enabled us to trace the knowledge innovations shaping the digital age while simultaneously drawing on critical theory of technology to consider what Selwyn (2010) describes as the 'state of the actual' (p. 69) with respect to young children's play and learning in the digital age – in essence a cultural and critical perspective on young children's play and learning in the digital age. We suggest that working from a cultural and critical perspective means that teachers, policy-makers, researchers and administrators can frame responses to young children's play and learning in the digital age that are more carefully orientated towards how and why technologies are utilised by children in various settings. The digital age and the domestication of touchscreen technologies in young children's lives does not need to be received as a revolutionary 'bolt from the blue'. Nor need it be viewed as an imposition from beyond our cultural and societal environments in which the only viable response becomes moral panic.

The evolution of tablet computing, particularly the development of these resources for young children from the social-constructivist thinking of Alan Kay is a case in point. We have described how 20th-century understandings about learning underpin the 21st-century development of new technologies that are particularly well matched to the needs of young children. In developing his DynaBook concept, Kay (1972) drew on ideas about how children learn from thinkers such as Piaget, Vygotsky, Dewey, and Montessori. Bergen (2014) describes these as foundational thinkers who have been central to our understandings about play and learning for young children in Western-European culture for many years. Starting from this cultural knowledge Kay was able to influence the contemporary manifestation of the iPad. With tablet technologies now figuring in children's lives, a cultural and critical perspective enables the iPad to be viewed as a cultural resource for young children in which alternative forms of play and learning are responsive to the resource itself. A cultural and critical perspective does not displace the need for caution when using technologies – instead it enables consideration of the 'state of the actual' in relation to the resources. This means that attention is still necessarily paid to appropriate and healthy screen practices, ensuring children experience balanced amounts of technology time and opportunities for physical activity in their daily lives alongside new understanding about digital play and learning.

In this book we have drawn particularly on the notion of critical theory of technology as located in a body of knowledge known as theory of technology. In drawing on theory of technology we have been informed by the idea that cultural knowledge is not mono-theoretical, but rather multidisciplinary. We have suggested that varied perspectives on knowledge are required to address the complex and contextualised issues regarding technologies for young children in the digital age (see the discussion of Mode 2 knowledge in Chapter 4). In Chapter 1, following Gibbons (2010), we argued that it was important to consider the relationship between people and technologies in a society if we were to avoid approaching the big questions and developments of the digital age without any philosophical or theoretical tools with which to fashion a response. We made use of three 'theories' of technology throughout this book to consider this relationship and it is helpful to return to these now as a catalyst for understanding the notion of a cultural and critical orientation towards young children's play and learning in the digital age.

One way of viewing the technology/human relationship is to consider that technological innovation drives changes in behaviour and social practices. For example, technological determinism sees the move to 'on demand' viewing of television instead of following scheduled broadcasts as the result of the invention of portable computers and apps. Technological determinism focuses on the outcomes of innovation rather than the reasons for innovation and construes the user or consumer as either powerless to resist changes imposed by the invention of novel resources or the resources themselves as powerful sources for play and learning. A technological determinist orientation positions educators as either against or in favour of technologies. Those against may see themselves as constrained by curriculum policy to ensure that children acquire operational skills to make use of the tools of their society, or they may take an 'anti-technology' position in the hope of averting the seemingly inevitable negative consequences of technological innovation on young children's play and learning. Those in favour of technology use may view technologies as intrinsically enabling learning for children and promote their application in educational settings because technologies are considered the way of the future. The One Laptop Per Child initiative is a case in point (http://one. laptop.org/about/mission).

The second perspective on the relationship between technology and humans which we reviewed was the substantive theory of technology. This body of thought views technologies as shaping the cultural system of society, although the focus of humans on the benefits of the technology for achieving certain outcomes masks the ways in which the resources shape expectations about what become normal cultural practices. For example, while we appreciate the benefits of car travel we pay less attention to the consequences for town planning or environmental considerations. Similarly, adopting the substantive theory of technologies means that educators are likely to focus on the ways in which digital resources can assist children and adults to carry out particular functions, perhaps taking and storing photographs of construction projects or art work, without attention to the shift in cultural expectations about normal practices associated with this move. The increased uptake of Learning Stories (Carr & Lee, 2012) as a form of assessment has led to educators taking more photographs to document children's play. However, a consequence of the greater 'ease' with which digital photographs can be taken is more time is spent on recording and documenting children's play than is spent on the planning and analysis of the play itself (Bath, 2012). The technology becomes a substantive realisation of quality early-childhood provision through the process of digitally documented assessment.

The third theory of technology involves taking a critical perspective. This way of thinking about the relationship between humans and technology pays attention to the purposes and values associated with our technological engagements. It allows understanding of the cultural-historical reasons why a technology was developed and prompts consideration not only of the uses to which a technology can be put, but the amplification of mental labour and processes such that new knowledge is enabled in a way that continues to inform technological innovation for the next generation. For those involved in early childhood education, a critical theory of technology makes space for professional judgement about educational values and the purposes of technologies in context. Attending to context enables attention to be paid to the cultural-historical development of technologies by people within society. Thus, in this book the notion of a 'cultural and critical' perspective provides a nuanced response to play and learning with technologies so that children's relationship with technologies is understood as historically situated, contemporarily used and future orientated. When we see a child using an iPad we can simultaneously view this as a transformation of historical knowledge about the physics of matter and young children's learning, enabling a particular form of multi-modal play or learning with the capacity to inform future knowledge developments. Toddlers and technologies are not static moments *in* time, *they are of their* time.

Thinking about children's play and learning from a cultural and critical perspective can seem intellectually challenging. This is particularly so when the technological determinist arguments for and against technologies seem so temptingly easy to muster. Or when a substantive view appears to at least speak to how it is that technologies shape cultural practices and therefore provide a justification for their use. However, we understand the power of a cultural and critical perspective to be its capacity to understand human relationships with technologies as located in the ordinary transformation of culture over time. Cultural mediation suggests that technological innovation occurs throughout any period of time. The time in which we happen to be alive is characterised by innovations in touchscreen technologies, NUIs and networked technologies. As we use these innovations in the present day, new knowledge will evolve to transform the next generation of technologies and consequently develop a changed cultural niche for children of the future.

The digital age and early childhood education

We cannot know for sure what these future innovations are likely to be. Maybe voice commands and audio content will negate the use of traditional literacy processes? It could be that algorithms and artificial intelligence will require new forms of knowledge processing of very young children. In these dynamic circumstances offering tips for teachers or relying on techno-tales to inform policy and administrative guidance are not useful. Instead of tips and techno-tales rooted in past understandings and expectations, we suggest that adopting a culturally informed, critical perspective will allow educators and policy-makers to take a proactive position, asking what knowledge and experiences with digital technologies children need to play and learn in the digital age. Vygotsky (1997) argued 'ultimately only life educates, and the deeper that life, the real world, burrows into the school, the more dynamic and the more robust will be the educational process' (p. 345). It is our contention that those who are engaged in providing early educational experiences for young children or whose responsibility it is to shape early education policy should develop a cultural-historical understanding of the contemporary manifestation of the digital age in their society and be ready to take a critical perspective on the knowledge that children require now and the ways in which educational experiences can best meet their requirements. Thinking culturally and critically will enable educators to address questions that are now emerging but which seem difficult to approach without opportunities to articulate a professional response that recognises value positions and the state of the actual in the lives of young children. For instance, should young children learn about microprocessors? What about the role of network technologies in their daily lives? Does a four year old need to know how algorithms work?

Thinking culturally and critically about providing early years education in the digital age is challenging but educators are not without resources. In this book we have given an account of the cultural-historical development of the digital technologies that are part of the everyday lives of young children. But this is not the only pertinent knowledge base from which early years educators can start to develop pedagogic practices that respond to the digital age. They also have access to contemporary cultural-historical understandings about early years educational provision and support for young children's learning and development. Central to this cultural knowledge about early years education are four distinguishing features of an effective contemporary learning environment, identified in Chapter 4 as foundational to the Learning Sciences:

1. Building on the pre-existing knowledge base of learners.
2. Engaging learners in multiple types of learning, including active and observational learning.
3. Ensuring that learning is directed towards the development of understanding.
4. Creating culturally relevant learning through community connectedness.

(Bransford, Brown, & Cocking, 2000)

Educational provision for young children typically engages these features, particularly through the use of play-based learning which is child-centred, concerned with the process of learning, understanding and developing learning dispositions and reflects society's values and expectations. Starting from these core features early years educators and those concerned with shaping early years provision can begin to respond in a culturally and critically informed way to the digital age.

Play-based learning remains necessary in the digital age but perhaps new ideas are needed about what constitutes play and what children will play about. A cultural and critical perspective enables new thinking about play-based learning. For example, in Chapter 5 we argued that it is no longer feasible to distinguish between traditional forms of play and a new form of play which can be labelled as digital play. Observations of play episodes in contemporary times suggest that the concept of blended play offers a more fruitful approach for research and pedagogical development. The work of Edwards, Nuttall, Mantilla, Wood and Grieshaber (2015) articulated a further challenge. If educator understandings about what 'counts' as play-based learning are based on a cultural position that predates the digital age then they will struggle to incorporate digital technologies in their pedagogical practices. However, a cultural and critical perspective will take account of technologies in the everyday lives and cultural practices of children and their families and prompt professional reflection on the ways in which technological innovation can amplify the capacities of young learners; what it is that they need to know to make effective and productive use of the digital resources of their time and in the future.

For many years, early childhood education centred on the play-based interests of children as a source for curriculum formation. The research we presented in Chapter 8 suggests that early childhood education today necessarily encompasses the experience of the digital by children at home and in the community. Early years learning is traditionally connected with the child's interests, their home and community life. We suggest that in the digital age, early learning can and should continue to reflect children's interests at home and in the community. However, what this looks like for children will reconfigure the notion of 'interests' – as demonstrated in Chapter 8, there can be no assumption of universality about 'starting points' or the desire to engage with any particular technology or technological activity. Educators need to attend to the 'state of the actual' to identify what children can already do, what they want to do next, and the ways in which technologies can enhance and extend their individual curiosity and respond to their preferences.

Play-based learning in the digital age requires responses from educators that are contextually relevant to the state of the actual in family life and the social mediation of technologies that children experience with others, predominantly their parents and siblings. As we discussed in Chapter 8, most children's first experience of digital technologies will be in everyday family life. Digital technology may control the temperature of their home, track food supplies in the fridge and allow visual and auditory communication with distant family members. The boredom of queuing or waiting may be alleviated by playing a game on a smartphone or watching a programme downloaded into a tablet. Siblings may share YouTube clips or Facebook posts and phones may be the preferred tool for taking photographs. The evidence which we reviewed about family life and the mediation of parents and siblings and family culture should make it clear that there can be no simple expectations about the experiences and competencies with digital technologies which children bring to their educational settings. Family expectations, culture and relationships, as well as socio-economic circumstances, make a difference to children's digital experiences and these differences are compounded by individual preferences. Furthermore, the digital resources accessible at home are likely to be different from those provided in educational settings where there are particular expectations about sustainability, security and the appropriateness of genres and response modalities (Edwards, Henderson, Gronn, Scott, & Mirkhil, 2017). Adopting a cultural and critical perspective will allow educators to acknowledge the 'state of the actual' in the lives of the children they are responsible for and to formulate a curricular and pedagogic response that builds on the knowledge base of the learner and creates culturally relevant learning.

Ensuring that learning is directed towards the development of understanding (rather than the transmission of knowledge, particularly knowledge presented in the form of discrete disciplines), is characteristic of early years educational settings. In this context the capacity of technology to amplify mental labour that is such a feature of the digital age offers an immediate way in which early years educators can begin to engage with questions about current practices and activities and future innovations. Practices such as creating and consuming with YouTube Kids tutorials already demonstrate ways in which technological innovations can be involved in amplifying the capacities of young children. Thinking culturally and critically, teachers, researchers, policy-makers and administrators will be able to consider what amplification looks like and means for young children growing up in the digital age. This may include applying culturally located conceptual knowledge about learning to consider how and why technologies enable amplification e.g. understanding what constitutes networked technologies. Educators will want to consider why some apps are better than others at enabling amplification and make critically informed professional judgements when they select apps so that selection is based on the capacity for amplification, not just drill and skill or even the notion that some apps are better for children than others because they are 'open-ended'.

Practitioners' pedagogic knowledge will be important for play and learning in the digital age just as it has been in earlier times. Gee and Hayes (2011) offer a clear-cut statement on the importance of this personal scaffolding and the pedagogical contribution of educators:

> No technology – books, television, computers, video games or the Internet – by itself makes people good or bad, smart or stupid.... They can be forces for good or ill. A computer connected to the internet in the hands of a child with good mentoring is often a force for learning. It may not be in other circumstances. The real issue, then, is social, that is, who has and who does

not have mentoring, not technology alone. The same is true of books and of language.

(Gee & Hayes, 2011, p. 5)

Early work by Stephen and Plowman (e.g. Plowman & Stephen, 2007; Stephen & Plowman, 2008) made clear the important role that educators have in ensuring that young children have the kind of positive encounters with digital technologies that foster learning. Their studies challenged the technological deterministic assumption that the technology could take over the educator role. They demonstrated that, as well as needing their educators to provide a digital learning environment that was planned to take account of the actual in their everyday lives at home and in their educational setting and which responded to their individual preferences and interests, young children needed proximal pedagogical interactions. Children benefited from attuned demonstrations and modelling. They required support with material aspects of digital resources, with written text instructions and menus and sometimes with audio instructions or understanding the goal of a game. They needed an educator to draw their attention to similarities and differences in the information presented or displays viewed and to explain why a response was incorrect when the software only pointed to an error or gave the expected correct response after a set number of trials. Practitioners have existing repertoires of pedagogic interactions which they employ when engaged with traditional, non-digital learning opportunities. This professional knowledge awaits transformation for the digital age through a process of conceptual development and practical exploration informed by a cultural and critical perspective that takes account of the understandings of and relationships with technologies between children and educators.

The curriculum experienced in early childhood education settings reflects teacher beliefs, societal values and political positions about children and childhood and the need to acknowledge the range of value positions and expectations that families hold. From a cultural and critical perspective, a curriculum located in the digital age will not be entirely the same as that which served the purposes of the industrial age. Policy decisions about the early childhood curriculum and professional judgements about their implementation will be informed by what adults understand, think about and value with respect to the digital. Educators, like parents and policy-makers, are being required to make decisions about current actions and provisions, justified in part at least by their understanding of the skills and knowledge that will be valued in a future they cannot predict with confidence.

Cole (1996) made use of the concept of prolepsis to consider the thinking that influences adults as they make decisions about provision and practices to support learning, either at home or in educational settings. Prolepsis refers to the process by which adults think about which experiences are desirable for children in terms of their own understanding of the present and the links which they see between their own experience of childhood and adulthood. Prolepsis means that decisions about current environments are based on projections of past experiences and outcomes into the future (McPake & Plowman, 2010). However, the knowledge innovations we have described in this book mean that projections from the past are likely to be an insufficient guide to future lives in the digital age. Even young educators began their engagement with digital technologies before the advent of the iPad and have not had the same first-hand experience of growing up with tablet computers, smartphones and spreadable media as the children for whom they are now responsible. A similar difficulty faces those charged with developing policy and practice guidance; projections from past experiences are not a sufficient background from which to plan for future educational needs. Personalised experiences of the past are not a solid position from which to make decisions about present provision and future needs, particularly in an environment where moral panic about the intrusion of digital technologies into young lives confronts beliefs in the educational potential of new technologies. In such circumstances educators can be left struggling for direction or may choose to focus narrowly on developing children's operational skills with existing technologies in their setting.

A cultural and critical perspective on play and learning in the digital age offers a knowledge alternative. From this position those responsible for curriculum design may understand technologies as culturally generated and valued – just as traditional aspects of the early childhood learning environment were once culturally determined by the knowledge needs of industrial society. Early years educators already make value judgements about the kinds of literature to which children should be introduced in their educational settings. They seek to develop particular forms of social behaviour and challenge other ways of interacting, and they now contemporarily promote practices that enhance the sustainability of the physical environment and minimise negative environmental outcomes such as climate change. Such culturally sensitive and critical thinking and decision-making can be extended to children's experience of the digital age, considering what is valued behaviour and knowledge.

Throughout this book we have drawn attention to the ways in which knowledge changes, embedded in a particular cultural-historical context, have implications for curricular and pedagogic decision-making. Knowledge generates cultural change (expressed via technological innovation), which in turn changes the cultural niche for play and learning as experienced by young children. As we have already described, this process has challenged existing understandings of play as traditional play increasingly blurs with the digital. It also means that the 'transmission' of knowledge is no longer necessarily a primary pedagogic strategy in the digital age. Current culturally available technologies enable children to seek answers to questions or explore specified topics in ways that go beyond the traditional dependency on printed texts and the literacy tools associated with writing and reading the printed word. Children playing and learning in the digital age need to become familiar with digital tools for searching, storing and retrieving information and for evaluating sources and synthesising information across a number of mediums. Increasingly, a knowledge of how algorithms operate and an understanding of networked technologies will be critical in early childhood so that children are aware of how their spreadable media environments are created and understand that not everyone with whom they engage is exposed to the same media as they themselves experience.

Ensuring that children have opportunities to become competent with cultural tools such as reading and writing, understanding and manipulating number and measurement, including time and physical properties, has been central to the early childhood educational curriculum for many years. A cultural and critical approach suggests that relevance also lies in helping children to understand search engines, the concept of the internet and spreadable media tools such as blogs. Like reading, competency with some digital tools requires specific teaching. However, just as the educators' interest is not only with phonics skills or letter recognition per se, but with the possibilities for engaging with the world that this skill affords, so too with play and learning in the digital age. What children will be able to do as informed and able users of digital tools will be of more enduring significance. Furthermore, educational questions about play and learning for everyday life and knowledge development can themselves be expected to drive knowledge innovation in the future just as social, political and cultural contexts gave rise to innovation in the past. Kay's influential work on the DynaBook arose from a desire to support children's learning and drew on a range of knowledge resources about the process of learning and cognitive development in relation to the available technologies (including the then 'on the horizon' touchscreen interface). Knowledge collaboration between educators, researchers and designers is likely to lead to as yet unimagined ways of play and learning, perhaps drawing on the significance of artificial intelligence as the next frontier in cultural knowledge production for early childhood education.

Conclusion

In introducing this book we provided the example of a child and grandfather at play. We described their activity, engaging with a variety of technologies and practices as unremarkable. Unremarkable due to the role of culture in creating developmental contexts for young children. From this perspective we have suggested that technological innovations are always located in historical knowledge innovations and does not necessarily need to be experienced as 'bolts from the blue' or impositions from afar. Rather, technological innovations (such as that located in the story of the iPad) have evolved from the knowledge and desires of previous times to be available for use now – in our time. Beginning in the 20th century and continuing into the 21st century, developments in micro-processing, digitalisation, networked computing and user-technology interfaces have extended throughout society, creating what Masuda (1985) described as a new productive power characterised as the digital age. With this evolution of knowledge and technological capacities has come evolution in our cultural practices for communication, managing information, leisure, play and learning. Growing up in the digital age means being part of a culture in which digital technologies are employed for everyday practices. Playing and learning in our time means playing and learning in a digital culture – and this requires practices and affords opportunities that have evolved from the industrial age.

It is our contention that understanding play and learning in the digital age is most appropriately achieved through the multidisciplinary and context or problem-focused approach that underpins research and theory in the Learning Sciences. We see learning as helpfully informed by the Learning Sciences approach that applies knowledge from a range of pertinent disciplines to the complex and contextualised experience of learners in the digital age. Such an approach to learning and to pedagogic responsibilities demands that educators focus on their knowledge about learning and reflect critically on ways of responding in particular contexts and circumstances. We have argued that, just as our knowledge about learning is evolving in the digital age, so too our thinking about play in contemporary times is changing so that it is best understood as a blending of traditional play practices and what was earlier thought of as a discrete form of play labelled digital play. The cultural practices of play are being transformed in the digital age.

We have argued that a cultural-historical perspective on learning and play offers a way of making sense of current experiences. In Part III of this book we looked in some detail at the experiences of young children growing up in contemporary times where digital technologies are embedded in everyday life. Those responsible for the education and care of young children not only need to understand how and why digital culture has evolved so that they can understand the context in which they are placed but also need to be able to respond to this digital age. We have described three possible responses – technological determinism, a substantive focus and a critical perspective. We have advocated for the critical perspective as one that empowers educators to respond in ways that acknowledge and reflect the state of the actual, the everyday conditions of growing up in the digital age, and to do so in ways that are sensitive to the values, desires and expectations of families and communities.

A cultural and critical perspective therefore equips early years educators and those responsible for making decisions about early years educational policy and provision to understand and reflect on technological innovation and knowledge advances and to respond in culturally sensitive and appropriate ways that take account of past and future transformations. While we acknowledge that developing a culturally informed and critically aware perspective can be seen as a daunting task for the early years sector, we suggest that there is a body of knowledge about play, learning and pedagogy which is central to the culture of early years educational practice and which is ready for transformation to meet the needs of the young children today who are playing and learning in the digital age.

References

Bath, C. (2012). 'I can't read it; I don't know': young children's participation in the pedagogical documentation of English early childhood education and care settings. *International Journal of Early Years Education, 20*(2), 190–201.

Beer, D. (2009). Power through the algorithm? Participatory web cultures and the techno-logical unconscious. *New Media Society*, *11*, 985. doi: 10.1177/1461444809336551.

Bergen, D. (2014). Foundations of play theory. In L. Brooker, M. Blaise, and S. Edwards (Eds.), *The SAGE handbook of play and learning in early childhood* (pp. 9–20). London: SAGE.

Bransford, J. D., Brown, A. L., & Cocking, R. R. (2000). *How people learn: brain, mind, experience, and school.* Washington, D.C.: National Academy Press.

Carr, M., & Lee, W. (2012). *Learning stories: constructing learner identities in early educa-tion.* London: SAGE.

Cole, M. (1996). *Cultural psychology: a once and future discipline.* Cambridge, MA: Harvard University Press.

Davydov, V. (1982). Translated by S. Kerr. The influence of L. S. Vygotsky on education, theory, research and practice. *Educational Researcher*, *24*(3), 12–21.

Edwards, S., Henderson, M., Gronn, D., Scott, A., & Mirkhil, M. (2017). Digital disconnect or digital difference? A socio-ecological perspective on young children's technology use in the home and the early childhood centre. *Technology, Pedagogy and Education*, *26*(1), 1–17.

Edwards, S., Nuttall, J., Mantilla, A., Wood, E., & Grieshaber, S. (2015). Digital play: what do early childhood teachers see? In S. Bulfin, N. F. Johnson, & C. Bigum (Eds.), *Critical perspectives on early childhood education* (pp. 66–84). Palgrave Macmillan's Digital Education and Learning Series. New York, NY: Palgrave Macmillan.

Gee, J. P., & Hayes, E. R. (2011). *Language and learning in the digital age.* Abingdon: Routledge.

Gibbons, A. (2010). Reflections concerning technology: a case for the philosophy of tech-nology in early childhood teacher education and professional development programs. In S. Izumi-Taylor & S. Blake (Eds.), *Technology for early childhood education and socialization: developmental applications and methodologies* (pp. 1–19). Hershey, NY: IGI Global.

Kay, A. C. (1972, August). A personal computer for children of all ages. In *Proceedings of the ACM annual conference – Volume 1* (p. 1). ACM.

Masuda, Y. (1980). *The information society as post-industrial society.* Tokyo: Institute for the Information Society.

Masuda, Y. (1985). Three great social revolutions: agricultural, industrial, and informational. *Prometheus*, *3*(2), 269–274.

McPake, J., & Plowman, L. (2010). At home with the future: influences on young children's early experiences with digital technologies. In N. Yelland (Ed.), *Contemporary perspectives on early childhood education* (pp. 210–226). Maidenhead: McGraw-Hill Education.

Plowman, L., & Stephen, C. (2007). Guided interaction in pre-school settings. *Journal of Computer Assisted Learning*, *23*(1), 14–26.

Selwyn, N. (2010). Looking beyond learning: notes towards the critical study of educational technology. *Journal of Computer Assisted Learning*, *26*, 65–73.

Stephen, C., & Plowman, L. (2008). Enhancing learning with information and communica-tion technologies in pre-school. *Early Child Development and Care*, *178*(6), 637–654.

Vygotsky, L. S. (1997). *The collected works of LS Vygotsky: problems of the theory and history of psychology* (Vol. 3). New York: Springer Science & Business Media.

INDEX

Page numbers in **bold** denote figures.